P9-BJS-229

Mrs. Beeton's Book of Household Management

Mrs. Beeton's Book of Household Management

The 1861 Classic with Advice on Cooking, Cleaning, Childrearing, Entertaining, and More

---

Isabella Beeton

Foreword by Sarah A. Chrisman

Skyhorse Publishing

Editor's Note: Sections of the original book were cut during abridgment to create a conveniently sized edition for the curious, modern reader. Recipe ingredients were also formatted into columns for easier reading. However, in an attempt to preserve the historical nature of this book, edits for clarification were not made to the original Beeton text. All original errors are included.

Published Originally by S. O. Beeton in 24 Monthly Parts 1859–1861.

Illustrations on pages 2, 3, 6, 8, 28, 30, 51, 56, 103, 120, 122, 142, 154, 156, 196, 237, 270 courtesy of Sarah A. Chrisman and www.thisvictorianlife.com.

Illustrations on pages 7, 29, 30, 32, 37, 46, 106, 112, 209, 211, 229, 230, 231, originally published in the Montgomery Ward Catalogue and Buyer's Guide 1895.

First Published in a Bound Edition 1861.
First Skyhorse Publishing edition 2015.

10 9 8 7 6 5 4 3

Library of Congress Cataloging-in-Publication Data is available on file.

Cover design by Jane Sheppard
Cover illustration by Charles Dana Gibson

Print ISBN: 978-1-63450-242-9
Ebook ISBN: 978-1-5107-0066-6

Printed in the United States of America

Contents

Foreword ix

Preface xiii

Chapter I: THE MISTRESS 1

Chapter II: THE HOUSEKEEPER 27

Chapter III: ARRANGEMENT AND ECONOMY OF THE KITCHEN 33

Chapter IV: INTRODUCTION TO COOKERY 45

Chapter V: GENERAL DIRECTIONS FOR MAKING SOUPS 56

Chapter VI: RECIPES: FRUIT AND VEGETABLE SOUPS 65

Chapter VII: THE NATURAL HISTORY OF FISHES 78

Chapter VIII: RECIPES: FISH 91

Chapter IX: GENERAL REMARKS 102

Chapter X: RECIPES: SAUCES, PICKLES, GRAVIES, AND FORCEMEATS 104

Chapter XI: GENERAL REMARKS 113

Chapter XII: RECIPES 127

Chapter XIII: GENERAL OBSERVATIONS ON THE COMMON HOG 132

Chapter XIV: RECIPES: PORK AND HAM 136

Chapter XV: GENERAL OBSERVATIONS ON THE CALF 140

Chapter XVI: RECIPES: VEAL 144

Chapter XVII: GENERAL OBSERVATIONS ON BIRDS 147

Chapter XVIII: RECIPES: POULTRY AND RABBIT 150

Chapter XIX: GENERAL OBSERVATIONS ON GAME 157

Chapter XX: RECIPES: GAME 162

Chapter XXI: GENERAL OBSERVATIONS ON VEGETABLES 165

Chapter XXII: RECIPES: VEGETABLES 168

Chapter XXIII: GENERAL OBSERVATIONS ON PUDDINGS AND PASTRY 171

Chapter XXIV: RECIPES: PUDDINGS AND PASTRY 174

Chapter XXV: GENERAL OBSERVATIONS ON CREAMS, JELLIES, SOUFFLÉS, OMELETS, & SWEET DISHES 187

Chapter XXVI: RECIPES: VARIOUS SWEETS 190

Chapter XVII: GENERAL OBSERVATIONS ON PRESERVES, CONFECTIONARY, DESSERT DISHES, AND ICES 196

Chapter XXVIII: RECIPES: SWEET SAUCES AND JAMS 205

Chapter XXIX: GENERAL OBSERVATIONS ON MILK, BUTTER, CHEESE, AND EGGS 210

Chapter XXX: RECIPES: CHEESE AND EGGS 214

Chapter XXXI: GENERAL OBSERVATIONS ON BREAD AND CAKES 217

Chapter XXXII: RECIPES: BREADS AND CAKES 224

Chapter XXXIII: GENERAL OBSERVATIONS ON BEVERAGES 229

Chapter XXXIV: RECIPES: BEVERAGES 232

Chapter XXXV: DINNERS AND DINING 235

Chapter XXXVI: THE REARING, MANAGEMENT, AND DISEASES OF INFANCY AND CHILDHOOD 242

Chapter XXXVII: THE DOCTOR 269

Chapter XXXVIII: LEGAL MEMORANDA 286

Index 297

FOREWORD

What a culture reads tells us a lot about its people, and *Mrs. Beeton's Book of Household Management* was one of Victorian Britain's most popular books, selling over 60,000 copies in the first year after its publication back in 1861. The book was broad enough in scope to be of interest to everyone from the female managers of great estates down to their humble servants. Indeed, the pages listing servants' duties and wages were just as useful to the servants themselves as they were to their employers: the book was an unimpeachable reference as to what they should expect from the people they worked for, and of what, in turn, was expected of them. If a servant felt she was being cheated or that unreasonable demands were put on her, she could point to the book's authority when approaching her mistress. This gave her grievances far more weight than a simple complaint of feeling mistreated.

The book's primary audience, however, was the housewives of a burgeoning middle class. For these women, the book *was* their servant—and quite a good one. It offered them help with everything from setting a table to dealing with legal memoranda, and of course, chapter after chapter of detailed recipes.

Since Beeton's work is primarily remembered as a cookbook, modern Americans might be quite startled when they discover in its pages a complicated natural history of fishes juxtaposed against the seafood recipes. It seems even more jarring to twenty-first-century eyes to see very scientific analyses speckled with theological references. After fish are defined as "the fourth class in the system of Linnaeus . . . having long under-jaws, eggs without white, organs of sense, fins for supporters, bodies covered with concave scales, gills to supply the place of lungs for respiration and water for the natural element of their existence" the book describes the diversity of sea-life as "equally wonderful with those of any other works which have come from the hand of the Creator." However, when we remind ourselves that Mrs. Beeton's *Book* . . . came out just two years after Charles Darwin's *On the Origin of Species*, the context of all of this snaps into focus. We see for ourselves the fascination with science that characterized the period and extended to all members of society, including housewives; and we also witness their struggle to integrate newfound knowledge with lifelong faith. It's a fascinating window into their world, a glimpse into their very minds.

In a similar window into the time, Beeton's chagrin about the mistreatment of hogs by some farmers shows us the beginnings of animal welfare concerns, and one can only imagine how she would have felt about the conditions of food animals in modern factory farms.

Descriptions of medieval and ancient hunting tales might seem an interesting choice for introducing a chapter on game recipes, but when we remember how much the Victorians enjoyed incorporating classical imagery into their art, this too springs into context. Seeing an image of Hera carved into a Victorian bedframe or medieval beasts ornamenting nineteenth century parlor chairs reinforces this peek into a particular corner of many people's hearts at the time. When we put all these things together we gain a more thorough understanding of the culture.

Besides offering insights into the time the produced it, the book contains some advice whose practicality is timeless. Beeton begins by telling us, "As with the commander of an army . . . so it is with the mistress of a house." In other words, the woman in charge of a home has as much responsibility and deserves as much respect as any other manager, and her personality will imprint itself upon her home. Perusing the book further, we see her advice range from this profound wisdom down to words on very practical matters, such as the value of fruit to good health or that "stale" eggs are "things to be run from." Victorians in general—

and Victorian middle-class women in particular—exhibited a wonderful capacity for engaging with subjects ranging from the philosophical to the pragmatic. We could all benefit from the attitude exemplified by this wide-ranging, comprehensive book.

Mrs. Isabella Beeton, the icon of Victorian domesticity, was a real, flesh and blood woman. She and I actually share a birthday (March 12, if anyone wants to send me a cake), although admittedly we're separated by nearly a century and a half. Born in 1836, Isabella died tragically young, perishing of complications from childbirth a month shy of her twenty-ninth birthday. Her book lived on though, and as sad as it is to contemplate, perhaps her early death was precisely what allowed her spirit to be so adaptable. When living authors enjoy success, the public at best considers them idols with feet of clay. However, as a spirit and a symbol, Mrs. Beeton's memory attained divine status. Her *Book of Household Management* was virtually a bible for domestic life. Every woman who sought the guidance of its pages had an ideal image in her heart of its author. Throughout the nineteenth, twentieth, and into the twenty-first centuries, countless new editions of Beeton's book were continually reprinted, often dramatically altered to reinterpret her original vision as something more appropriate to the time and place of the latest edition. Her name has been attached to innumerable products throughout the years, and it seems likely she would be totally bewildered by items such as the "Mrs. Beeton's Cheese Ipad Mini Covers" which were recently for sale online. (I know they certainly mystified me.) The book in your hands now, though, is one she would recognize. She wrote it herself.

—Sarah A. Chrisman
author, *Victorian Secrets*
and *This Victorian Life*

PREFACE

I must frankly own, that if I had known, beforehand, that this book would have cost me the labour which it has, I should never have been courageous enough to commence it. What moved me, in the first instance, to attempt a work like this, was the discomfort and suffering which I had seen brought upon men and women by household mismanagement. I have always thought that there is no more fruitful source of family discontent than a housewife's badly-cooked dinners and untidy ways. Men are now so well served out of doors,—at their clubs, well-ordered taverns, and dining-houses, that in order to compete with the attractions of these places, a mistress must be thoroughly acquainted with the theory and practice of cookery, as well as be perfectly conversant with all the other arts of making and keeping a comfortable home.

In this book I have attempted to give, under the chapters devoted to cookery, an intelligible arrangement to every recipe, a list of the *ingredients*, a plain statement of the *mode* of preparing each dish, and a careful estimate of its *cost*, the *number of people* for whom it is *sufficient*, and the time when it is *seasonable*. For the matter of the recipes, I am indebted, in some measure, to many correspondents of the "Englishwoman's Domestic Magazine," who have obligingly placed at my disposal their formulas for many original preparations. A large private circle has also rendered me considerable service. A diligent study of the works of the best modern writers on cookery was also necessary to the faithful fulfilment of my task. Friends in England, Scotland, Ireland, France, and Germany, have also very materially aided me. I have paid great attention to those recipes which come under the head of "COLD MEAT COOKERY." But in the department belonging to the Cook I have striven, too, to make my work something more than a Cookery Book, and have, therefore, on the best authority that I could obtain, given an account of the natural history of the animals and vegetables which we use as food. I have followed the animal from his birth to his appearance on the table; have described the manner of feeding him, and of slaying him, the position of his various joints, and, after giving the recipes, have described the modes of carving Meat, Poultry, and Game. Skilful artists have designed the numerous drawings which appear in this work, and which illustrate, better than any description, many important and interesting items. The coloured plates are a novelty not without value.

Towards the end of the work will be found valuable chapters on the "Management of Children"——"The Doctor," the latter principally referring to accidents and emergencies, some of which are certain to occur in the experience of every one of us; and the last chapter contains "Legal Memoranda," which will be serviceable in cases of doubt as to the proper course to be adopted in the relations between Landlord and Tenant, Tax-gatherer and Tax-payer, and Tradesman and Customer.

These chapters have been contributed by gentlemen fully entitled to confidence; those on medical subjects by an experienced surgeon, and the legal matter by a solicitor.

I wish here to acknowledge the kind letters and congratulations I have received during the progress of this work, and have only further to add, that I trust the result of the four years' incessant labour which I have expended will not be altogether unacceptable to some of my countrymen and countrywomen.

ISABELLA BEETON.

CHAPTER I

THE MISTRESS

"Strength, and honour are her clothing; and she shall rejoice in time to come. She openeth her mouth with wisdom; and in her tongue is the law of kindness. She looketh well to the ways of her household; and eateth not the bread of idleness. Her children arise up, and call her blessed; her husband also, and he praiseth her."—*Proverbs*, xxxi. 25-28.

AS WITH THE COMMANDER OF AN ARMY, or the leader of any enterprise, so is it with the mistress of a house. Her spirit will be seen through the whole establishment; and just in proportion as she performs her duties intelligently and thoroughly, so will her domestics follow in her path. Of all those acquirements, which more particularly belong to the feminine character, there are none which take a higher rank, in our estimation, than such as enter into a knowledge of household duties; for on these are perpetually dependent the happiness, comfort, and well-being of a family. In this opinion we are borne out by the author of "The Vicar of Wakefield," who says: "The modest virgin, the prudent wife, and the careful matron, are much more serviceable in life than petticoated philosophers, blustering heroines, or virago queens. She who makes her husband and her children happy, who reclaims the one from vice and trains up the other to virtue, is a much greater character than ladies described in romances, whose whole occupation is to murder mankind with shafts from their quiver, or their eyes."

EARLY RISING IS ONE OF THE MOST ESSENTIAL QUALITIES which enter into good Household Management, as it is not only the parent of health, but of innumerable other advantages. Indeed, when a mistress is an early riser, it is almost certain that her house will be orderly and well-managed. On the contrary, if she remain in bed till a late hour, then the domestics, who, as we have before observed, invariably partake somewhat of their mistress's character, will surely become sluggards. To self-indulgence all are more or less disposed, and it is not to be expected that servants are freer from this fault than the heads of houses. The great Lord Chatham thus gave his advice in reference to this subject:—"I would have inscribed on the curtains of your bed, and the walls of your chamber, 'If you do not rise early, you can make progress in nothing.'"

CLEANLINESS IS ALSO INDISPENSABLE TO HEALTH, and must be studied both in regard to the person and the house, and all that it contains. Cold or tepid baths should be employed every morning, unless, on account of illness or other circumstances, they should be deemed objectionable.

FRUGALITY AND ECONOMY ARE HOME VIRTUES, without which no household can prosper. Dr. Johnson says: "Frugality may be termed the daughter of Prudence, the sister of Temperance, and the parent of Liberty. He that is extravagant will quickly become poor, and poverty will enforce dependence and invite corruption." The necessity of practising economy should be evident to every one, whether in the possession of an income no more than sufficient for a family's requirements, or of a large fortune, which puts financial adversity out of the question. We must always remember that it is a great merit in housekeeping to manage a little well. "He is a good waggoner," says Bishop Hall, "that can turn in a little room. To live well in abundance is the praise of the estate, not of the person. I will study more how to give a good account of my little, than how to make it more." In this there is true wisdom, and it may be added, that those who can manage a little well, are most likely to succeed in their management of larger matters. Economy and frugality must never, however, be allowed to degenerate into parsimony and meanness.

FRIENDSHIPS SHOULD NOT BE HASTILY FORMED, nor the heart given, at once, to every new-comer. There are ladies who uniformly smile at, and approve everything and everybody, and who possess neither the courage to reprehend vice, nor the generous warmth to defend virtue. The friendship of such persons is without attachment, and their love without affection or even preference. They imagine that every one who has any penetration is ill-natured, and look coldly on a discriminating judgment. It should be remembered, however, that this discernment does not always proceed from an uncharitable temper, but that those who possess a long experience and thorough knowledge of the world, scrutinize the conduct and dispositions of people before they trust themselves to the first fair appearances. Addison, who was not deficient in a knowledge of mankind, observes that "a friendship, which makes the least noise, is very often the most useful; for which reason, I should prefer a prudent friend to a zealous one." And Joanna Baillie tells us that

"Friendship is no plant of hasty growth,
Though planted in esteem's deep-fixed soil,
The gradual culture of kind intercourse
Must bring it to perfection."

HOSPITALITY IS A MOST EXCELLENT VIRTUE; but care must be taken that the love of company, for its own sake, does not become a prevailing passion; for then the habit is no longer hospitality, but dissipation. Reality and truthfulness in this, as in all other duties of life, are the points to be studied; for, as Washington Irving well says, "There is an emanation from the heart in genuine hospitality, which cannot be described, but is immediately felt, and puts the stranger at once at his ease." With respect to the continuance of friendships, however, it may be found necessary, in some cases, for a mistress to relinquish, on assuming the responsibility of a household, many of those commenced in the earlier part of her life. This will be the more requisite, if the number still retained be quite equal to her means and opportunities.

IN CONVERSATION, TRIFLING OCCURRENCES, such as small disappointments, petty annoyances, and other every-day incidents, should never be mentioned to your friends. The extreme injudiciousness of repeating these will be at once apparent, when we reflect on the unsatisfactory discussions which they too frequently occasion, and on the load of advice which they are the cause of being tendered, and which is, too often, of a kind neither to be useful nor agreeable. Greater events, whether of joy or sorrow, should be communicated to friends; and, on such occasions, their sympathy gratifies and comforts. If the mistress be a wife, never let an account of her husband's failings pass her lips; and in cultivating the power of conversation, she should keep the versified advice of Cowper continually in her memory, that it

"Should flow like water after summer showers,
Not as if raised by mere mechanic powers."

GOOD TEMPER SHOULD BE CULTIVATED by every mistress, as upon it the welfare of the household may be said to turn; indeed, its influence can hardly be over-estimated, as it has the effect of moulding the characters of those around her, and of acting most beneficially on the happiness of the domestic circle. Every head of a household should strive to be cheerful, and should never fail to show a deep interest in all that appertains to the well-being of those who claim the protection of her roof. Gentleness, not partial and temporary, but universal and regular, should pervade her conduct; for where such a spirit is habitually manifested, it not only delights her children, but makes her domestics attentive and respectful; her visitors are also pleased by it, and their happiness is increased.

ON THE IMPORTANT SUBJECT OF DRESS AND FASHION we cannot do better than quote an opinion from the eighth volume of the "Englishwoman's Domestic Magazine." The writer there says, "Let people write, talk, lecture, satirize, as they may, it cannot be denied that, whatever is the prevailing mode in attire, let it intrinsically be ever so absurd, it

will never *look* as ridiculous as another, or as any other, which, however convenient, comfortable, or even becoming, is totally opposite in style to that generally worn."

IN PURCHASING ARTICLES OF WEARING APPAREL, whether it be a silk dress, a bonnet, shawl, or riband, it is well for the buyer to consider three things: I. That it be not too expensive for her purse. II. That its colour harmonize with her complexion, and its size and pattern with her figure. III. That its tint allow of its being worn with the other garments she possesses. The quaint Fuller observes, that the good wife is none of our dainty dames, who love to appear in a variety of suits every day new, as if a gown, like a stratagem in war, were to be used but once. But our good wife sets up a sail according to the keel of her husband's estate; and, if of high parentage, she doth not so remember what she was by birth, that she forgets what she is by match.

THE DRESS OF THE MISTRESS should always be adapted to her circumstances, and be varied with different occasions. Thus, at breakfast she should be attired in a very neat and simple manner, wearing no ornaments. If this dress should decidedly pertain only to the breakfast-hour, and be specially suited for such domestic occupations as usually follow that meal, then it would be well to exchange it before the time for receiving visitors, if the mistress be in the habit of doing so. It is still to be remembered, however, that, in changing the dress, jewellery and ornaments are not to be worn until the full dress for dinner is assumed.

The advice of Polonius to his son Laertes, in Shakspeare's tragedy of "Hamlet," is most excellent; and although given to one of the male sex, will equally apply to a "fayre ladye:"—

"Costly thy habit as thy purse can buy,
But not express'd in fancy; rich, not gaudy;
For the apparel oft proclaims the man."

CHARITY AND BENEVOLENCE ARE DUTIES which a mistress owes to herself as well as to her fellow-creatures; and there is scarcely any income so small, but something may be spared from it, even if it be but "the widow's mite." It is to be always remembered, however, that it is

the *spirit* of charity which imparts to the gift a value far beyond its actual amount, and is by far its better part.

True Charity, a plant divinely nursed,
Fed by the love from which it rose at first,
Thrives against hope, and, in the rudest scene,
Storms but enliven its unfading green;
Exub'rant is the shadow it supplies,
Its fruit on earth, its growth above the skies.

Visiting the houses of the poor is the only practical way really to understand the actual state of each family; and although there may be difficulties in following out this plan in the metropolis and other large cities, yet in country towns and rural districts these objections do not obtain. Great advantages may result from visits paid to the poor; for there being, unfortunately, much ignorance, generally, amongst them with respect to all household knowledge, there will be opportunities for advising and instructing them, in a pleasant and unobtrusive manner, in cleanliness, industry, cookery, and good management.

IN MARKETING, THAT THE BEST ARTICLES ARE THE CHEAPEST, may be laid down as a rule; and it is desirable, unless an experienced and confidential housekeeper be kept, that the mistress should herself purchase all provisions and stores needed for the house. If the mistress be a young wife, and not accustomed to order "things for the house," a little practice and experience will soon teach her who are the best tradespeople to deal with, and what are the best provisions to buy. Under each particular head of FISH, MEAT, POULTRY, GAME, &c., will be described the proper means of ascertaining the quality of these comestibles.

A HOUSEKEEPING ACCOUNT-BOOK should invariably be kept, and kept punctually and precisely. The plan for keeping household accounts, which we should recommend, would be to make an entry, that is, write down into a daily diary every amount paid on that particular day, be it ever so small; then, at the end of the month, let these various payments be ranged under their specific heads of Butcher, Baker, &c.; and thus will be seen the proportions paid to each tradesman, and any one month's expenses may be contrasted with another. The housekeeping accounts should be balanced not less than once a month; so that you may see that the money you have in hand tallies with your account of it in your diary. Judge Haliburton never wrote truer words than when he said, "No man is rich whose expenditure exceeds his means, and no one is poor whose incomings exceed his outgoings."

> When, in a large establishment, a housekeeper is kept, it will be advisable for the mistress to examine her accounts regularly. Then any increase of expenditure which may be apparent, can easily be explained, and the housekeeper will have the satisfaction of knowing whether her efforts to manage her department well and economically, have been successful.

ENGAGING DOMESTICS is one of those duties in which the judgment of the mistress must be keenly exercised. There are some respectable registry-offices, where good servants may sometimes be hired; but the plan rather to be recommended is, for the mistress to make inquiry amongst her circle of friends and acquaintances, and her tradespeople. The latter generally know those in their neighbourhood, who are wanting situations, and will communicate with them, when a personal interview with some of them will enable the mistress to form some idea of the characters of the applicants, and to suit herself accordingly.

> We would here point out an error—and a grave one it is—into which some mistresses fall. They do not, when engaging a servant, expressly tell her all the duties which she will be expected to perform. This is an act of omission severely to be reprehended. Every portion of work which the maid will have to do, should be plainly stated by the mistress, and understood by the servant. If this plan is not carefully adhered to, domestic contention is almost certain to ensue, and this may not be easily settled; so that a change of servants, which is so much to be deprecated, is continually occurring.

THE FOLLOWING TABLE OF THE AVERAGE YEARLY WAGES paid to domestics, with the various members of the household placed in the order in which they are usually ranked, will serve as a guide to regulate the expenditure of an establishment:—

When not found in When found in
Livery. Livery.

The House Steward From £10 to £80 —
The Valet "25 to 50 From £20 to £30
The Butler "25 to 50 —
The Cook "20 to 40 —
The Gardener "20 to 40 —
The Footman "20 to 40 "15 to 25

The Under Butler "15 to 30 "15 to 25
The Coachman — "20 to 35
The Groom "15 to 30 "12 to 20
The Under Footman — "12 to 20
The Page or Footboy "8 to 18 "6 to 14
The Stableboy "6 to 12 —

When no extra When an extra
allowance is made for allowance is made for
Tea, Sugar, and Beer. Tea, Sugar, and Beer.

The Housekeeper From £20 to £15 From £18 to £40
The Lady's-maid "12 to 25 "10 to 20
The Head Nurse "15 to 30 "13 to 26
The Cook "11 to 30 "12 to 26
The Upper Housemaid "12 to 20 "10 to 17
The Upper Laundry-maid "12 to 18 "10 to 15
The Maid-of-all-work "9 to 14 "7-½ to 11
The Under Housemaid "8 to 12 "6-½ to 10
The Still-room Maid "9 to 14 "8 to 13
The Nursemaid "8 to 12 "5 to 10
The Under Laundry-maid "9 to 11 "8 to 12
The Kitchen-maid "9 to 14 "8 to 12
The Scullery-maid "5 to 9 "4 to 8

These quotations of wages are those usually given in or near the metropolis; but, of course, there are many circumstances connected with locality, and also having reference to the long service on the one hand, or the inexperience on the other, of domestics, which may render the wages still higher or lower than those named above.

All the domestics mentioned in the above table would enter into the establishment of a wealthy nobleman. The number of servants, of course, would become smaller in proportion to the lesser size of the establishment; and we may here enumerate a scale of servants suited to various incomes, commencing with—

About £1,000 a year—A cook, upper housemaid, nursemaid, under housemaid, and a man servant.
About £750 a year—A cook, housemaid, nursemaid, and footboy.
About £500 a year—A cook, housemaid, and nursemaid.
About £300 a year—A maid-of-all-work and nursemaid.
About £200 or £150 a year—A maid-of-all-work (and girl occasionally).

HAVING THUS INDICATED some of the more general duties of the mistress, relative to the moral government of her household, we will now give a few specific instructions on matters having a more practical relation to the position which she is supposed to occupy in the eye of the world. To do this the more clearly, we will begin with her earliest duties, and take her completely through the occupations of a day.

HAVING RISEN EARLY, as we have already advised, and having given due attention to the bath, and made a careful toilet, it will be well at once to see that the children have received their proper ablutions, and are in every way clean and comfortable. The first meal of the day, breakfast, will then be served, at which all the family should be punctually present, unless illness, or other circumstances, prevent.

AFTER BREAKFAST IS OVER, it will be well for the mistress to make a round of the kitchen and other offices, to see that all are in order, and that the morning's work has been properly performed by the various domestics. The orders for the day should then be given, and any questions which the domestics desire to ask, respecting their several departments, should be answered, and any special articles they may require, handed to them from the store-closet.

> In those establishments where there is a housekeeper, it will not be so necessary for the mistress, personally, to perform the above-named duties.

AFTER THIS GENERAL SUPERINTENDENCE of her servants, the mistress, if a mother of a young family, may devote herself to the instruction of some of its younger members, or to the examination of the state of their wardrobe, leaving the later portion of the morning for reading, or for some amusing recreation. "Recreation," says Bishop Hall, "is intended to the mind as whetting is to the scythe, to sharpen the edge of it, which would otherwise grow dull and blunt. He, therefore, that spends his whole time in recreation is ever whetting, never mowing; his grass may grow and his steed starve; as, contrarily, he that always toils and never recreates, is ever mowing, never whetting, labouring much to little purpose. As good no scythe as no edge. Then only doth the work go forward, when the scythe is so seasonably and moderately whetted that it may cut, and so cut, that it may have the help of sharpening."

> Unless the means of the mistress be very circumscribed, and she be obliged to devote a great deal of her time to the making of her children's clothes, and other economical pursuits, it is right that she should give some time to the pleasures of literature, the innocent delights of the garden, and to the improvement of any special abilities for music, painting, and other elegant arts, which she may, happily, possess.

THESE DUTIES AND PLEASURES BEING PERFORMED AND ENJOYED, the hour of luncheon will have arrived. This is a very necessary meal between an early breakfast and a late dinner, as a healthy person, with good exercise, should have a fresh supply of food once in four hours. It should be a light meal; but its solidity must, of course, be, in some degree, proportionate to the time it is intended to enable you to wait for your dinner, and the amount of exercise you take in the mean time. At this time, also, the servants' dinner will be served.

> In those establishments where an early dinner is served, that will, of course, take the place of the luncheon. In many houses, where a nursery dinner is provided for the children and about one o'clock, the mistress and the elder portion of the family make their luncheon at the same time from the same joint, or whatever may be provided. A mistress will arrange, according to circumstances, the serving of the meal; but the more usual plan is for the lady of the house to have the joint brought to her table, and afterwards carried to the nursery.

AFTER LUNCHEON, MORNING CALLS AND VISITS may be made and received. These may be divided under three heads: those of ceremony, friendship, and congratulation or condolence. Visits of ceremony, or courtesy, which occasionally merge into those of friendship, are to be paid under various circumstances. Thus, they are uniformly required after dining at a friend's house, or after a ball, picnic, or any other party. These visits should be short, a stay of from fifteen to twenty minutes being quite sufficient. A lady paying a visit may remove her boa or neckerchief; but neither her shawl nor bonnet.

When other visitors are announced, it is well to retire as soon as possible, taking care to let it appear that their arrival is not the cause. When they are quietly seated, and the bustle of their entrance is over, rise from your chair, taking a kind leave of the hostess, and bowing politely to the guests. Should you call at an inconvenient time, not having ascertained the luncheon hour, or from any other inadvertence, retire as soon as possible, without, however, showing that you feel yourself an intruder. It is not difficult for any well-bred or even good-tempered person, to know what to say on such an occasion, and, on politely withdrawing, a promise can be made to call again, if the lady you have called on, appear really disappointed.

IN PAYING VISITS OF FRIENDSHIP, it will not be so necessary to be guided by etiquette as in paying visits of ceremony; and if a lady be pressed by her friend to remove her shawl and bonnet, it can be done if it will not interfere with her subsequent arrangements. It is, however, requisite to call at suitable times, and to avoid staying too long, if your friend is engaged. The courtesies of society should ever be maintained, even in the domestic circle, and amongst the nearest friends. During these visits, the manners should be easy and cheerful, and the subjects of conversation such as may be readily terminated. Serious discussions or arguments are to be altogether avoided, and there is much danger and impropriety in expressing opinions of those persons and characters with whom, perhaps, there is but a slight acquaintance.

It is not advisable, at any time, to take favourite dogs into another lady's drawing-room, for many persons have an absolute dislike to such animals; and besides this, there is always a chance of a breakage of some article occurring, through their leaping and bounding here and there, sometimes very much to the fear and annoyance of the hostess. Her children, also, unless they are particularly well-trained and orderly, and she is on exceedingly friendly terms with the hostess, should not accompany a lady in making morning calls. Where a lady, however, pays her visits in a carriage, the children can be taken in the vehicle, and remain in it until the visit is over.

FOR MORNING CALLS, it is well to be neatly attired; for a costume very different to that you generally wear, or anything approaching an evening dress, will be very much out of place. As a general rule, it may be said, both in reference to this and all other occasions, it is better to be under-dressed than over-dressed.

A strict account should be kept of ceremonial visits, and notice how soon your visits have been returned. An opinion may thus be formed as to whether your frequent visits are, or are not, desirable. There are, naturally, instances when the circumstances of old age or ill health will preclude any return of a call; but when this is the case, it must not interrupt the discharge of the duty.

IN PAYING VISITS OF CONDOLENCE, it is to be remembered that they should be paid within a week after the event which occasions them. If the acquaintance, however, is but slight, then immediately after the family has appeared at public worship. A lady should send in her card, and if her friends be able to receive her, the visitor's manner and conversation should be subdued and in harmony with the character of her visit. Courtesy would dictate that a mourning card should be used, and that visitors, in paying condoling visits, should be dressed in black, either silk or plain-coloured apparel. Sympathy with the affliction of the family, is thus expressed, and these attentions are, in such cases, pleasing and soothing.

> In all these visits, if your acquaintance or friend be not at home, a card should be left. If in a carriage, the servant will answer your inquiry and receive your card; if paying your visits on foot, give your card to the servant in the hall, but leave to go in and rest should on no account be asked. The form of words, "Not at home," may be understood in different senses; but the only courteous way is to receive them as being perfectly true. You may imagine that the lady of the house is really at home, and that she would make an exception in your favour, or you may think that your acquaintance is not desired; but, in either case, not the slightest word is to escape you, which would suggest, on your part, such an impression.

IN RECEIVING MORNING CALLS, the foregoing description of the etiquette to be observed in paying them, will be of considerable service. It is to be added, however, that the occupations of drawing, music, or reading should be suspended on the entrance of morning visitors. If a lady, however, be engaged with light needlework, and none other is appropriate in the drawing-room, it may not be, under some circumstances, inconsistent with good breeding to quietly continue it during conversation, particularly if the visit be protracted, or the visitors be gentlemen.

THE MORNING CALLS BEING PAID OR RECEIVED, and their etiquette properly attended to, the next great event of the day in most establishments is "The Dinner;" and we only propose here to make a few general remarks on this important topic, as, in future pages, the whole "Art of Dining" will be thoroughly considered, with reference to its economy, comfort, and enjoyment.

IN GIVING OR ACCEPTING AN INVITATION FOR DINNER, the following is the form of words generally made use of. They, however, can be varied in proportion to the intimacy or position of the hosts and guests:—

> Mr. and Mrs. A—— present their compliments to Mr. and Mrs. B——, and request the honour, [or hope to have the pleasure] of their company to dinner on Wednesday, the 6th of December next.

A—— STREET,
November 13th, 1859. R. S. V. P.

The letters in the corner imply "*Répondez, s'il vous plaît;*" meaning, "an answer will oblige." The reply, accepting the invitation, is couched in the following terms:—

> Mr. and Mrs. B—— present their compliments to Mr. and Mrs. A—, and will do themselves the honour of, [or will have much pleasure in] accepting their kind invitation to dinner on the 6th of December next.

B—— SQUARE, *November 18th, 1859.*

Cards, or invitations for a dinner-party, should be issued a fortnight or three weeks (sometimes even a month) beforehand, and care should be taken by the hostess, in the selection of the invited guests, that they should be suited to each other. Much also of the pleasure of a dinner-party will depend on the arrangement of the guests at table, so as to form a due admixture of talkers and listeners, the grave and the gay. If an invitation to dinner is accepted, the guests should be punctual, and the mistress ready in her drawing-room to receive them. At some periods it has been considered fashionable to come late to dinner, but lately *nous avons changé tout cela.*

THE HALF-HOUR BEFORE DINNER has always been considered as the great ordeal through which the mistress, in giving a dinner-party, will either pass with flying colours, or, lose many of her laurels. The anxiety to receive her guests,—her hope that all will be present in due time,—her trust in the skill of her cook, and the attention of the other domestics, all tend to make these few minutes a trying time. The mistress, however, must display no kind of agitation, but show her tact in suggesting light and cheerful subjects of conversation, which will be much aided by the introduction of any particular new book, curiosity of art, or article of vertu, which may pleasantly engage the attention of the company. "Waiting for Dinner," however, is a trying time, and there are few who have not felt—

"How sad it is to sit and pine,
The long *half-hour* before we dine!
Upon our watches oft to look,
Then wonder at the clock and cook,
* * * * *
"And strive to laugh in spite of Fate!
But laughter forced soon quits the room,
And leaves it in its former gloom.
But lo! the dinner now appears,
The object of our hopes and fears,
The end of all our pain!"

DINNER BEING ANNOUNCED, the host offers his arm to, and places on his right hand at the dinner-table, the lady to whom he desires to pay most respect, either on account of her age, position, or from her being the greatest stranger in the party. If this lady be married and her husband present, the latter takes the hostess to her place at table, and seats himself at her right hand. The rest of the company follow in couples, as specified by the master and mistress of the house, arranging the party according to their rank and other circumstances which may be known to the host and hostess.

> It will be found of great assistance to the placing of a party at the dinner-table, to have the names of the guests neatly (and correctly) written on small cards, and placed at that part of the table where it is desired they should sit. With respect to the number of guests, it has often been said, that a private dinner-party should consist of not less than the number of the Graces, or more than that of the Muses. A party of ten or twelve is, perhaps, in a general way, sufficient to enjoy themselves and be enjoyed. White kid gloves are worn by ladies at dinner-parties, but should be taken off before the business of dining commences.

THE GUESTS BEING SEATED AT THE DINNER-TABLE, the lady begins to help the soup, which is handed round, commencing with the gentleman on her right and on her left, and continuing in the same order till all are served. It is generally established as a rule, not to ask for soup or fish twice, as, in so doing, part of the company may be kept waiting too long for the second course, when, perhaps, a little revenge is taken by looking at the awkward consumer of a second portion. This rule, however, may, under various circumstances, not be considered as binding.

> It is not usual, where taking wine is *en règle*, for a gentleman to ask a lady to take wine until the fish or soup is finished, and then the gentleman honoured by sitting on the right of the hostess, may politely inquire if she will do him the honour of taking wine with him. This will act as a signal to the rest of the company, the gentleman of the house most probably requesting the same pleasure of the ladies at his right and left. At many tables, however, the custom or fashion of drinking wine in this manner, is abolished, and the servant fills the glasses of the guests with the various wines suited to the course which is in progress.

WHEN DINNER IS FINISHED, THE DESSERT is placed on the table, accompanied with finger-glasses. It is the custom of some gentlemen to wet a corner of the napkin; but the hostess, whose behaviour will set the tone to all the ladies present, will merely wet the tips of her fingers, which will serve all the purposes required. The French and other continentals have a habit of gargling the mouth; but it is a custom which no English gentlewoman should, in the slightest degree, imitate.

WHEN FRUIT HAS BEEN TAKEN, and a glass or two of wine passed round, the time will have arrived when the hostess will rise, and thus give the signal for the ladies to leave the gentlemen, and retire to the drawing-room. The gentlemen of the party will rise at the same time, and he who is nearest the door, will open it for the ladies, all remaining courteously standing until the last lady has withdrawn. Dr. Johnson has a curious paragraph on the effects of a dinner on men. "Before dinner," he says, "men meet with great inequality of understanding; and those who are conscious of their inferiority have the modesty not to talk. When they have drunk wine, every man feels himself happy, and loses that modesty, and grows impudent and vociferous; but he is not improved, he is only not sensible of his defects." This is rather severe, but there may be truth in it.

> In former times, when the bottle circulated freely amongst the guests, it was necessary for the ladies to retire earlier than they do at present, for the gentlemen of the company soon became unfit to conduct themselves with that decorum which is essential in the presence of ladies. Thanks, however, to the improvements in modern society, and the high example shown to the nation by its most illustrious personages, temperance is, in these happy days, a striking feature in the character of a gentleman. Delicacy of conduct towards the female sex has increased with the esteem in which they are now universally held, and thus, the very early withdrawing of the ladies from the dining-room is to be deprecated. A lull in the conversation will seasonably indicate the moment for the ladies' departure.

AFTER-DINNER INVITATIONS MAY BE GIVEN; by which we wish to be understood, invitations for the evening. The time of the arrival of these visitors will vary according to their engagements, or sometimes will be varied in obedience to the caprices of fashion. Guests invited for the evening are, however, generally considered at liberty to arrive whenever it will best suit themselves,—usually between nine and twelve, unless earlier hours are specifically named. By this arrangement, many fashionable people and others, who have numerous engagements to fulfil, often contrive to make their appearance at two or three parties in the course of one evening.

THE ETIQUETTE OF THE DINNER-PARTY TABLE being disposed of, let us now enter slightly into that of an evening party or ball. The invitations issued and accepted for either of these, will be written in the same style as those already described for a dinner-party. They should be sent out *at least* three weeks before the day fixed for the event, and should be replied to within a week of their receipt. By attending to these courtesies, the guests will have time to consider their engagements and prepare their dresses, and the hostess will, also, know what will be the number of her party.

> If the entertainment is to be simply an evening party, this must be specified on the card or note of invitation. Short or verbal invitations, except where persons are exceedingly intimate, or are very near relations, are very far from proper, although, of course, in this respect and in many other respects, very much always depends on the manner in which the invitation is given. True politeness, however, should be studied even amongst the nearest friends and relations; for the mechanical forms of good breeding are of great consequence, and too much familiarity may have, for its effect, the destruction of friendship.

AS THE LADIES AND GENTLEMEN ARRIVE, each should be shown to a room exclusively provided for their reception; and in that set apart for the ladies, attendants should be in waiting to assist in uncloaking, and helping to arrange the hair and toilet of those who require it. It will be found convenient, in those cases where the number of guests is large, to provide numbered tickets, so that they can be attached to the cloaks and shawls of each lady, a duplicate of which should be handed to the guest. Coffee is sometimes provided in this, or an ante-room, for those who would like to partake of it.

AS THE VISITORS ARE ANNOUNCED BY THE SERVANT, it is not necessary for the lady of the house to advance each time towards the door, but merely to rise from her seat to receive their courtesies and congratulations. If, indeed, the hostess wishes to show particular favour to some peculiarly honoured guests, she may introduce them to others, whose acquaintance she may imagine will be especially suitable and agreeable. It is very often the practice of the master of the house to introduce one gentleman to another, but occasionally the lady performs this office; when it will, of course, be polite for the persons thus introduced to take their seats together for the time being.

> The custom of non-introduction is very much in vogue in many houses, and guests are thus left to discover for themselves the position and qualities of the people around them. The servant, indeed, calls out the names of all the visitors as they arrive, but, in many instances, mispronounces them; so that it will not be well to follow this information, as if it were an unerring guide. In our opinion, it is a cheerless and depressing custom, although, in thus speaking, we do not allude to the large assemblies of the aristocracy, but to the smaller parties of the middle classes.

A SEPARATE ROOM OR CONVENIENT BUFFET should be appropriated for refreshments, and to which the dancers may retire; and cakes and biscuits, with wine negus, lemonade, and ices, handed round. A supper is also mostly provided at the private parties of the middle classes; and this requires, on the part of the hostess, a great deal of attention and supervision. It usually takes place between the first and second parts of the programme of the dances, of which there should be several prettily written or printed copies distributed about the ball-room.

WHEN ANY OF THE CARRIAGES OF THE GUESTS ARE ANNOUNCED, or the time for their departure arrived, they should make a slight intimation to the hostess, without, however, exciting any observation, that they are about to depart. If this cannot be done, however, without creating too much bustle, it will be better for the visitors to retire quietly without taking their leave. During the course of the week, the hostess will expect to receive from every guest a call, where it is possible, or cards expressing the gratification experienced from her entertainment. This attention is due to every lady for the pains and trouble she has been at, and tends to promote social, kindly feelings.

HAVING THUS DISCOURSED of parties of pleasure, it will be an interesting change to return to the more domestic business of the house, although all the details we have been giving of dinner-parties, balls, and the like, appertain to the department of the mistress. Without a knowledge of the etiquette to be observed on these occasions, a mistress would be unable to enjoy and appreciate those friendly pleasant meetings which give, as it were, a fillip to life, and make the quiet happy home of an English gentlewoman appear the more delightful and enjoyable. In their proper places, all that is necessary to be known respecting the dishes and appearance of the breakfast, dinner, tea, and supper tables, will be set forth in this work.

A FAMILY DINNER AT HOME, compared with either giving or going to a dinner-party, is, of course, of much more frequent occurrence, and many will say, of much greater importance. Both, however, have to be considered with a view to their nicety and enjoyment; and the latter more particularly with reference to economy. These points will be especially noted in the following pages on "Household Cookery." Here we will only say, that for both mistress and servants, as well in large as small households, it will be found, by far, the better plan, to cook and serve the dinner, and to lay the tablecloth and the sideboard, with the same cleanliness, neatness, and scrupulous exactness, whether it be for the mistress herself alone, a small family, or for "company." If this rule be strictly adhered to, all will find themselves increase in managing skill; whilst a knowledge of their daily duties will become familiar, and enable them to meet difficult occasions with ease, and overcome any amount of obstacles.

OF THE MANNER OF PASSING EVENINGS AT HOME, there is none pleasanter than in such recreative enjoyments as those which relax the mind from its severer duties, whilst they stimulate it with a gentle delight. Where there are young people forming a part of the evening circle, interesting and agreeable pastime should especially be promoted. It is of incalculable benefit to them that their homes should possess all the attractions of healthful amusement, comfort, and happiness; for if they do not find pleasure there, they will seek it elsewhere. It ought, therefore, to enter into the domestic policy of every parent, to make her children feel that home is the happiest place in the world; that to imbue them with this delicious home-feeling is one of the choicest gifts a parent can bestow.

CHAPTER II

THE HOUSEKEEPER

AS SECOND IN COMMAND IN THE HOUSE, except in large establishments, where there is a house steward, the housekeeper must consider herself as the immediate representative of her mistress, and bring, to the management of the household, all those qualities of honesty, industry, and vigilance, in the same degree as if she were at the head of her *own* family. Constantly on the watch to detect any wrong-doing on the part of any of the domestics, she will overlook all that goes on in the house, and will see that every department is thoroughly attended to, and that the servants are comfortable, at the same time that their various duties are properly performed.

> Cleanliness, punctuality, order, and method, are essentials in the character of a good housekeeper. Without the first, no household can be said to be well managed. The second is equally all-important; for those who are under the housekeeper will take their "cue" from her; and in the same proportion as punctuality governs her movements, so will it theirs. Order, again, is indispensable; for by it we wish to be understood that "there should be a place for everything, and everything in its place." Method, too, is most necessary; for when the work is properly contrived, and each part arranged in regular succession, it will be done more quickly and more effectually.

A NECESSARY QUALIFICATION FOR A HOUSEKEEPER is, that she should thoroughly understand accounts. She will have to write in her books an accurate registry of all sums paid for any and every purpose, all the current expenses of the house, tradesmen's bills, and other extraneous matter. As we have mentioned under the head of the Mistress, a housekeeper's accounts should be periodically balanced, and examined by the head of the house. Nothing tends more to the satisfaction of both employer and employed, than this arrangement. "Short reckonings make long friends," stands good in this case, as in others.

It will be found an excellent plan to take an account of every article which comes into the house connected with housekeeping, and is not paid for at the time. The book containing these entries can then be compared with the bills sent in by the various tradesmen, so that any discrepancy can be inquired into and set right. An intelligent housekeeper will, by this means, too, be better able to judge of the average consumption of each article by the household; and if that quantity be, at any time, exceeded, the cause may be discovered and rectified, if it proceed from waste or carelessness.

ALTHOUGH IN THE DEPARTMENT OF THE COOK, the housekeeper does not generally much interfere, yet it is necessary that she should possess a good knowledge of the culinary art, as, in many instances, it may be requisite for her to take the superintendence of the kitchen. As a rule, it may be stated, that the housekeeper, in those establishments where there is no house steward or man cook, undertakes the preparation of the confectionary, attends to the preserving and pickling of fruits and vegetables; and, in a general way, to the more difficult branches of the art of cookery.

> Much of these arrangements will depend, however, on the qualifications of the cook; for instance, if she be an able artiste, there will be but little necessity for the housekeeper to interfere, except in the already noticed articles of confectionary, &c. On the contrary, if the cook be not so clever an adept in her art, then it will be requisite for the housekeeper to give more of her attention to the business of the kitchen, than in the former case. It will be one of the duties of the housekeeper to attend to the marketing, in the absence of either a house steward or man cook.

THE DAILY DUTIES OF A HOUSEKEEPER are regulated, in a great measure, by the extent of the establishment she superintends. She should, however, rise early, and see that all the domestics are duly performing their work, and that everything is progressing satisfactorily for the preparation of the breakfast for the household and family. After breakfast, which, in large establishments, she will take in the "housekeeper's room" with the lady's-maid, butler, and valet, and where they will be waited on by the still-room maid, she will, on various days set apart for each purpose, carefully examine the household linen, with a view to its being repaired, or to a further quantity being put in hand to

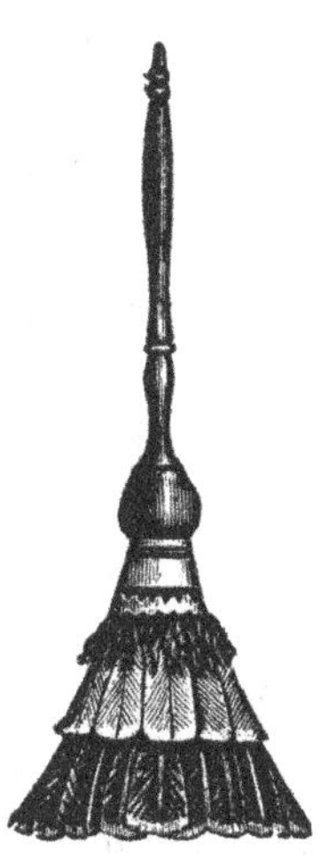

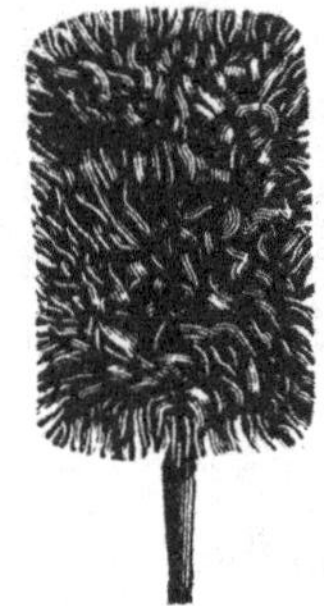

be made; she will also see that the furniture throughout the house is well rubbed and polished; and will, besides, attend to all the necessary details of marketing and ordering goods from the tradesmen.

The housekeeper's room is generally made use of by the lady's-maid, butler, and valet, who take there their breakfast, tea, and supper. The lady's-maid will also use this apartment as a sitting-room, when not engaged with her lady, or with some other duties, which would call her elsewhere. In different establishments, according to their size and the rank of the family, different rules of course prevail. For instance, in the mansions of those of very high rank, and where there is a house steward, there are two distinct tables kept, one in the steward's room for the principal members of the household, the other in the servants' hall, for the other domestics. At the steward's dinner-table, the steward and housekeeper preside; and here, also, are present the lady's-maid, butler, valet, and head gardener. Should any visitors be staying with the family, their servants, generally the valet and lady's-maid, will be admitted to the steward's table.

AFTER DINNER, the housekeeper, having seen that all the members of the establishment have regularly returned to their various duties, and that all the departments of the household are in proper working order, will have many important matters claiming her attention. She will, possibly, have to give the finishing touch to some article of confectionary, or be occupied with some of the more elaborate processes of the still-room. There may also be the dessert to arrange, ice-creams to make; and all these employments call for no ordinary degree of care, taste, and attention.

> The still-room was formerly much more in vogue than at present; for in days of "auld lang syne," the still was in constant requisition for the supply of sweet-flavoured waters for the purposes of cookery, scents and aromatic substances used in the preparation of the toilet, and cordials in cases of accidents and illness. There are some establishments, however, in which distillation is still carried on, and in these, the still-room maid has her old duties to perform. In a general way, however, this domestic is immediately concerned with the housekeeper. For the latter she lights the fire, dusts her room, prepares the breakfast-table, and waits at the different meals taken in the housekeeper's room. A still-room maid may learn a very great deal of useful knowledge from her intimate connection with the housekeeper, and if she be active and intelligent, may soon fit herself for a better position in the household.

IN THE EVENING, the housekeeper will often busy herself with the necessary preparations for the next day's duties. Numberless small, but still important arrangements, will have to be made, so that everything may move smoothly. At times, perhaps, attention will have to be paid to the breaking of lump-sugar, the stoning of raisins, the washing, cleansing,

and drying of currants, &c. The evening, too, is the best time for setting right her account of the expenditure, and duly writing a statement of moneys received and paid, and also for making memoranda of any articles she may require for her storeroom or other departments.

Periodically, at some convenient time,—for instance, quarterly or half-yearly, it is a good plan for the housekeeper to make an inventory of everything she has under her care, and compare this with the lists of a former period; she will then be able to furnish a statement, if necessary, of the articles which, on account of time, breakage, loss, or other causes, it has been necessary to replace or replenish.

IN CONCLUDING THESE REMARKS on the duties of the housekeeper, we will briefly refer to the very great responsibility which attaches to her position. Like "Caesar's wife," she should be "above suspicion," and her honesty and sobriety unquestionable; for there are many temptations to which she is exposed. In a physical point of view, a housekeeper should be healthy and strong, and be particularly clean in her person, and her hands, although they may show a degree of roughness, from the nature of some of her employments, yet should have a nice inviting appearance. In her dealings with the various tradesmen, and in her behaviour to the domestics under her, the demeanour and conduct of the housekeeper should be such as, in neither case, to diminish, by an undue familiarity, her authority or influence.

Note—It will be useful for the mistress and housekeeper to know the best seasons for various occupations connected with Household Management; and we, accordingly, subjoin a few hints which we think will prove valuable.

CHAPTER III

ARRANGEMENT AND ECONOMY OF THE KITCHEN

"THE DISTRIBUTION OF A KITCHEN," says Count Rumford, the celebrated philosopher and physician, who wrote so learnedly on all subjects connected with domestic economy and architecture, "must always depend so much on local circumstances, that general rules can hardly be given respecting it; the principles, however, on which this distribution ought, in all cases, to be made, are simple and easy to be understood," and, in his estimation, these resolve themselves into symmetry of proportion in the building and convenience to the cook. The requisites of a good kitchen, however, demand something more special than is here pointed out. It must be remembered that it is the great laboratory of every household, and that much of the "weal or woe," as far as regards bodily health, depends upon the nature of the preparations concocted within its walls. A good kitchen, therefore, should be erected with a view to the following particulars. 1. Convenience of distribution in its parts, with largeness of dimension. 2. Excellence of light, height of ceiling, and good ventilation. 3. Easiness of access, without passing through the house. 4. Sufficiently remote from the principal apartments of the house, that the members, visitors, or guests of the family, may not perceive the odour incident to cooking, or hear the noise of culinary operations. 5. Plenty of fuel and water, which, with the scullery, pantry, and storeroom, should be so near it, as to offer the smallest possible trouble in reaching them.

THE SIMPLICITY OF THE PRIMITIVE AGES has frequently been an object of poetical admiration, and it delights the imagination to picture men living upon such fruits as spring spontaneously from the earth, and desiring no other beverages to slake their thirst, but such as fountains and rivers supply. Thus we are told, that the ancient inhabitants of Argos lived principally on pears; that the Arcadians revelled in acorns, and the Athenians in figs. This, of course, was in the golden age, before ploughing began, and when mankind enjoyed all kinds of plenty without having to earn their bread "by the sweat of their brow." This delightful period, however, could not last for ever, and the earth became barren, and continued unfruitful till Ceres came and taught the art of sowing, with several other useful inventions. The first whom she taught to till the ground was Triptolemus, who communicated his instructions to his countrymen the Athenians. Thence the art was carried into Achaia, and thence into Arcadia. Barley was the first grain that was used, and the invention of bread-making is ascribed to Pan.

> The use of fire, as an instrument of cookery, must have been coeval with this invention of bread, which, being the most necessary of all kinds of food, was frequently used in a sense so comprehensive as to include both meat and drink. It was, by the Greeks, baked under the ashes.

IN THE PRIMARY AGES it was deemed unlawful to eat flesh, and when mankind began to depart from their primitive habits, the flesh of swine was the first that was eaten. For several ages, it was pronounced unlawful to slaughter oxen, from an estimate of their great value in assisting men to cultivate the ground; nor was it usual to kill young animals, from a sentiment which considered it cruel to take away the life of those that had scarcely tasted the joys of existence.

> At this period no cooks were kept, and we know from Homer that his ancient heroes prepared and dressed their

> victuals with their own hands. Ulysses, for example, we are told, like a modern charwoman, excelled at lighting a fire, whilst Achilles was an adept at turning a spit. Subsequently, heralds, employed in civil and military affairs, filled the office of cooks, and managed marriage feasts; but this, no doubt, was after mankind had advanced in the art of living, a step further than *roasting*, which, in all places, was the ancient manner of dressing meat.

FROM KITCHEN RANGES to the implements used in cookery is but a step. With these, every kitchen should be well supplied, otherwise the cook must not be expected to "perform her office" in a satisfactory manner. Of the culinary utensils of the ancients, our knowledge is very limited; but as the art of living, in every civilized country, is pretty much the same, the instruments for cooking must, in a great degree, bear a striking resemblance to each other. On referring to classical antiquities, we find mentioned, among household utensils, leather bags, baskets constructed of twigs, reeds, and rushes; boxes, basins, and bellows; bread-moulds, brooms, and brushes; caldrons, colanders, cisterns, and chafing-dishes; cheese-rasps, knives, and ovens of the Dutch kind; funnels and frying-pans; handmills, soup-ladles, milk-pails, and oil-jars; presses, scales, and sieves; spits of different sizes, but some of them large enough to roast an ox; spoons, fire-tongs, trays, trenchers, and drinking-vessels; with others for carrying food, preserving milk, and holding cheese. This enumeration, if it does nothing else, will, to some extent, indicate the state of the simpler kinds of mechanical arts among the ancients.

IN THE MANUFACTURE OF THESE UTENSILS, bronze metal seems to have been much in favour with the ancients. It was chosen not only for their domestic vessels, but it was also much used for their public sculptures and medals. It is a compound, composed of from six to twelve parts of tin to one hundred of copper. It gives its name to figures and all pieces of sculpture made of it. Brass was another favourite metal, which is composed of copper and zinc. It is more fusible than copper, and not so apt to tarnish. In a pure state it is not malleable, unless when hot, and after it has been melted twice it will not bear the hammer. To render it capable of being wrought, it requires 7 lb. of lead to be put to 1 cwt. of its own material.

> The Corinthian brass of antiquity was a mixture of silver, gold, and copper. A fine kind of brass, supposed to be made by the cementation of copper plates with calamine, is, in Germany, hammered out into leaves, and is called Dutch metal in this country. It is employed in the same way as gold leaf. Brass is much used for watchworks, as well as for wire.

The braziers, ladles, stewpans, saucepans, gridirons, and colanders of antiquity might generally pass for those of the English manufacture of the present day, in so far as shape is concerned. In proof of this we have placed together the following similar articles of ancient and modern pattern, in order that the reader may, at a single view, see wherein any difference that is between them, consists.

AMONGST THE MOST ESSENTIAL REQUIREMENTS of the kitchen are scales or weighing-machines for family use. These are found to have existed among the ancients, and must, at a very early age, have been both publicly and privately employed for the regulation of quantities. The modern English weights were adjusted by the 27th chapter of Magna Charta, or the great charter forced, by the barons, from King John at Runnymede, in Surrey. Therein it is declared that the weights, all over England, shall be the same, although for different commodities there were

two different kinds, Troy and Avoirdupois. The origin of both is taken from a grain of wheat gathered in the middle of an ear. The standard of measures was originally kept at Winchester, and by a law of King Edgar was ordained to be observed throughout the kingdom.

WITHOUT FUEL, A KITCHEN might be pronounced to be of little use; therefore, to discover and invent materials for supplying us with the means of domestic heat and comfort, has exercised the ingenuity of man. Those now known have been divided into five classes; the first comprehending the fluid inflammable bodies; the second, peat or turf; the third, charcoal of wood; the fourth, pit-coal charred; and the fifth, wood or pit-coal in a crude state, with the capacity of yielding a copious and bright flame. The first may be said seldom to be employed for the purposes of cookery; but *peat*, especially amongst rural populations, has, in all ages, been regarded as an excellent fuel. It is one of the most important productions of an alluvial soil, and belongs to the vegetable rather than the mineral kingdom. It may be described as composed of wet, spongy black earth, held together by decayed vegetables. Formerly it covered extensive tracts in England, but has greatly disappeared before the genius of agricultural improvement. *Charcoal* is a kind of artificial coal, used principally where a strong and clear fire is desired. It is a black, brittle, insoluble, inodorous, tasteless substance, and, when newly-made, possesses the remarkable property of absorbing certain quantities of the different gases. Its dust, when used as a polishing powder, gives great brilliancy to metals. It consists of wood half-burned, and is manufactured by cutting pieces of timber into nearly the same size, then disposing them in heaps, and covering them with earth, so as to prevent communication with the air, except when necessary to make them burn. When they have been sufficiently charred, the fire is extinguished by stopping the vents through which the air is admitted. Of *coal* there are various species; as, pit, culm, slate, cannel, Kilkenny, sulphurous, bovey, jet, &c. These have all their specific differences, and are employed for various purposes; but are all, more or less, used as fuel.

TIMES WHEN THINGS ARE IN SEASON.

JANUARY

Fish—Barbel, brill, carp, cod, crabs, crayfish, dace, eels, flounders, haddocks, herrings, lampreys, lobsters, mussels, oysters, perch, pike, plaice, prawns, shrimps, skate, smelts, soles, sprats, sturgeon, tench, thornback, turbot, whitings.

Meat—Beef, house lamb, mutton, pork, veal, venison.

Poultry—Capons, fowls, tame pigeons, pullets, rabbits, turkeys.

Game—Grouse, hares, partridges, pheasants, snipe, wild-fowl, woodcock.

Vegetables—Beetroot, broccoli, cabbages, carrots, celery, chervil, cresses, cucumbers (forced), endive, lettuces, parsnips, potatoes, savoys, spinach, turnips,—various herbs.

Fruit—Apples, grapes, medlars, nuts, oranges, pears, walnuts, crystallized preserves (foreign), dried fruits, such as almonds and raisins; French and Spanish plums; prunes, figs, dates.

FEBRUARY

Fish—Barbel, brill, carp, cod may be bought, but is not so good as in January, crabs, crayfish, dace, eels, flounders, haddocks, herrings, lampreys, lobsters, mussels, oysters, perch, pike, plaice, prawns, shrimps, skate, smelts, soles, sprats, sturgeon, tench, thornback, turbot, whiting.

Meat—Beef, house lamb, mutton, pork, veal.

Poultry—Capons, chickens, ducklings, tame and wild pigeons, pullets with eggs, turkeys, wild-fowl, though now not in full season.

Game—Grouse, hares, partridges, pheasants, snipes, woodcock.

Vegetables—Beetroot, broccoli (purple and white), Brussels sprouts, cabbages, carrots, celery, chervil, cresses, cucumbers (forced), endive, kidney-beans, lettuces, parsnips, potatoes, savoys, spinach, turnips,—various herbs.

Fruit—Apples (golden and Dutch pippins), grapes, medlars, nuts, oranges, pears (Bon Chrétien), walnuts, dried fruits (foreign), such as almonds and raisins; French and Spanish plums; prunes, figs, dates, crystallized preserves.

MARCH

Fish—Barbel, brill, carp, crabs, crayfish, dace, eels, flounders, haddocks, herrings, lampreys, lobsters, mussels, oysters, perch, pike, plaice, prawns, shrimps, skate, smelts, soles, sprats, sturgeon, tench, thornback, turbot, whiting.

Meat—Beef, house lamb, mutton, pork, veal.

Poultry—Capons, chickens, ducklings, tame and wild pigeons, pullets with eggs, turkeys, wild-fowl, though now not in full season.

Game—Grouse, hares, partridges, pheasants, snipes, woodcock.

Vegetables—Beetroot, broccoli (purple and white), Brussels sprouts, cabbages, carrots, celery, chervil, cresses, cucumbers (forced), endive, kidney-beans, lettuces, parsnips, potatoes, savoys, sea-kale, spinach, turnips,—various herbs.

Fruit—Apples (golden and Dutch pippins), grapes, medlars, nuts, oranges, pears (Bon Chrétien), walnuts, dried fruits (foreign), such as almonds and raisins; French and Spanish plums; prunes, figs, dates, crystallized preserves.

APRIL

Fish—Brill, carp, cockles, crabs, dory, flounders, ling, lobsters, red and gray mullet, mussels, oysters, perch, prawns, salmon (but rather scarce and expensive), shad, shrimps, skate, smelts, soles, tench, turbot, whitings.

Meat—Beef, lamb, mutton, veal.

Poultry—Chickens, ducklings, fowls, leverets, pigeons, pullets, rabbits.

Game—Hares.

Vegetables—Broccoli, celery, lettuces, young onions, parsnips, radishes, small salad, sea-kale, spinach, sprouts,—various herbs.

Fruit—Apples, nuts, pears, forced cherries, &c. for tarts, rhubarb, dried fruits, crystallized preserves.

MAY

Fish—Carp, chub, crabs, crayfish, dory, herrings, lobsters, mackerel, red and gray mullet, prawns, salmon, shad, smelts, soles, trout, turbot.

Meat—Beef, lamb, mutton, veal.

Poultry—Chickens, ducklings, fowls, green geese, leverets, pullets, rabbits.

Vegetables—Asparagus, beans, early cabbages, carrots, cauliflowers, creases, cucumbers, lettuces, pease, early potatoes, salads, sea-kale,—various herbs.

Fruit—Apples, green apricots, cherries, currants for tarts, gooseberries, melons, pears, rhubarb, strawberries.

JUNE

Fish—Carp, crayfish, herrings, lobsters, mackerel, mullet, pike, prawns, salmon, soles, tench, trout, turbot.

Meat—Beef, lamb, mutton, veal, buck venison.

Poultry—Chickens, ducklings, fowls, green geese, leverets, plovers, pullets, rabbits, turkey poults, wheatears.

Vegetables—Artichokes, asparagus, beans, cabbages, carrots, cucumbers, lettuces, onions, parsnips, pease, potatoes, radishes, small salads, sea-kale, spinach,—various herbs.

Fruit—Apricots, cherries, currants, gooseberries, melons, nectarines, peaches, pears, pineapples, raspberries, rhubarb, strawberries.

JULY

Fish—Carp, crayfish, dory, flounders, haddocks, herrings, lobsters, mackerel, mullet, pike, plaice, prawns, salmon, shrimps, soles, sturgeon, tench, thornback.

Meat—Beef, lamb, mutton, veal, buck venison.

Poultry—Chickens, ducklings, fowls, green geese, leverets, plovers, pullets, rabbits, turkey poults, wheatears, wild ducks (called flappers).

Vegetables—Artichokes, asparagus, beans, cabbages, carrots, cauliflowers, celery, cresses, endive, lettuces, mushrooms, onions, pease, radishes, small salading, sea-kale, sprouts, turnips, vegetable marrow,—various herbs.

Fruit—Apricots, cherries, currants, figs, gooseberries, melons, nectarines, pears, pineapples, plums, raspberries, strawberries, walnuts in high season, and pickled.

AUGUST

Fish—Brill, carp, chub, crayfish, crabs, dory, eels, flounders, grigs, herrings, lobsters, mullet, pike, prawns, salmon, shrimps, skate, soles, sturgeon, thornback, trout, turbot.

Meat—Beef, lamb, mutton, veal, buck venison.

Poultry—Chickens, ducklings, fowls, green geese, pigeons, plovers, pullets, rabbits, turkey poults, wheatears, wild ducks.

Game—Leverets, grouse, blackcock.

Vegetables—Artichokes, asparagus, beans, carrots, cabbages, cauliflowers, celery, cresses, endive, lettuces, mushrooms, onions, pease, potatoes, radishes, sea-bale, small salading, sprouts, turnips, various kitchen herbs, vegetable marrows.

Fruit—Currants, figs, filberts, gooseberries, grapes, melons, mulberries, nectarines, peaches, pears, pineapples, plums, raspberries, walnuts.

SEPTEMBER

Fish—Brill, carp, cod, eels, flounders, lobsters, mullet, oysters, plaice, prawns, skate, soles, turbot, whiting, whitebait.

Meat—Beef, lamb, mutton, pork, veal.

Poultry—Chickens, ducks, fowls, geese, larks, pigeons, pullets, rabbits, teal, turkeys.

Game—Blackcock, buck venison, grouse, hares, partridges, pheasants.

Vegetables—Artichokes, asparagus, beans, cabbage sprouts, carrots, celery, lettuces, mushrooms, onions, pease, potatoes, salading, sea-kale, sprouts, tomatoes, turnips, vegetable marrows,—various herbs.

Fruit—Bullaces, damsons, figs, filberts, grapes, melons, morella-cherries, mulberries, nectarines, peaches, pears, plums, quinces, walnuts.

OCTOBER

Fish—Barbel, brill, cod, crabs, eels, flounders, gudgeons, haddocks, lobsters, mullet, oysters, plaice, prawns, skate, soles, tench, turbot, whiting.

Meat—Beef, mutton, pork, veal, venison.

Poultry—Chickens, fowls, geese, larks, pigeons, pullets, rabbits, teal, turkeys, widgeons, wild ducks.

Game—Blackcock, grouse, hares, partridges, pheasants, snipes, woodcocks, doe venison.

Vegetables—Artichokes, beets, cabbages, cauliflowers, carrots, celery, lettuces, mushrooms, onions, potatoes, sprouts, tomatoes, turnips, vegetable marrows,—various herbs.

Fruit—Apples, black and white bullaces, damsons, figs, filberts, grapes, pears, quinces, walnuts.

NOVEMBER

Fish—Brill, carp, cod, crabs, eels, gudgeons, haddocks, oysters, pike, soles, tench, turbot, whiting.

Meat—Beef, mutton, veal, doe venison.

Poultry—Chickens, fowls, geese, larks, pigeons, pullets, rabbits, teal, turkeys, widgeons, wild duck.

Game—Hares, partridges, pheasants, snipes, woodcocks.

Vegetables—Beetroot, cabbages, carrots, celery, lettuces, late cucumbers, onions, potatoes, salading, spinach, sprouts,—various herbs.

Fruit—Apples, bullaces, chestnuts, filberts, grapes, pears, walnuts.

DECEMBER

Fish—Barbel, brill, carp, cod, crabs, eels, dace, gudgeons, haddocks, herrings, lobsters, oysters, porch, pike, shrimps, skate, sprats, soles, tench, thornback, turbot, whiting.

Meat—Beef, house lamb, mutton, pork, venison.

Poultry—Capons, chickens, fowls, geese, pigeons, pullets, rabbits, teal, turkeys, widgeons, wild ducks.

Game—Hares, partridges, pheasants, snipes, woodcocks.

Vegetables—Broccoli, cabbages, carrots, celery, leeks, onions, potatoes, parsnips, Scotch kale, turnips, winter spinach.

Fruit—Apples, chestnuts, filberts, grapes, medlars, oranges, pears, walnuts, dried fruits, such as almonds and raisins, figs, dates, &c.,—crystallized preserves.

CHAPTER IV

INTRODUCTION TO COOKERY

AS IN THE FINE ARTS, the progress of mankind from barbarism to civilization is marked by a gradual succession of triumphs over the rude materialities of nature, so in the art of cookery is the progress gradual from the earliest and simplest modes, to those of the most complicated and refined. Plain or rudely-carved stones, tumuli, or mounds of earth, are the monuments by which barbarous tribes denote the events of their history, to be succeeded, only in the long course of a series of ages, by beautifully-proportioned columns, gracefully-sculptured statues, triumphal arches, coins, medals, and the higher efforts of the pencil and the pen, as man advances by culture and observation to the perfection of his facilities. So is it with the art of cookery. Man, in his primitive state, lives upon roots and the fruits of the earth, until, by degrees, he is driven to seek for new means, by which his wants may be supplied and enlarged. He then becomes a hunter and a fisher. As his species increases, greater necessities come upon him, when he gradually abandons the roving life of the savage for the more stationary pursuits of the herdsman. These beget still more settled habits, when he begins the practice of agriculture, forms ideas of the rights of property, and has his own, both defined and secured. The forest, the stream, and the sea are now no longer his only resources for food. He sows and he reaps, pastures and breeds cattle, lives on the cultivated produce of his fields, and revels in the luxuries of the dairy; raises flocks for clothing, and assumes, to all intents and purposes, the habits of permanent life and the comfortable condition of a farmer. This is the fourth stage of social progress, up to which the useful or mechanical arts have been incidentally developing themselves, when trade and commerce begin. Through these various phases, *only to live* has been the great object of mankind; but, by-and-by, comforts are multiplied, and accumulating riches create new wants. The object, then, is not only to *live*, but to live economically, agreeably, tastefully, and well. Accordingly, the art of cookery commences; and although the fruits of the earth, the fowls of the air, the beasts of the field, and the fish of the sea, are still the only food of mankind, yet these are so prepared, improved, and dressed by skill and ingenuity, that they are the means of immeasurably extending the boundaries of human enjoyments. Everything that is edible, and passes under the hands of the cook, is more or less changed, and assumes new forms. Hence the influence of that functionary is immense upon the happiness of a household.

In order that the duties of the Cook may be properly performed, and that he may be able to reproduce esteemed dishes with certainty, all terms of

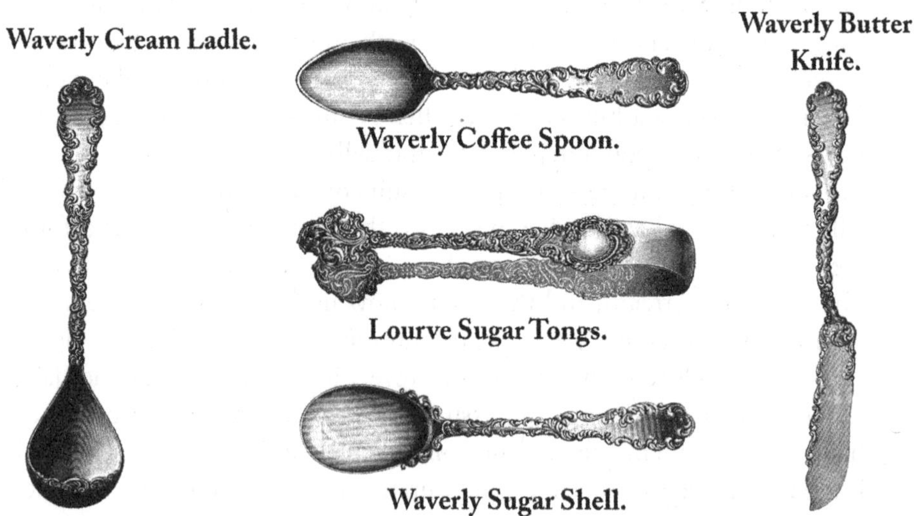

Waverly Cream Ladle.

Waverly Coffee Spoon.

Waverly Butter Knife.

Lourve Sugar Tongs.

Waverly Sugar Shell.

indecision should be banished from his art. Accordingly, what is known only to him, will, in these pages, be made known to others. In them all those indecisive terms expressed by a bit of this, some of that, a small piece of that, and a handful of the other, shall never be made use of, but all quantities be precisely and explicitly stated. With a desire, also, that all ignorance on this most essential part of the culinary art should disappear, and that a uniform system of weights and measures should be adopted, we give an account of the weights which answer to certain measures.

A TABLE-SPOONFUL is frequently mentioned in a recipe, in the prescriptions of medical men, and also in medical, chemical, and gastronomical works. By it is generally meant and understood a measure or bulk equal to that which would be produced by *half an ounce* of water.

A DESSERT-SPOONFUL is the half of a table-spoonful; that is to say, by it is meant a measure or bulk equal to a *quarter of an ounce* of water.

A TEA-SPOONFUL is equal in quantity to a *drachm* of water.

A DROP—This is the name of a vague kind of measure, and is so called on account of the liquid being *dropped* from the mouth of a bottle. Its quantity, however, will vary, either from the consistency of the liquid or the size and shape of the mouth of the bottle. The College of Physicians determined the quantity of a drop to be *one grain*, 60 drops making one fluid drachm. Their drop, or sixtieth part of a fluid drachm, is called a *minim*.

THE DUTIES OF THE COOK, THE KITCHEN AND THE SCULLERY MAIDS, are so intimately associated, that they can hardly be treated of separately. The cook, however, is at the head of the kitchen; and in proportion to her possession of the qualities of cleanliness, neatness, order, regularity, and celerity of action, so will her influence appear in the conduct of those who are under her; as it is upon her that the whole responsibility of the business of the kitchen rests, whilst the others must lend her, both a ready and a willing assistance, and be especially tidy in their appearance, and active, in their movements.

> In the larger establishments of the middle ages, cooks, with the authority of feudal chiefs, gave their orders from a high chair in which they ensconced themselves, and commanded a view of all that was going on throughout their several domains. Each held a long wooden spoon, with which he tasted, without leaving his seat, the various comestibles that were cooking on the stoves, and which he frequently used as a rod of punishment on the backs of those whose idleness and gluttony too largely predominated over their diligence and temperance.

HER FIRST DUTY, in large establishments and where it is requisite, should be to set her dough for the breakfast rolls, provided this has not been done on the previous night, and then to engage herself with those numerous little preliminary occupations which may not inappropriately be termed laying out her duties for the day. This will bring in the breakfast hour of eight, after which, directions must be given, and preparations made, for the different dinners of the household and family.

BY THE TIME THAT THE COOK has performed the duties mentioned above, and well swept, brushed, and dusted her kitchen, the breakfast-bell will most likely summon her to the parlour, to "bring in" the breakfast. It is the cook's department, generally, in the smaller establishments, to wait at breakfast, as the housemaid, by this time, has gone up-stairs into the bedrooms, and has there applied herself to her various duties. The cook usually answers the bells and single knocks at the door in the early part of the morning, as the tradesmen, with whom it is her more special business to speak, call at these hours.

IT IS IN HER PREPARATION OF THE DINNER that the cook begins to feel the weight and responsibility of her situation, as she must take upon herself all the dressing and the serving of the principal dishes, which her skill and ingenuity have mostly prepared. Whilst these, however, are cooking, she must be busy with her pastry, soups, gravies, ragouts, &c. Stock, or what the French call *consommé*, being the basis of most made dishes, must be always at hand, in conjunction with her sweet herbs and spices for seasoning. "A place for everything, and everything in its place," must be her rule, in order that time may not be wasted in looking for things when they are wanted, and in order that the whole apparatus of cooking may move with the regularity and precision of a well-adjusted machine;—all must go on simultaneously. The vegetables and sauces must be ready with the dishes they are to accompany, and in order that they may be suitable, the smallest oversight must not be made in their preparation. When the dinner-hour has arrived, it is the duty of the cook to dish-up such dishes as may, without injury, stand, for some time, covered on the hot plate or in the hot closet; but such as are of a more important or *recherché* kind, must be delayed until the order "to serve" is given from the drawing-room. Then comes haste; but there must be no hurry,—all must work with order. The cook takes charge of the fish, soups, and poultry; and the kitchen-maid of the vegetables, sauces, and gravies. These she puts into their appropriate dishes, whilst the scullery-maid waits on and assists the cook. Everything must be timed so as to prevent its getting cold, whilst great care should be taken, that, between the first and second courses, no more time is allowed to elapse than is necessary, for fear that the company in the dining-room lose all relish for what has yet to come of the dinner. When the dinner has been served, the most important feature in the daily life of the cook is at an end. She must, however, now begin to look to the contents of her larder, taking care to keep everything sweet and clean, so that no disagreeable smells may arise from the gravies, milk, or meat that may be there. These are the principal duties of a cook in a first-rate establishment.

WHILST THE COOK IS ENGAGED WITH HER MORNING DUTIES, the kitchen-maid is also occupied with hers. Her first duty, after the fire is lighted, is to sweep and clean the kitchen, and the various offices belonging to it. This she does every morning, besides cleaning the stone steps at the entrance of the house, the halls, the passages, and the stairs which lead to the kitchen. Her general duties, besides these, are to wash and scour all these places twice a week, with the tables, shelves, and cupboards. She has also to dress the nursery and servants'-hall dinners, to prepare all fish, poultry, and vegetables, trim meat joints and cutlets, and do all such duties as may be considered to enter into the cook's department in a subordinate degree.

MODERN COOKERY stands so greatly indebted to the gastronomic propensities of our French neighbours, that many of their terms are adopted and applied by English artists to the same as well as similar preparations of their own. A vocabulary of these is, therefore, indispensable in a work of this kind. Accordingly, the following will be found sufficiently complete for all ordinary purposes:—

EXPLANATION OF FRENCH TERMS USED IN MODERN HOUSEHOLD COOKERY.

Aspic—A savoury jelly, used as an exterior moulding for cold game, poultry, fish, &c. This, being of a transparent nature, allows the bird which

it covers to be seen through it. This may also be used for decorating or garnishing.

Assiette (plate)—*Assiettes* are the small *entrées* and *hors-d'oeuvres*, the quantity of which does not exceed what a plate will hold. At dessert, fruits, cheese, chestnuts, biscuits, &c., if served upon a plate, are termed *assiettes*—ASSIETTE VOLANTE is a dish which a servant hands round to the guests, but is not placed upon the table. Small cheese soufflés and different dishes, which ought to be served very hot, are frequently made*assielles volantes*.

Au-Bleu—Fish dressed in such a manner as to have a *bluish* appearance.

Bain-Marie—An open saucepan or kettle of nearly boiling water, in which a smaller vessel can be set for cooking and warming. This is very useful for keeping articles hot, without altering their quantity or quality. If you keep sauce, broth, or soup by the fireside, the soup reduces and becomes too strong, and the sauce thickens as well as reduces; but this is prevented by using the *bain-marie*, in which the water should be very hot, but not boiling.

Béchamel—French white sauce, now frequently used in English cookery.

Blanch—To whiten poultry, vegetables, fruit, &c., by plunging them into boiling water for a short time, and afterwards plunging them into cold water, there to remain until they are cold.

Blanquette—A sort of fricassee.

Bouilli—Beef or other meat boiled; but, generally speaking, boiled beef is understood by the term.

Bouillie—A French dish resembling hasty-pudding.

Bouillon—A thin broth or soup.

Braise—To stew meat with fat bacon until it is tender, it having previously been blanched.

Braisière—A saucepan having a lid with ledges, to put fire on the top.

Brider—To pass a packthread through poultry, game, &c., to keep together their members.

Caramel (burnt sugar)—This is made with a piece of sugar, of the size of a nut, browned in the bottom of a saucepan; upon which a cupful of stock is gradually poured, stirring all the time a glass of broth, little by little. It may be used with the feather of a quill, to colour meats, such as the upper part of fricandeaux; and to impart colour to sauces. Caramel made with water instead of stock may be used to colour *compôtes* and other*entremets.*

Casserole—A crust of rice, which, after having been moulded into the form of a pie, is baked, and then filled with a fricassee of white meat or a purée of game.

Compote—A stew, as of fruit or pigeons.

Consommé—Rich stock, or gravy.

Croquette—Ball of fried rice or potatoes.

Croutons—Sippets of bread.

Daubière—An oval stewpan, in which *daubes* are cooked; *daubes* being meat or fowl stewed in sauce.

Désosser—To *bone*, or take out the bones from poultry, game, or fish. This is an operation requiring considerable experience.

Entrées—Small side or corner dishes, served with the first course.

Entremets—Small side or corner dishes, served with the second course.

Escalopes—Collops; small, round, thin pieces of tender meat, or of fish, beaten with the handle of a strong knife to make them tender.

Feuilletage—Puff-paste.

Flamber—To singe fowl or game, after they have been picked.

Foncer—To put in the bottom of a saucepan slices of ham, veal, or thin broad slices of bacon.

Galette—A broad thin cake.

Gâteau—A cake, correctly speaking; but used sometimes to denote a pudding and a kind of tart.

Glacer—To glaze, or spread upon hot meats, or larded fowl, a thick and rich sauce or gravy, called *glaze.* This is laid on with a feather or brush, and in confectionary the term means to ice fruits and pastry with sugar, which glistens on hardening.

Hors-D'oeuvres—Small dishes, or *assiettes volantes* of sardines, anchovies, and other relishes of this kind, served to the guests during the first course. (*See* ASSIETTES VOLANTES.)

Lit—A bed or layer; articles in thin slices are placed in layers, other articles, or seasoning, being laid between them.

Maigre—Broth, soup, or gravy, made without meat.

Matelote—A rich fish-stew, which is generally composed of carp, eels, trout, or barbel. It is made with wine.

Mayonnaise—Cold sauce, or salad dressing.

Meringue—A kind of icing, made of whites of eggs and sugar, well beaten.

Miroton—Larger slices of meat than collops; such as slices of beef for a vinaigrette, or ragout or stew of onions.

Mouiller—To add water, broth, or other liquid, during the cooking.

Paner—To cover over with very fine crumbs of bread, meats, or any other articles to be cooked on the gridiron, in the oven, or frying-pan.

Piquer—To lard with strips of fat bacon, poultry, game, meat, &c. This should always be done according to the vein of the meat, so that in carving you slice the bacon across as well as the meat.

Poêlée—Stock used instead of water for boiling turkeys, sweetbreads, fowls, and vegetables, to render them less insipid. This is rather an expensive preparation.

Purée—Vegetables, or meat reduced to a very smooth pulp, which is afterwards mixed with enough liquid to make it of the consistency of very thick soup.

Ragout—Stew or hash.

Remoulade—Salad dressing.

Rissoles—Pastry, made of light puff-paste, and cut into various forms, and fried. They may be filled with fish, meat, or sweets.

Roux—Brown and white; French thickening.

Salmi—Ragout of game previously roasted.

Sauce Piquante—A sharp sauce, in which somewhat of a vinegar flavour predominates.

Sauter—To dress with sauce in a saucepan, repeatedly moving it about.

Tamis—Tammy, a sort of open cloth or sieve through which to strain broth and sauces, so as to rid them of small bones, froth, &c.

Tourte—Tart. Fruit pie.

Trousser—To truss a bird; to put together the body and tie the wings and thighs, in order to round it for roasting or boiling, each being tied then with packthread, to keep it in the required form.

Vol-Au-Vent—A rich crust of very fine puff-paste, which may be filled with various delicate ragouts or fricassees, of fish, flesh, or fowl. Fruit may also be inclosed in a *vol-au-vent*.

CHAPTER V

GENERAL DIRECTIONS FOR MAKING SOUPS

LEAN, JUICY BEEF, MUTTON, AND VEAL, form the basis of all good soups; therefore it is advisable to procure those pieces which afford the richest succulence, and such as are fresh-killed. Stale meat renders them bad, and fat is not so well adapted for making them. The principal art in composing good rich soup, is so to proportion the several ingredients that the flavour of one shall not predominate over another, and that all the articles of which it is composed, shall form an agreeable whole. To accomplish this, care must be taken that the roots and herbs are perfectly well cleaned, and that the water is proportioned to the quantity of meat and other ingredients. Generally a quart of water may be allowed to a pound of meat for soups, and half the quantity for gravies. In making soups or gravies, gentle stewing or simmering is incomparably the best. It may be remarked, however, that a really good soup can never be made but in a well-closed vessel, although, perhaps, greater wholesomeness is obtained by an occasional exposure to the air. Soups will, in general, take from three to six hours doing, and are much better prepared the day before they are wanted. When the soup is cold, the fat may be much more easily and completely removed; and when it is poured off, care must be taken not to disturb the settlings at the bottom of the vessel, which are so fine that they will escape through a sieve. A tamis is the best strainer, and if the soup is strained while it is hot, let the tamis or cloth be previously soaked in cold water. Clear soups must be perfectly transparent, and thickened soups about the consistence of cream. To thicken and give body to soups and gravies, potato-mucilage, arrow-root, bread-raspings, isinglass, flour and butter, barley, rice, or oatmeal, in a little water rubbed well together, are used. A piece of boiled beef pounded to a pulp, with a bit of butter and flour, and rubbed through a sieve, and gradually incorporated with the soup, will be found an excellent addition. When the soup appears to be *too thin* or *too weak*, the cover of the boiler should be taken off, and the contents allowed to boil till some of the watery parts have evaporated; or some of the thickening materials, above mentioned, should be added. When soups and gravies are kept from day to day in hot weather, they should be warmed up every day, and put into fresh scalded pans or tureens, and placed in a cool cellar. In temperate weather, every other day may be sufficient.

VARIOUS HERBS AND VEGETABLES are required for the purpose of making soups and gravies. Of these the principal are,—Scotch barley, pearl barley, wheat flour, oatmeal, bread-raspings, pease, beans, rice, vermicelli, macaroni, isinglass, potato-mucilage, mushroom or mushroom ketchup, champignons, parsnips, carrots, beetroot, turnips, garlic, shalots, and onions. Sliced onions, fried with butter and flour till they are browned, and then rubbed through a sieve, are excellent to heighten the colour and flavour of brown soups and sauces, and form the basis of many of the fine relishes furnished by the cook. The older and drier the onion, the stronger will be its flavour. Leeks, cucumber, or burnet vinegar; celery or celery-seed pounded. The latter, though equally strong, does not impart the delicate sweetness of the fresh vegetable; and when used as a substitute, its flavour should be corrected by the addition of a bit of sugar. Cress-seed, parsley, common thyme, lemon thyme, orange thyme, knotted marjoram, sage, mint, winter savoury, and basil. As fresh green basil is seldom to be procured, and its fine flavour is soon lost, the best way of preserving the extract is by pouring wine on the fresh leaves.

FOR THE SEASONING OF SOUPS, bay-leaves, tomato, tarragon, chervil, burnet, allspice, cinnamon, ginger, nutmeg, clove, mace, black and white pepper, essence of anchovy, lemon-peel, and juice, and Seville orange-juice, are all taken. The latter imparts a finer flavour than the lemon, and the acid is much milder. These materials, with wine, mushroom ketchup, Harvey's sauce, tomato sauce, combined in various proportions, are, with other ingredients, manipulated into an almost endless variety of excellent soups and gravies. Soups, which are intended to constitute the principal part of a meal, certainly ought not to be flavoured like sauces, which are only designed to give a relish to some particular dish.

SOUP, BROTH AND BOUILLON

IT HAS BEEN ASSERTED, that English cookery is, nationally speaking, far from being the best in the world. More than this, we have been frequently told by brilliant foreign writers, half philosophers, half *chefs*, that we are the *worst* cooks on the face of the earth, and that the proverb which alludes to the divine origin of food, and the precisely opposite origin of its preparers, is peculiarly applicable to us islanders. Not, however, to the inhabitants of the whole island; for, it is stated in a work which treats of culinary operations, north of the Tweed, that the "broth" of Scotland claims, for excellence and wholesomeness, a very close second place to the *bouillon*, or common soup of France. "*Three* hot meals of broth and meat, for about the price of ONE roasting joint," our Scottish brothers and sisters get, they say; and we hasten to assent to what we think is now a very well-ascertained fact. We are glad to note, however, that soups of vegetables, fish, meat, and game, are now very frequently found in the homes of the English middle classes, as well as in the mansions of the wealthier and more aristocratic; and we take this to be one evidence, that we are on the right road to an improvement in our system of cookery. One great cause of many of the spoilt dishes and badly-cooked meats which are brought to our tables, arises, we think, and most will agree with us, from a non-acquaintance with "common, every-day things." Entertaining this view, we intend to preface the chapters of this work with a simple scientific *résumé* of all those causes and circumstances which relate to the food we have to prepare, and the theory and chemistry of the various culinary operations. Accordingly, this is the proper place to treat of the quality of the flesh of animals, and describe some of the circumstances which influence it for good or bad. We will, therefore, commence with the circumstance of *age*, and examine how far this affects the quality of meat.

THE CHEMISTRY AND ECONOMY OF SOUP-MAKING

STOCK BEING THE BASIS of all meat soups, and, also, of all the principal sauces, it is essential to the success of these culinary operations, to know the most complete and economical method of extracting, from a certain quantity of meat, the best possible stock or broth. The theory and philosophy of this process we will, therefore, explain, and then proceed to show the practical course to be adopted.

AS ALL MEAT is principally composed of fibres, fat, gelatine, osmazome, and albumen, it is requisite to know that the FIBRES are inseparable, constituting almost all that remains of the meat after it has undergone a long boiling.

FAT is dissolved by boiling; but as it is contained in cells covered by a very fine membrane, which never dissolves, a portion of it always adheres to the fibres. The other portion rises to the surface of the stock, and is that which has escaped from the cells which were not whole, or which have burst by boiling.

GELATINE is soluble: it is the basis and the nutritious portion of the stock. When there is an abundance of it, it causes the stock, when cold, to become a jelly.

OSMAZOME is soluble even when cold, and is that part of the meat which gives flavour and perfume to the stock. The flesh of old animals contains more *osmazome* than that of young ones. Brown meats contain more than white, and the former make the stock more fragrant. By roasting meat, the osmazome appears to acquire higher properties; so, by putting the remains of roast meats into your stock-pot, you obtain a better flavour.

ALBUMEN is of the nature of the white of eggs; it can be dissolved in cold or tepid water, but coagulates when it is put into water not quite at the boiling-point. From this property in albumen, it is evident that if the meat is put into the stock-pot when the water boils, or after this is made to boil up quickly, the albumen, in both cases, hardens. In the first it rises to the surface, in the second it remains in the meat, but in both it prevents the gelatine and osmazome from dissolving; and hence a thin and tasteless stock will be obtained. It ought to be known, too, that the coagulation of the albumen in the meat, always takes place, more or less, according to the size of the piece, as the parts farthest from the surface always acquire *that degree* of heat which congeals it before entirely dissolving it.

BONES ought always to form a component part of the stock-pot. They are composed of an earthy substance,—to which they owe their solidity,—of gelatine, and a fatty fluid, something like marrow. *Two ounces* of them contain as much gelatine as *one pound* of meat; but in them, this is so incased in the earthy substance, that boiling water can dissolve only the surface of whole bones. By breaking them, however, you can dissolve more, because you multiply their surfaces; and by reducing them to powder or paste, you can dissolve them entirely; but you must not grind them dry. We have said (99) that gelatine forms the basis of stock; but this, though very nourishing, is entirely without taste; and to make the stock savoury, it must contain *osmazome*. Of this, bones do not contain a particle; and that is the reason why stock made entirely of them, is not liked; but when you add meat to the broken or pulverized bones, the osmazome contained in it makes the stock sufficiently savoury.

In concluding this part of our subject, the following condensed hints and directions should be attended to in the economy of soup-making:—

I. BEEF MAKES THE BEST STOCK; veal stock has less colour and taste; whilst mutton sometimes gives it a tallowy smell, far from agreeable, unless the meat has been previously roasted or broiled. Fowls add very little to the flavour of stock, unless they be old and fat. Pigeons, when they are old, add the most flavour to it; and a rabbit or partridge is also a great improvement. From the freshest meat the best stock is obtained.

II. IF THE MEAT BE BOILED solely to make stock, it must be cut up into the smallest possible pieces; but, generally speaking, if it is desired to have good stock and a piece of savoury meat as well, it is necessary to put a rather large piece into the stock-pot, say sufficient for two or three days, during which time the stock will keep well in all weathers. Choose the freshest meat, and have it cut as thick as possible; for if it is a thin, flat piece, it will not look well, and will be very soon spoiled by the boiling.

III. NEVER WASH MEAT, as it deprives its surface of all its juices; separate it from the bones, and tie it round with tape, so that its shape may be preserved, then put it into the stock-pot, and for each pound of meat, let there be one pint of water; press it down with the hand, to allow the air, which it contains, to escape, and which often raises it to the top of the water.

IV. PUT THE STOCK-POT ON A GENTLE FIRE, so that it may heat gradually. The albumen will first dissolve, afterwards coagulate; and as it is in this state lighter than the liquid, it will rise to the surface; bringing with it all its impurities. It is this which makes *the scum*. The rising of the hardened albumen has the same effect in clarifying stock as the white of eggs; and, as a rule, it may be said that the more scum there is, the clearer will be the stock. Always take care that the fire is very regular.

V. REMOVE THE SCUM when it rises thickly, and do not let the stock boil, because then one portion of the scum will be dissolved, and the other go to the bottom of the pot; thus rendering it very difficult to obtain a clear broth. If the fire is regular, it will not be necessary to add cold water in order to make the scum rise; but if the fire is too large at first, it will then be necessary to do so.

VI. WHEN THE STOCK IS WELL SKIMMED, and begins to boil, put in salt and vegetables, which may be two or three carrots, two turnips, one parsnip, a bunch of leeks and celery tied together. You can add, according to taste, a piece of cabbage, two or three cloves stuck in an onion, and a tomato. The latter gives a very agreeable flavour to the stock. If fried onion be added, it ought, according to the advice of a famous French *chef*, to be tied in a little bag: without this precaution, the colour of the stock is liable to be clouded.

VII. BY THIS TIME we will now suppose that you have chopped the bones which were separated from the meat, and those which were left from the roast meat of the day before. Remember, as was before pointed out, that the more these are broken, the more gelatine you will have. The best way to break them up is to pound them roughly in an iron mortar, adding, from time to time, a little water, to prevent them getting heated. It is a great saving thus to make use of the bones of meat, which, in too many English families, we fear, are entirely wasted; for it is certain, as previously stated (No. 102), that two ounces of bone contain as much gelatine (which is the nutritive portion of stock) as one pound of meat. In their broken state tie them up in a bag, and put them in the stock-pot; adding the gristly parts of cold meat, and trimmings, which can be used for no other purpose. If, to make up the weight, you have received from the butcher a piece of mutton or veal, broil it slightly over a clear fire before putting it in the stock-pot, and be very careful that it does not contract the least taste of being smoked or burnt.

VIII. ADD NOW THE VEGETABLES, which, to a certain extent, will stop the boiling of the stock. Wait, therefore, till it simmers well up again, then draw it to the side of the fire, and keep it gently simmering till it is served, preserving, as before said, your fire always the same. Cover the stock-pot well, to prevent evaporation; do not fill it up, even if you take out a little stock, unless the meat is exposed; in which case a little boiling water may be added, but only enough to cover it. After six hours' slow and gentle simmering, the stock is done; and it should not be continued on the fire, longer than is necessary, or it will tend to insipidity.

Note—It is on a good stock, or first good broth and sauce, that excellence in cookery depends. If the preparation of this basis of the culinary art is intrusted to negligent or ignorant persons, and the stock is not well skimmed, but indifferent results will be obtained. The stock will never be clear; and when it is obliged to be clarified, it is deteriorated both in quality and flavour. In the proper management of the stock-pot an immense deal of trouble is saved, inasmuch as one stock, in a small dinner, serves for all purposes. Above all things, the greatest economy, consistent with excellence, should be practised, and the price of everything which enters the kitchen correctly ascertained. The *theory* of this part of Household Management may appear trifling; but its practice is extensive, and therefore it requires the best attention.

CHAPTER VI

RECIPES: FRUIT AND VEGETABLE SOUPS

It will be seen, by reference to the following Recipes, that an entirely original and most intelligible system has been pursued in explaining the preparation of each dish. We would recommend the young housekeeper, cook, or whoever may be engaged in the important task of "getting ready" the dinner, or other meal, to follow precisely the order in which the recipes are given. Thus, let them first place on their table all the INGREDIENTS necessary; then the modus operandi, or MODE of preparation, will be easily managed. By a careful reading, too, of the recipes, there will not be the slightest difficulty in arranging a repast for any number of persons, and an accurate notion will be gained of the TIME the cooling of each dish will occupy, of the periods at which it is SEASONABLE, as also of its AVERAGE COST.

The addition of the natural history, and the description of the various properties of the edible articles in common use in every family, will be serviceable both in a practical and an educational point of view.

STOCKS FOR ALL KINDS OF SOUPS

MEDIUM STOCK

Ingredients

4 lbs. of shin of beef
4 lbs. of knuckle of veal
2 lbs. of each any bones, trimmings of poultry, or fresh meat
½ a lb. of lean bacon or ham
2 oz. of butter
2 large onions, each stuck with 3 cloves
1 turnip
3 carrots
½ a leek
1 head of celery
2 oz. of salt
½ a teaspoonful of whole pepper
1 large blade of mace
1 small bunch of savoury herbs
4 quarts and ½ pint of cold water

Mode—Cut up the meat and bacon or ham into pieces about 3 inches square; rub the butter on the bottom of the stewpan; put in ½ a pint of water, the meat, and all the other ingredients. Cover the stewpan, and place it on a sharp fire, occasionally stirring its contents. When the bottom of the pan becomes covered with a pale, jelly-like substance, add 4 quarts of cold water, and simmer very gently for 5 hours. As we have said before, do not let it boil quickly. Skim off every particle of grease whilst it is doing, and strain it through a fine hair sieve.

This is the basis of many of the soups afterwards mentioned, and will be found quite strong enough for ordinary purposes.

Time—5-½ hours. *Average cost*, 9d. per quart.

WHITE STOCK

(*To be Used in the Preparation of White Soups.*)

Ingredients

4 lbs. of knuckle of veal
any poultry trimmings
4 slices of lean ham
1 carrot, 2 onions
1 head of celery
12 white peppercorns
1 oz. of salt
1 blade of mace
1 oz. butter
4 quarts of water

Mode—Cut up the veal, and put it with the bones and trimmings of poultry, and the ham, into the stewpan, which has been rubbed with the butter. Moisten with ½ a pint of water, and simmer till the gravy begins to flow. Then add the 4 quarts of water and the remainder of the ingredients; simmer for 5 hours. After skimming and straining it carefully through a very fine hair sieve, it will be ready for use.

Time—5-½ hours. *Average cost*, 9d. per quart.

Note—When stronger stock is desired, double the quantity of veal, or put in an old fowl. The liquor in which a young turkey has been boiled, is an excellent addition to all white stock or soups.

BROWNING FOR STOCK

Ingredients

2 oz. of powdered sugar
½ a pint of water

Mode—Place the sugar in a stewpan over a slow fire until it begins to melt, keeping it stirred with a wooden spoon until it becomes black, then add the water, and let it dissolve. Cork closely, and use a few drops when required.

Note—In France, burnt onions are made use of for the purpose of browning. As a general rule, the process of browning is to be discouraged, as apt to impart a slightly unpleasant flavour to the stock, and, consequently, all soups made from it.

BARLEY SOUP

Ingredients

2 lbs. of shin of beef
¼ lb. of pearl barley
a large bunch of parsley
4 onions
6 potatoes
salt and pepper
4 quarts of water

Mode—Put in all the ingredients, and simmer gently for 3 hours.

Time—3 hours. *Average cost*, 2-½d. per quart.

Seasonable all the year, but more suitable for winter.

BARLEY—This, in the order of cereal grasses, is, in Britain, the next plant to wheat in point of value, and exhibits several species and varieties. From what country it comes originally, is not known, but it was cultivated in the earliest ages of antiquity, as the Egyptians were afflicted with the loss of it in the ear, in the time of Moses. It was a favourite grain with the Athenians, but it was esteemed as an ignominious food by the Romans. Notwithstanding this, however, it was much used by them, as it was in former times by the English, and still is, in the Border counties, in Cornwall, and also in Wales. In other parts of England, it is used mostly for malting purposes. It is less nutritive than wheat; and in 100 parts, has of starch

79, gluten 6, saccharine matter 7, husk 8. It is, however, a lighter and less stimulating food than wheat, which renders a decoction of it well adapted for invalids whose digestion is weak.

CABBAGE SOUP

Ingredients

1 large cabbage
3 carrots
2 onions
4 or 5 slices of lean bacon
salt and pepper to taste
2 quarts of medium stock

Mode—Scald the cabbage, exit it up and drain it. Line the stewpan with the bacon, put in the cabbage, carrots, and onions; moisten with skimmings from the stock, and simmer very gently, till the cabbage is tender; add the stock, stew softly for half an hour, and carefully skim off every particle of fat. Season and serve.

Time—1-½ hour. *Average cost,* 1s. per quart.

Seasonable in winter.

Sufficient for 8 persons.

CHANTILLY SOUP

Ingredients

1 quart of young green peas
a small bunch of parsley
2 young onions
2 quarts of medium stock

Mode—Boil the peas till quite tender, with the parsley and onions; then rub them through a sieve, and pour the stock to them. Do not let it boil after the peas are added, or you will spoil the colour. Serve very hot.

Time—Half an hour. *Average* cost, 1s. 6d. per quart.

Seasonable from June to the end of August.

Sufficient for 8 persons.

Note—Cold peas pounded in a mortar, with a little stock added to them, make a very good soup in haste.

> **PARSLEY**—Among the Greeks, in the classic ages, a crown of parsley was awarded, both in the Nemaean and Isthmian games, and the voluptuous Anacreon pronounces this beautiful herb the emblem of joy and festivity. It has an elegant leaf, and is extensively used in the culinary art. When it was introduced to Britain is not known. There are several varieties,—the *plain*-leaved and the *curled*-leaved, *celery*-parsley, *Hamburg* parsley, and *purslane*. The curled is the best, and, from the form of its leaf, has a beautiful appearance on a dish as a garnish. Its flavour is, to many, very agreeable in soups; and although to rabbits, hares, and sheep it is a luxury, to parrots it is a poison. The celery-parsley is used as a celery, and the Hamburg is cultivated only for its roots, which are used as parsnips or carrots, to eat with meat. The purslane is a native of South America, and is not now much in use.

CHESTNUT (SPANISH) SOUP

Ingredients

¾ lb. of Spanish chestnuts
¼ pint of cream
seasoning to taste of salt
cayenne, and mace
1 quart of stock

Mode—Take the outer rind from the chestnuts, and put them into a large pan of warm water. As soon as this becomes too hot for the fingers to remain in it, take out the chestnuts, peel them quickly, and immerse them in cold water, and wipe and weigh them. Now cover them with good stock, and stew them gently for rather more than ¾ of an hour, or until they break when touched with a fork; then drain, pound, and rub them through a fine sieve reversed; add sufficient stock, mace, cayenne, and salt, and stir it often until it boils, and put in the cream. The stock in which the chestnuts are boiled can be used for the soup, when its sweetness is not objected to, or it may, in part, be added to it; and the rule is, that ¾ lb. of chestnuts should be given to each quart of soup.

Time—rather more than 1 hour. *Average cost* per quart, 1s. 6d.
Seasonable from October to February.
Sufficient for 4 persons.

THE CHESTNUT—This fruit is said, by some, to have originally come from Sardis, in Lydia; and by others, from Castanea, a city of Thessaly, from which it takes its name. By the ancients it was much used as a food, and is still common in France and Italy, to which countries it is, by some, considered indigenous. In the southern part of the European continent, it is eaten both raw and roasted. The tree was introduced into Britain by the Romans; but it only flourishes in the warmer parts of the island, the fruit rarely arriving at maturity in Scotland. It attains a great age, as well as an immense size. As a food, it is the least oily and most farinaceous of all the nuts, and, therefore, the easiest of digestion. The tree called the *horse chestnut* is very different, although its fruit very much resembles that of the other. Its "nuts," though eaten by horses and some other animals, are unsuitable for human food.

COCOA-NUT SOUP

Ingredients

6 oz. of grated cocoa-nut
6 oz. of rice flour
½ a teaspoonful of mace
seasoning to taste of cayenne and salt
¼ of a pint of boiling cream
3 quarts of medium stock

Mode—Take the dark rind from the cocoa-nut, and grate it down small on a clean grater; weigh it, and allow, for each quart of stock, 2 oz. of the cocoa-nut. Simmer it gently for 1 hour in the stock, which should then be strained closely from it, and thickened for table.

Time—2-¼ hours. *Average cost* per quart, 1s. 3d.

Seasonable in Autumn.

Sufficient for 10 persons.

THE COCOA-NUT—This is the fruit of one of the palms, than which it is questionable if there is any other species of tree marking, in itself, so abundantly the goodness of Providence, in making provision for the wants of man. It grows wild in the Indian seas, and in the eastern parts of Asia; and thence it has been introduced into every part of the tropical regions. To the natives of those climates, its bark supplies the material for creating their dwellings; its leaves, the means of roofing them; and the leaf-stalks, a kind of gauze for covering their windows, or protecting the baby in the cradle. It is also made into lanterns, masks to screen the face from the heat of the sun, baskets, wicker-work, and even a kind of paper for writing on. Combs, brooms, torches, ropes, matting, and sailcloth are made of its fibers. With these, too, beds are made and cushions stuffed. Oars are supplied by the leaves; drinking-cups, spoons, and other domestic utensils by the shells of the nuts; milk by its juice, of which, also, a kind of honey and sugar are prepared. When fermented, it furnishes the means of intoxication; and when the fibres are burned, their ashes supply an alkali for making soap. The buds of the tree bear a striking resemblance to cabbage when boiled; but when they are cropped, the tree dies. In a fresh state, the kernel is eaten raw, and its juice is a most agreeable and refreshing beverage. When the nut is imported to this country, its fruit is, in general, comparatively dry, and is considered indigestible. The tree is one of the least productive of the palm tribe.

SOUP A LA JULIENNE

Ingredients

½ pint of carrots
½ pint of turnips
¼ pint of onions
2 or 3 leeks
½ head of celery
1 lettuce
a little sorrel and chervil
if liked, 2 oz. of butter
2 quarts of stock

Mode—Cut the vegetables into strips of about 1-¼ inch long, and be particular they are all the same size, or some will be hard whilst the others will be done to a pulp. Cut the lettuce, sorrel, and chervil into larger pieces; fry the carrots in the butter, and pour the stock boiling to them. When this is done, add all the other vegetables, and herbs, and stew gently for at least an hour. Skim off all the fat, pour the soup over thin slices of bread, cut round about the size of a shilling, and serve.

Time—1-½ hour. *Average cost*, 1s. 3d. per quart.

Seasonable all the year.

Sufficient for 8 persons.

ONION SOUP

Ingredients

6 large onions
2 oz. of butter
salt and pepper to taste
¼ pint of cream
1 quart of stock

Mode—Chop the onions, put them in the butter, stir them occasionally, but do not let them brown. When tender, put the stock to them, and season; strain the soup, and add the boiling cream.

Time—1-½ hour. *Average cost*, 1s. per quart.

Seasonable in winter.

Sufficient for 4 persons.

THE ONION—Like the cabbage, this plant was erected into an object of worship by the idolatrous Egyptians 2,000 years before the Christian era, and it still forms a favourite food in the country of these people, as well as in other parts of Africa. When it was first introduced to England, has not been ascertained; but it has long been in use, and esteemed as a favourite seasoning plant to various dishes. In warmer climates it is much milder in its flavour; and such as are grown in Spain and Portugal, are, comparatively speaking, very large, and are often eaten both in a boiled and roasted state. The Strasburg is the most esteemed; and, although all the species have highly nutritive properties, they impart such a disagreeable odour to the breath, that they are often rejected even where they are liked. Chewing a little raw parsley is said to remove this odour.

PEA SOUP (GREEN)

Ingredients

3 pints of green peas
¼ lb. of butter
2 or three thin slices of ham
6 onions sliced
4 shredded lettuces
the crumb of 2 French rolls
2 handfuls of spinach
1 lump of sugar
2 quarts of common stock

Mode—Put the butter, ham, 1 quart of the peas, onions, and lettuces, to a pint of stock, and simmer for an hour; then add the remainder of the stock, with the crumb of the French rolls, and boil for another hour. Now boil the spinach, and squeeze it very dry. Rub the soup through a sieve, and the spinach with it, to colour it. Have ready a pint of *young* peas boiled; add them to the soup, put in the sugar, give one boil, and serve. If necessary, add salt.

Time—2-½ hours. *Average cost*, 1s. 9d. per quart.

Seasonable from June to the end of August.

Sufficient for 10 persons.

Note—It will be well to add, if the peas are not quite young, a little sugar. Where economy is essential, water may be used instead of stock for this soup, boiling in it likewise the pea-shells; but use a double quantity of vegetables.

VEGETABLE SOUP

Ingredients

7 oz. of carrot
10 oz. of parsnip
10 oz. of potato, cut into thin slices
1-¼ oz. of butter
5 teaspoonfuls of flour
a teaspoonful of made mustard
salt and pepper to taste
the yolks of 2 eggs
rather more than 2 quarts of water.

Mode—Boil the vegetables in the water 2-½ hours; stir them often, and if the water boils away too quickly, add more, as there should be 2 quarts of soup when done. Mix up in a basin the butter and flour, mustard, salt, and pepper, with a teacupful of cold water; stir in the soup, and boil 10 minutes. Have ready the yolks of the eggs in the tureen; pour on, stir well, and serve.

Time—3 hours. *Average cost*, 4d. per quart.

Seasonable in winter.

Sufficient for 8 persons.

STEW SOUP

Ingredients

2 lbs. of beef
5 onions, 5 turnips
¾ lb. of *rice*
a large bunch of parsley
a few sweet herbs, pepper and salt
2 quarts of water

Mode—Cut the beef up in small pieces, add the other ingredients, and boil gently for 2½ hours. Oatmeal or potatoes would be a great improvement.

Time—2½ hours. *Average cost*, 6d. per quart.

Seasonable in winter.

Sufficient for 6 persons.

FISH STOCK

Ingredients

- 2 lbs. of beef or veal (these can be omitted)
- any kind of white fish trimmings, of fish which are to be dressed for table
- 2 onions
- the rind of ½ a lemon
- a bunch of sweet herbs
- 2 carrots
- 2 quarts of water

Mode—Cut up the fish, and put it, with the other ingredients, into the water. Simmer for 2 hours; skim the liquor carefully, and strain it. When a richer stock is wanted, fry the vegetables and fish before adding the water.

Time—2 hours. *Average cost*, with meat, 10d. per quart; without, 3d.

Note—Do not make fish stock long before it is wanted, as it soon turns sour.

CHAPTER VII

THE NATURAL HISTORY OF FISHES

IN NATURAL HISTORY, FISHES form the fourth class in the system of Linnaeus, and are described as having long under-jaws, eggs without white, organs of sense, fins for supporters, bodies covered with concave scales, gills to supply the place of lungs for respiration, and water for the natural element of their existence. Had mankind no other knowledge of animals than of such as inhabit the land and breathe their own atmosphere, they would listen with incredulous wonder, if told that there were other kinds of beings which existed only in the waters, and which would die almost as soon as they were taken from them. However strongly these facts might be attested, they would hardly believe them, without the operation of their own senses, as they would recollect the effect produced on their own bodies when immersed in water, and the impossibility of their sustaining life in it for any lengthened period of time. Experience, however, has taught them, that the "great deep" is crowded with inhabitants of various sizes, and of vastly different constructions, with modes of life entirely distinct from those which belong to the animals of the land, and with peculiarities of design, equally wonderful with those of any other works which have come from the hand of the Creator. The history of these races, however, must remain for ever, more or less, in a state of darkness, since the depths in which they live, are beyond the power of human exploration, and since the illimitable expansion of their domain places them almost entirely out of the reach of human accessibility.

IN STUDYING THE CONFORMATION OF FISHES, we naturally conclude that they are, in every respect, well adapted to the element in which they have their existence. Their shape has a striking resemblance to the lower part of a ship; and there is no doubt that the form of the fish originally suggested the form of the ship. The body is in general slender, gradually diminishing towards each of its extremities, and flattened on each of its sides. This is precisely the form of the lower part of the hull of a ship; and it enables both the animal and the vessel, with comparative ease, to penetrate and divide the resisting medium for which they have been adapted. The velocity of a ship, however, in sailing before the wind, is by no means to be compared to that of a fish. It is well known that the largest fishes will, with the greatest ease, overtake a ship in full sail, play round it without effort, and shoot ahead of it at pleasure. This arises from their great flexibility, which, to compete with mocks the labours of art, and enables them to migrate thousands of miles in a season, without the slightest indications of languor or fatigue.

THE PRINCIPAL INSTRUMENTS EMPLOYED BY FISHES to accelerate their motion, are their air-bladder, fins, and tail. By means of the air-bladder they enlarge or diminish the specific gravity of their bodies. When they wish to sink, they compress the muscles of the abdomen, and eject the air contained in it; by which, their weight, compared with that of the water, is increased, and they consequently descend. On the other hand, when they wish to rise, they relax the compression of the abdominal muscles, when the air-bladder fills and distends, and the body immediately ascends to the surface. How simply, yet how wonderfully, has the Supreme Being adapted certain means to the attainment of certain ends! Those fishes which are destitute of the air-bladder are heavy in the water, and have no great "alacrity" in rising. The larger proportion of them remain at the bottom, unless they are so formed as to be able to strike their native element downwards with sufficient force to enable them to ascend. When the air-bladder of a fish is burst, its power of ascending to the surface has for ever passed away. From a knowledge of this fact, the fishermen of cod are enabled to preserve them alive for a considerable time in their well-boats. The means they adopt to accomplish this, is to perforate the sound, or air-bladder, with a needle, which disengages the air, when the fishes immediately descend to the bottom of the well, into which they are thrown. Without this operation, it would be impossible to keep the cod under water whilst they had life. In swimming, the *fins* enable fishes to preserve their upright position, especially those of the belly, which act like two feet. Without those, they would swim with their bellies upward, as it is in their backs that the centre of gravity lies. In ascending and descending, these are likewise of great assistance, as they contract and expand accordingly. The *tail* is an instrument of great muscular force, and largely assists the fish in all its motions. In some instances it acts like the rudder of a ship, and enables it to turn sideways; and when moved from side to side with a quick vibratory motion, fishes are made, in the same manner as the "screw" propeller makes a steamship, to dart forward with a celerity proportioned to the muscular force with which it is employed.

THE RESPIRATION OF FISHES is effected by means of those comb-like organs which are placed on each side of the neck, and which are called gills. It is curious to watch the process of breathing as it is performed by the finny tribes. It seems to be so continuous, that it might almost pass for an illustration of the vexed problem which conceals the secret of perpetual motion. In performing it, they fill their mouths with water, which they drive backwards with a force so great as to open the large flap, to allow it to escape behind. In this operation all, or a great portion, of the air contained in the water, is left among the feather-like processes of the gills, and is carried into the body, there to perform its part in the animal economy. In proof of this, it has been ascertained that, if the water in which fishes are put, is, by any means, denuded of its air, they immediately seek the surface, and begin to gasp for it. Hence, distilled water is to them what a vacuum made by an air-pump, is to most other animals. For this reason, when a fishpond, or other aqueous receptacle in which fishes are kept, is entirely frozen over, it is necessary to make holes in the ice, not so especially for the purpose of feeding them, as for that of giving them air to breathe.

ALTHOUGH NATURALISTS HAVE DIVIDED FISHES into two great tribes, the *osseous* and the *cartilaginous*, yet the distinction is not very precise; for the first have a great deal of cartilage, and the second, at any rate, a portion of calcareous matter in their bones. It may, therefore, be said that the bones of fishes form a kind of intermediate substance between true bones and cartilages. The backbone extends through the whole length of the body, and consists of vertebrae, strong and thick towards the head, but weaker and more slender as it approaches the tail. Each species has a determinate number of vertebrae, which are increased in size in proportion with the body. The ribs are attached to the processes of the vertebrae, and inclose the breast and abdomen. Some kinds, as the rays, have no ribs; whilst others, as the sturgeon and eel, have very short ones. Between the pointed processes of the vertebrae are situated the bones which support the dorsal (back) and the anal (below the tail) fins, which are connected with the processes by a ligament. At the breast are the sternum or breastbone, clavicles or collar-bones, and the scapulae or shoulder-blades, on which the pectoral or breast fins are placed. The bones which support the ventral or belly fins are called the *ossa pelvis*. Besides these principal bones, there are often other smaller ones, placed between the muscles to assist their motion.

WITH RESPECT TO THE FOOD OF FISHES, this is almost universally found in their own element. They are mostly carnivorous, though they seize upon almost anything that comes in their way: they even devour their own offspring, and manifest a particular predilection for all living creatures. Those, to which Nature has meted out mouths of the greatest capacity, would seem to pursue everything with life, and frequently engage in fierce conflicts with their prey. The animal with the largest mouth is usually the victor; and he has no sooner conquered his foe than he devours him. Innumerable shoals of one species pursue those of another, with a ferocity which draws them from the pole to the equator, through all the varying temperatures and depths of their boundless domain. In these pursuits a scene of universal violence is the result; and many species must have become extinct, had not Nature accurately proportioned the means of escape, the production, and the numbers, to the extent and variety of the danger to which they are exposed. Hence the smaller species are not only more numerous, but more productive than the larger; whilst their instinct leads them in search of food and safety near the shores, where, from the shallowness of the waters, many of their foes are unable to follow them.

IN REFERENCE TO THE LONGEVITY OF FISHES, it is affirmed to surpass that of all other created beings; and it is supposed they are, to a great extent, exempted from the diseases to which the flesh of other animals is heir. In place of suffering from the rigidity of age, which is the cause of the natural decay of those that "live and move and have their being" on the land, their bodies continue to grow with each succeeding supply of food, and the conduits of life to perform their functions unimpaired. The age of fishes has not been properly ascertained, although it is believed that the most minute of the species has a longer lease of life than man. The mode in which they die has been noted by the Rev. Mr. White, the eminent naturalist of Selbourne. As soon as the fish sickens, the head sinks lower and lower, till the animal, as it were, stands upon it. After this, as it becomes weaker, it loses its poise, till the tail turns over, when it comes to the surface, and floats with its belly upwards. The reason for its floating in this manner is on account of the body being no longer balanced by the fins of the belly, and the broad muscular back preponderating, by its own gravity, over the belly, from this latter being a cavity, and consequently lighter.

FISHES ARE EITHER SOLITARY OR GREGARIOUS, and some of them migrate to great distances, and into certain rivers, to deposit their spawn. Of sea-fishes, the cod, herring, mackerel, and many others, assemble in immense shoals, and migrate through different tracts of the ocean; but, whether considered in their solitary or gregarious capacity, they are alike wonderful to all who look through Nature up to Nature's God, and consider, with due humility, yet exalted admiration, the sublime variety, beauty, power, and grandeur of His productions, as manifested in the Creation.

FISH AS AN ARTICLE OF HUMAN FOOD

AS THE NUTRITIVE PROPERTIES OF FISH are deemed inferior to those of what is called butchers' meat, it would appear, from all we can learn, that, in all ages, it has held only a secondary place in the estimation of those who have considered the science of gastronomy as a large element in the happiness of mankind. Among the Jews of old it was very little used, although it seems not to have been entirely interdicted, as Moses prohibited only the use of such as had neither scales nor fins. The Egyptians, however, made fish an article of diet, notwithstanding that it was rejected by their priests. Egypt, however, is not a country favourable to the production of fish, although we read of the people, when hungry, eating it raw; of epicures among them having dried it in the sun; and of its being salted and preserved, to serve as a repast on days of great solemnity.

> The modern Egyptians are, in general, extremely temperate in regard to food. Even the richest among them take little pride, and, perhaps, experience as little

> delight, in the luxuries of the table. Their dishes mostly consist of pilaus, soups, and stews, prepared principally of onions, cucumbers, and other cold vegetables, mixed with a little meat cut into small pieces. On special occasions, however, a whole sheep is placed on the festive board; but during several of the hottest months of the year, the richest restrict themselves entirely to a vegetable diet. The poor are contented with a little oil or sour milk, in which they may dip their bread.

THE GEOGRAPHICAL SITUATION OF GREECE was highly favourable for the development of a taste for the piscatory tribes; and the skill of the Greek cooks was so great, that they could impart every variety of relish to the dish they were called upon to prepare. Athenaeus has transmitted to posterity some very important precepts upon their ingenuity in seasoning with salt, oil, and aromatics.

> At the present day the food of the Greeks, through the combined influence of poverty and the long fasts which their religion imposes upon them, is, to a large extent, composed of fish, accompanied with vegetables and fruit. Caviare, prepared from the roes of sturgeons, is the national ragout, which, like all other fish dishes, they season with aromatic herbs. Snails dressed in garlic are also a favourite dish.

AS THE ROMANS, in a great measure, took their taste in the fine arts from the Greeks, so did they, in some measure, their piscine appetites. The eel-pout and the lotas's liver were the favourite fish dishes of the Roman epicures; whilst the red mullet was esteemed as one of the most delicate fishes that could be brought to the table.

> With all the elegance, taste, and refinement of Roman luxury, it was sometimes promoted or accompanied by acts of great barbarity. In proof of this, the mention of the red mullet suggests the mode in which it was sometimes treated for the, to us, *horrible* entertainment of the *fashionable* in Roman circles. It may be premised, that as England has, Rome, in her palmy days, had, her fops, who had, no doubt, through the medium of their cooks, discovered that when the scales of the red mullet were removed, the flesh presented a fine pink-colour. Having discovered this, it was further observed that at the death of the animal, this colour passed through a succession of beautiful shades, and, in order that these might be witnessed and enjoyed in their fullest perfection, the poor mullet was served alive in a glass vessel.

THE LOVE OF FISH among the ancient Romans rose to a real mania. Apicius offered a prize to any one who could invent a new brine compounded of the liver of red mullets; and Lucullus had a canal cut through a mountain, in the neighbourhood of Naples, that fish might be the more easily transported to the gardens of his villa. Hortensius, the orator, wept over the death of a turbot which he had fed with his own hands; and the daughter of Druses adorned one that she had, with rings of gold. These were, surely, instances of misplaced affection; but there is no accounting for tastes. It was but the other day that we read in the "*Times*" of a wealthy*living* English hermit, who delights in the companionship of rats!

> The modern Romans are merged in the general name of Italians, who, with the exception of macaroni, have no specially characteristic article of food.

FROM ROME TO GAUL is, considering the means of modern locomotion, no great way; but the ancient sumptuary laws of that kingdom give us little information regarding the ichthyophagous propensities of its inhabitants. Louis XII. engaged six fishmongers to furnish his board with fresh-water animals, and Francis I. had twenty-two, whilst Henry the Great extended his requirements a little further, and had twenty-four. In the time of Louis XIV. the cooks had attained to such a degree of perfection in their art, that they could convert the form and flesh of the trout, pike, or carp, into the very shape and flavour of the most delicious game.

> The French long enjoyed a European reputation for their skill and refinement in the preparing of food. In place of plain joints, French cookery delights in the marvels of what are called made dishes, ragouts, stews, and fricassees, in which no trace of the original materials of which they are compounded is to be found.

FROM GAUL WE CROSS TO BRITAIN, where it has been asserted, by, at least, one authority, that the ancient inhabitants ate no fish. However this may be, we know that the British shores, particularly those of the North Sea, have always been well supplied with the best kinds of fish, which we may reasonably infer was not unknown to the inhabitants, or likely to be lost upon them for the lack of knowledge as to how they tasted. By the time of Edward II., fish had, in England, become a dainty, especially the sturgeon, which was permitted to appear on no table but that of the king. In the fourteenth century, a decree of King John informs us that the people ate both seals and porpoises; whilst in the days of the Troubadours, whales were fished for and caught in the Mediterranean Sea, for the purpose of being used as human food.

> Whatever checks the ancient British may have had upon their piscatory appetites, there are happily none of any great consequence upon the modern, who delight in wholesome food of every kind. Their taste is, perhaps, too much inclined to that which is accounted solid and substantial; but they really eat more moderately, even of animal food, than either the French or the Germans. Roast beef, or other viands cooked in the plainest manner, are, with them, a sufficient luxury; yet they delight in living *well*, whilst it is easy to prove how largely their affections are developed by even the prospect of a substantial cheer. In proof of this we will just observe, that if a great dinner is to be celebrated, it is not uncommon for the appointed stewards and committee to meet and have a preliminary dinner among themselves, in order to arrange the great one, and after that, to have another dinner to discharge the bill which the great one cost. This enjoyable disposition we take to form a very large item in the aggregate happiness of the nation.

THE GENERAL USE OF FISH, as an article of human food among civilized nations, we have thus sufficiently shown, and will conclude this portion of our subject with the following hints, which ought to be remembered by all those who are fond of occasionally varying their dietary with a piscine dish:—

I. Fish shortly before they spawn are, in general, best in condition. When the spawning is just over, they are out of season, and unfit for human food.

II. When fish is out of season, it has a transparent, bluish tinge, however much it may be boiled; when it is in season, its muscles are firm, and boil white and curdy.

III. As food for invalids, white fish, such as the ling, cod, haddock, coal-fish, and whiting, are the best; flat fish, as soles, skate, turbot, and flounders, are also good.

IV. Salmon, mackerel, herrings, and trout soon spoil or decompose after they are killed; therefore, to be in perfection, they should be prepared for the table on the day they are caught. With flat fish, this is not of such consequence, as they will keep longer. The turbot, for example, is improved by being kept a day or two.

GENERAL DIRECTIONS FOR DRESSING FISH

- IN DRESSING FISH, of any kind, the first point to be attended to, is to see that it be perfectly clean. It is a common error to wash it too much; as by doing so the flavour is diminished. If the fish is to be boiled, a little salt and vinegar should be put into the water, to give it firmness, after it is cleaned. Cod-fish, whiting, and haddock, are far better if a little salted, and kept a day; and if the weather be not very hot, they will be good for two days.

- WHEN FISH IS CHEAP AND PLENTIFUL, and a larger quantity is purchased than is immediately wanted, the overplus of such as will bear it should be potted, or pickled, or salted, and hung up; or it may be fried, that it may serve for stewing the next day. Fresh-water fish, having frequently a muddy smell and taste, should be soaked in strong salt and water, after it has been well cleaned. If of a sufficient size, it may be scalded in salt and water, and afterwards dried and dressed.

- FISH SHOULD BE PUT INTO COLD WATER, and set on the fire to do very gently, or the outside will break before the inner part is done. Unless the fishes are small, they should never be put into warm water; nor should water, either hot or cold, be poured *on* to the fish, as it is liable to break the skin: if it should be necessary to add a little water whilst the fish is cooking, it ought to be poured in gently at the side of the vessel. The fish-plate may be drawn up, to see if the fish be ready, which may be known by its easily separating from the bone. It should then be immediately taken out of the water, or it will become woolly. The fish-plate should be set crossways over the kettle, to keep hot for serving, and a clean cloth over the fish, to prevent its losing its colour.

- IN GARNISHING FISH, great attention is required, and plenty of parsley, horseradish, and lemon should be used. If fried parsley be used, it must be washed and picked, and thrown into fresh water. When the lard or dripping boils, throw the parsley into it immediately from the water, and instantly it will be green and crisp, and must be taken up with a slice. When well done, and with very good sauce, fish is more appreciated than almost any other dish. The liver and roe, in some instances, should be placed on the dish, in order that they may be distributed in the course of serving; but to each recipe will be appended the proper mode of serving and garnishing.

- IF FISH IS TO BE FRIED OR BROILED, it must be dried in a nice soft cloth, after it is well cleaned and washed. If for frying, brush it over with egg, and sprinkle it with some fine crumbs of bread. If done a second time with the egg and bread, the fish will look so much the better. If required to be very nice, a sheet of white blotting-paper must be placed to receive it, that it may be free from all grease. It must also be of a beautiful colour, and all the crumbs appear distinct. Butter gives a bad colour; lard and clarified dripping are most frequently used; but oil is the best, if the expense be no objection. The fish should be put into the lard when boiling, and there should be a sufficiency of this to cover it.

- WHEN FISH IS BROILED, it must be seasoned, floured, and laid on a very clean gridiron, which, when hot, should be rubbed with a bit of suet, to prevent the fish from sticking. It must be broiled over a very clear fire, that it may not taste smoky; and not too near, that it may not be scorched.

- IN CHOOSING FISH, it is well to remember that it is possible it may be *fresh*, and yet not *good*. Under the head of each particular fish in this work, are appended rules for its choice and the months when it is in season. Nothing can be of greater consequence to a cook than to have the fish good; as if this important course in a dinner does not give satisfaction, it is rarely that the repast goes off well.

CHAPTER VIII

RECIPES: FISH

Nothing is more difficult than to give the average prices of Fish, inasmuch as a few hours of bad weather at sea will, in the space of one day, cause such a difference in its supply, that the same fish—a turbot for instance—which may be bought to-day for six or seven shillings, will, to-morrow, be, in the London markets, worth, perhaps, almost as many pounds. The average costs, therefore, which will be found appended to each recipe, must be understood as about the average price for the different kinds of fish, when the market is supplied upon an average, and when the various sorts are of an average size and quality.

GENERAL RULE IN CHOOSING FISH—*A proof of freshness and goodness in most fishes, is their being covered with scales; for, if deficient in this respect, it is a sign of their being stale, or having been ill-used.*]

CODFISH

Cod may be boiled whole; but a large head and shoulders are quite sufficient for a dish, and contain all that is usually helped, because, when the thick part is done, the tail is insipid and overdone. The latter, cut in slices, makes a very good dish for frying; or it may be salted down and served with egg sauce and parsnips. Cod, when boiled quite fresh, is watery; salting a little, renders it firmer.

THE COD TRIBE—The Jugular, characterized by bony gills, and ventral fins before the pectoral ones, commences the second of the Linnaean orders of fishes, and is a numerous tribe, inhabiting only the depths of the ocean, and seldom visiting the fresh waters. They have a smooth head, and the gill membrane has seven rays. The body is oblong, and covered with deciduous scales. The fins are all inclosed in skin, whilst their rays are unarmed. The ventral fins are slender, and terminate in a point. Their habits are gregarious, and they feed on smaller fish and other marine animals.

TO DRESS CRAB

Ingredients

1 crab
2 tablespoonfuls of vinegar
1 ditto of oil
salt
white pepper, and cayenne, to taste.

Mode—Empty the shells, and thoroughly mix the meat with the above ingredients, and put it in the large shell. Garnish with slices of cut lemon and parsley. The quantity of oil may be increased when it is much liked.

Average cost, from 10d. to 2s.

Seasonable all the year; but not so good in May, June, and July.

Sufficient for 3 persons.

TO CHOOSE CRAB—The middle-sized crab is the best; and the crab, like the lobster, should be judged by its weight; for if light, it is watery.

FISH CAKE

Ingredients

The remains of any cold fish
1 onion
1 faggot of sweet herbs
salt and pepper to taste
1 pint of water
equal quantities of bread crumbs and cold potatoes
½ teaspoonful of parsley
1 egg
bread crumbs

Mode—Pick the meat from the bones of the fish, which latter put, with the head and fins, into a stewpan with the water; add pepper and salt, the onion and herbs, and stew slowly for gravy about 2 hours; chop the fish fine, and mix it well with bread crumbs and cold potatoes, adding the parsley and seasoning; make the whole into a cake with the white of an egg, brush it over with egg, cover with bread crumbs, and fry of a light brown; strain the gravy, pour it over, and stew gently for ¼ hour, stirring it carefully once or twice. Serve hot, and garnish with slices of lemon and parsley.

Time—½ hour, after the gravy is made.

BAKED HADDOCKS

Ingredients

A nice forcemeat
butter to taste
egg
bread crumbs

Mode—Scale and clean the fish, without cutting it open much; put in a nice delicate forcemeat, and sew up the slit. Brush it over with egg, sprinkle over bread crumbs, and baste frequently with butter. Garnish with parsley and cut lemon, and serve with a nice brown gravy, plain melted butter, or anchovy sauce. The egg and bread crumbs can be omitted, and pieces of butter placed over the fish.

Time—Large haddock, ¾ hour; moderate size, ¼ hour.

Seasonable from August to February.

Average cost, from 9d. upwards.

Note—Haddocks may be filleted, rubbed over with egg and bread crumbs, and fried a nice brown; garnish with crisped parsley.

> **THE HADDOCK**—This fish migrates in immense shoals, and arrives on the Yorkshire coast about the middle of winter. It is an inhabitant of the northern seas of Europe, but does not enter the Baltic, and is not known in the Mediterranean. On each side of the body, just beyond the gills, it has a dark spot, which superstition asserts to be the impressions of the finger and thumb of St. Peter, when taking the tribute money out of a fish of this species.

TO BOIL LOBSTERS

Ingredients

¼ lb. of salt to each gallon of water

Mode—Buy the lobsters alive, and choose those that are heavy and full of motion, which is an indication of their freshness. When the shell is incrusted, it is a sign they are old: medium-sized lobsters are the best. Have ready a stewpan of boiling water, salted in the above proportion; put in the lobster, and keep it boiling quickly from 20 minutes to ¾ hour, according to its size, and do not forget to skim well. If it boils too long, the meat becomes thready, and if not done enough, the spawn is not red: this must be obviated by great attention. Hub the shell over with a little butter or sweet oil, which wipe off again.

Time—Small lobster, 20 minutes to ½ hour; large ditto, ½ to ⅓ hour.

Average cost, medium size, 1s. 6d. to 2s. 6d.

Seasonable all the year, but best from March to October.

> **THE LOBSTER**—This is one of the crab tribe, and is found on most of the rocky coasts of Great Britain. Some are caught with the hand, but the larger number in pots, which serve all the purposes of a trap, being made of osiers, and baited with garbage. They are shaped like a wire mousetrap; so that when the lobsters once enter them, they cannot get out again. They are fastened to a cord and sunk in the sea, and their place marked by a buoy. The fish is very prolific, and deposits of its eggs in the sand, where they are soon hatched. On the coast of Norway, they are very abundant, and it is from there that the English metropolis is mostly supplied. They are rather indigestible, and, as a food, not so nurtritive as they are generally supposed to be.

BAKED PIKE

Ingredients

1 or 2 pike
a nice delicate stuffing
1 egg
bread crumbs
¼ lb. butter

Mode—Scale the fish, take out the gills, wash, and wipe it thoroughly dry; stuff it with forcemeat, sew it up, and fasten the tail in the mouth by means of a skewer; brush it over with egg, sprinkle with bread crumbs, and baste with butter, before putting it in the oven, which must be well heated. When the pike is of a nice brown colour, cover it with buttered paper, as the outside would become too dry. If 2 are dressed, a little variety may be made by making one of them green with a little chopped parsley mixed with the bread crumbs. Serve anchovy or Dutch sauce, and plain melted butter with it.

Time—According to size, 1 hour, more or less.

Average cost—Seldom bought.

Seasonable from September to March.

Note—Pike *à la génévese* may be stewed in the same manner as salmon *à la génévese*.

TO BOIL PRAWNS OR SHRIMPS

Ingredients

¼ lb. salt to each gallon of water

Mode—Prawns should be very red, and have no spawn under the tail; much depends on their freshness and the way in which they are cooked. Throw them into boiling water, salted as above, and keep them boiling for about 7 or 8 minutes. Shrimps should be done in the same way; but less time must be allowed. It may easily be known when they are done by their changing colour. Care should be taken that they are not over-boiled, as they then become tasteless and indigestible.

Time—Prawns, about 8 minutes; shrimps, about 5 minutes.

Average cost, prawns, 2s. per lb.; shrimps, 6d. per pint.

Seasonable all the year.

TO FRY SMELTS

Ingredients

Egg and bread crumbs
a little flour
boiling lard

Mode—Smelts should be very fresh, and not washed more than is necessary to clean them. Dry them in a cloth, lightly flour, dip them in egg, and sprinkle over with very fine bread crumbs, and put them into boiling lard. Fry of a nice pale brown, and be careful not to take off the light roughness of the crumbs, or their beauty will be spoiled. Dry them before the fire on a drainer, and servo with plain melted butter. This fish is often used as a garnishing.

Time—5 minutes.

Average cost, 2s. per dozen.

Seasonable from October to May.

> **THE SMELT**—This is a delicate little fish, and is in high esteem. Mr. Yarrell asserts that the true smelt is entirety confined to the western and eastern coasts of Britain. It very rarely ventures far from the shore, and is plentiful in November, December, and January.

BAKED SOLES

Ingredients

2 soles
¼ lb. of butter
egg
bread crumbs
minced parsley
1 glass of sherry
lemon-juice
cayenne and salt to taste

Mode—Clean, skin, and well wash the fish, and dry them thoroughly in a cloth. Brush them over with egg, sprinkle with bread crumbs mixed with a little minced parsley, lay them in a large flat baking-dish, white side uppermost; or if it will not hold the two soles, they may each be laid on a dish by itself; but they must not be put one on the top of the other. Melt the butter, and pour it over the whole, and bake for 20 minutes. Take a portion of the gravy that flows from the fish, add the wine, lemon-juice, and seasoning, give it one boil, skim, pour it *under* the fish, and serve.

Time—20 minutes. *Average cost*, 1s. to 2s. per pair.

Seasonable at any time.

Sufficient for 4 or 5 persons.

TO CHOOSE SOLES—This fish should be both thick and firm. If the skin is difficult to be taken off, and the flesh looks grey, it is good.

THE SOLE—This ranks next to the turbot in point of excellence among our flat fish. It is abundant on the British coasts, but those of the western shores are much superior in size to those taken on the northern. The finest are caught in Torbay, and frequently weigh 8 or 10 lbs. per pair. Its flesh being firm,

ADDENDUM AND ANECDOTE

It will be seen, from the number and variety of the recipes which we have been enabled to give under the head of FISH, that there exists in the salt ocean, and fresh-water rivers, an abundance of aliment, which the present state of gastronomic art enables the cook to introduce to the table in the most agreeable forms, and oftentimes at a very moderate cost.

Less nutritious as a food than the flesh of animals, more succulent than vegetables, fish may be termed a middle dish, suited to all temperaments and constitutions; and one which those who are recovering from illness may partake of with safety and advantage.

As to which is the best fish, there has been much discussion. The old Latin proverb, however, *de gustibus non disputandum*, and the more modern Spanish one, *sobre los gustos no hai disputa*, declare, with equal force, that where *taste* is concerned, no decision can be arrived at. Each person's palate may be differently affected—pleased or displeased; and there is no standard by which to judge why a red mullet, a sole, or a turbot, should be better or worse than a salmon, trout, pike, or a tiny tench.

Fish, as we have explained, is less nourishing than meat; for it is lighter in weight, size for size, and contains no ozmazome. Shell-fish, oysters particularly, furnish but little nutriment; and this is the reason why so many of the latter can be eaten without injury to the system.

In Brillat Savarin's [Footnote: Brillat Savarin was a French lawyer and judge of considerable eminence and great talents, and wrote, under the above title, a book on gastronomy, full of instructive information, enlivened with a fund of pleasantly-told anecdote.] clever and amusing volume, "The Physiology of Taste," he says, that towards the end of the eighteenth century it was a most common thing for a well-arranged entertainment in Paris to commence with oysters, and that many guests were not contented without swallowing twelve dozen. Being anxious to know the weight of this advanced-guard, he ascertained that a dozen oysters, fluid included, weighed 4 ounces,—thus, the twelve dozen would weigh about 3 lbs.; and there can be no doubt, that the same persons who made no worse a dinner on account of having partaken of the oysters, would have been completely satisfied if they had eaten the same weight of chicken or mutton. An anecdote, perfectly well authenticated, is narrated of a French gentleman (M. Laperte), residing at Versailles, who was extravagantly fond of oysters, declaring he never had enough. Savarin resolved to procure him the satisfaction, and gave him an invitation to dinner, which was duly accepted. The guest arrived, and his host kept company with him in swallowing the delicious bivalves up to the tenth dozen, when, exhausted, he gave up, and let M. Laperte go on alone. This gentleman managed to eat thirty-two dozen within an hour, and would doubtless have got through more, but the person who opened them is described as not being very skilful. In the interim Savarin was idle, and at length, tired with his painful state of inaction, he said to Laperte, whilst the latter was still in full career, "Mon cher, you will not eat as many oysters to-day as you meant; let us dine." They dined, and the insatiable oyster-eater acted at the repast as if he had fasted for a week.

FISH CARVING

GENERAL DIRECTIONS FOR CARVING FISH

In carving fish, care should be taken to help it in perfect flakes, as, if these are broken, the beauty of the fish is lost. The carver should be acquainted, too, with the choicest parts and morsels; and to give each guest an equal share of these *titbits* should be his maxim. Steel knives and forks should on no account be used in helping fish, as these are liable to impart to it a very disagreeable flavour. Where silver fish-carvers are considered too dear to be bought, good electro-plated ones answer very well, and are inexpensive. The prices set down for them by Messrs. Slack, of the Strand, are from a guinea upwards.

SALMON

First run the knife quite down to the bone, along the side of the fish, from *a* to *b*, and also from *c* to *d*. Then help the thick part lengthwise, that is, in the direction of the lines from *a* to *b*; and the thin part breadthwise, that is, in the direction of the lines from *e* to *f*, as shown in the engraving. A slice of the thick part should always be accompanied by a smaller piece of the thin from the belly, where lies the fat of the fish.

Note—Many persons, in carving salmon, make the mistake of slicing the thick part of this fish in the opposite direction to that we have stated; and thus, by the breaking of the flakes, the beauty of its appearance is destroyed.

BOILED OR FRIED SOLE

The usual way of helping this fish is to cut it quite through, bone and all, distributing it in nice and not too large pieces. A moderately-sized sole will be sufficient for three slices; namely, the head, middle, and tail. The guests should be asked which of these they prefer. A small one will only give two slices. If the sole is very large, the upper side may be raised from the bone, and then divided into pieces; and the under side afterwards served in the same way.

In helping FILLETED SOLES, one fillet is given to each person. (For mode of serving, see Coloured Plate A.)

CHAPTER IX

GENERAL REMARKS

AN ANECDOTE IS TOLD of the prince de Soubise, who, intending to give an entertainment, asked for the bill of fare. His *chef* came, presenting a list adorned with vignettes, and the first article of which, that met the prince's eye, was "fifty hams." "Bertrand," said the prince, "I think you must be extravagant; Fifty hams! do you intend to feast my whole regiment?" "No, Prince, there will be but one on the table, and the surplus I need for my Espagnole, blondes, garnitures, &c." "Bertrand, you are robbing me: this item will not do." "Monseigneur," said the *artiste*, "you do not appreciate me. Give me the order, and I will put those fifty hams in a crystal flask no longer than my thumb." The prince smiled, and the hams were passed. This was all very well for the prince de Soubise; but as we do not write for princes and nobles alone, but that our British sisters may make the best dishes out of the least expensive ingredients, we will also pass the hams, and give a few general directions concerning Sauces, &c.

THE PREPARATION AND APPEARANCE OF SAUCES AND GRAVIES are of the highest consequence, and in nothing does the talent and taste of the cook more display itself. Their special adaptability to the various viands they are to accompany cannot be too much studied, in order that they may harmonize and blend with them as perfectly, so to speak, as does a pianoforte accompaniment with the voice of the singer.

THE GENERAL BASIS OF MOST GRAVIES and some sauces is the same stock as that used for soups; and, by the employment of these,

STORE SAUCES, VARIOUS PICKLES AND BOTTLED FRUITS FOR TARTS AND COMPÔTES.

with, perhaps, an additional slice of ham, a little spice, a few herbs, and a slight flavouring from some cold sauce or ketchup, very nice gravies may be made for a very small expenditure. A milt (either of a bullock or sheep), the shank-end of mutton that has already been dressed, and the necks and feet of poultry, may all be advantageously used for gravy, where much is not required. It may, then, be established as a rule, that there exists no necessity for good gravies to be expensive, and that there is no occasion, as many would have the world believe, to buy ever so many pounds of fresh meat, in order to furnish an ever so little quantity of gravy

BROWN SAUCES, generally speaking, should scarcely be so thick as white sauces; and it is well to bear in mind, that all those which are intended to mask the various dishes of poultry or meat, should be of a sufficient consistency to slightly adhere to the fowls or joints over which they are poured. For browning and thickening sauces, &c., browned flour may be properly employed.

CHAPTER X

RECIPES: SAUCES, PICKLES, GRAVIES, AND FORCEMEATS

APPLE SAUCE FOR GEESE, PORK, &c

Ingredients

6 good-sized apples
sifted sugar to taste
a piece of butter the size of a walnut
water

Mode—Pare, core, and quarter the apples, and throw them into cold water to preserve their whiteness. Put them in a saucepan, with sufficient water to moisten them, and boil till soft enough to pulp. Beat them up, adding sugar to taste, and a small piece of butter This quantity is sufficient for a good-sized tureen.

Time—According to the apples, about ¾ hour. *Average cost*, 4d.

Sufficient, this quantity, for a goose or couple of ducks.

ASPARAGUS SAUCE

Ingredients

1 bunch of green asparagus
Salt
1 oz. of fresh butter
1 small bunch of parsley
3 or 4 green onions
1 large lump of sugar
4 tablespoonfuls of sauce tournée

Mode—Break the asparagus in the tender part, wash well, and put them into boiling salt and water to render them green. When they are tender, take them out, and put them into cold water; drain them on a cloth till all moisture is absorbed from them. Put the butter in a stewpan, with the parsley and onions; lay in the asparagus, and fry the whole over a sharp fire for 5 minutes. Add salt, the sugar and sauce tournée, and simmer for another 5 minutes. Rub all through a tammy, and if not a very good colour, use a little spinach green. This sauce should be rather sweet.

CUSTARD SAUCE FOR SWEET PUDDINGS OR TARTS

Ingredients

1 pint of milk
2 eggs
3 oz. of pounded sugar
1 tablespoonful of brandy

Mode—Put the milk in a very clean saucepan, and let it boil. Beat the eggs, stir to them the milk and pounded sugar, and put the mixture into a jug. Place the jug in a saucepan of boiling water; keep stirring well until it thickens, but do not allow it to boil, or it will curdle. Serve the sauce in a tureen, stir in the brandy, and grate a little nutmeg over the top. This sauce may be made very much nicer by using cream instead of milk; but the above recipe will be found quite good enough for ordinary purposes.

Average cost, 6d. per pint.

Sufficient, this quantity, for 2 fruit tarts, or 1 pudding.

FRIED BREAD CRUMBS

Cut the bread into thin slices, place them in a cool oven overnight, and when thoroughly dry and crisp, roll them down into fine crumbs. Put some lard, or clarified dripping, into a frying-pan; bring it to the boiling-point, throw in the crumbs, and fry them very quickly. Directly they are done, lift them out with a slice, and drain them before the fire from all greasy moisture. When quite crisp, they are ready for use. The fat they are fried in should be clear, and the crumbs should not have the slightest appearance or taste of having been, in the least degree, burnt.

GENERAL STOCK FOR GRAVIES

Either of the stocks, Nos. 104, 105, or 107, will be found to answer very well for the basis of many gravies, unless these are wanted very rich indeed. By the addition of various store sauces, thickening and flavouring, the stocks here referred to may be converted into very good gravies. It should be borne in mind, however, that the goodness and strength of spices, wines, flavourings, &c., evaporate, and that they lose a great deal of their fragrance, if added to the gravy a long time before they are wanted. If this point is attended to, a saving of one half the quantity of these ingredients will be effected, as, with long boiling, the flavour almost entirely passes away. The shank-bones of mutton, previously well soaked, will be found a great assistance in enriching gravies; a kidney or melt, beef skirt, trimmings of meat, &c. &c., answer very well when only a small quantity is wanted, and, as we have before observed, a good gravy need not necessarily be so very expensive; for economically-prepared dishes are oftentimes found as savoury and wholesome as dearer ones. The cook should also remember that the fragrance of gravies should not be overpowered by too much spice, or any strong essences, and that they should always be warmed in a *bain marie*, after they are flavoured, or else in a jar or jug placed in a saucepan full of boiling water. The remains of roast-meat gravy should always be saved; as, when no meat is at hand, a very nice gravy in haste may be made from it, and when added to hashes, ragoûts, &c., is a great improvement.

BROWN GRAVY

Ingredients

2 oz. of butter
2 large onions
2 lbs. of shin of beef
2 small slices of lean bacon (if at hand)
salt and whole pepper to taste
3 cloves, 2 quarts of water
For thickening, 2 oz. of butter
3 oz. of flour

Mode—Put the butter into a stewpan; set this on the fire, throw in the onions cut in rings, and fry them a light brown; then add the beef and bacon, which should be cut into small square pieces; season, and pour in a teacupful of water; let it boil for about ten minutes, or until it is of a nice brown colour, occasionally stirring the contents. Now fill up with water in the above proportion; let it boil up, when draw it to the side of the fire to simmer very gently for 1-½ hour; strain, and when cold, take off all the fat. In thickening this gravy, melt 3 oz. of butter in a stewpan, add 2 oz. of flour, and stir till of a light-brown colour; when cold, add it to the strained gravy, and boil it up quickly. This thickening may be made in larger quantities, and kept in a stone jar for use when wanted.

Time—Altogether, 2 hours. *Average cost*, 4d. per pint.

CLOVES—This very agreeable spice is the unexpanded flower-buds of the *Caryophyllus aromaticus*, a handsome, branching tree, a native of the Malacca Islands. They take their name from the Latin word *clavus*, or the French *clou*, both meaning a nail, and to which the clove has a considerable resemblance. Cloves were but little known to the ancients, and Pliny appears to be the only writer who mentions them; and he says, vaguely enough, that some were brought to Rome, very similar to grains of pepper, but somewhat longer; that they were only to be found in India, in a wood consecrated to the gods; and that they served in the manufacture of perfumes. The Dutch, as in the case of the nutmeg, endeavoured, when they gained possession of the Spice Islands, to secure a monopoly of cloves, and, so that the cultivation of the tree might be confined to Amboyna, their chief island, bribed the surrounding chiefs to cut down all trees found elsewhere. The Amboyna, or royal clove, is said to be the best, and is rare; but other kinds, nearly equally good, are produced in other parts of the world, and they come to Europe from Mauritius, Bourbon, Cayenne, and Martinique, as also from St. Kitts, St. Vincent's, and Trinidad. The clove contains about 20 per cent. of volatile aromatic oil, to which it owes its peculiar pungent flavour, its other parts being composed of woody fibre, water, gum, and resin.

HORSERADISH SAUCE, to serve with Roast Beef.

Ingredients

4 tablespoonfuls of grated horseradish
1 teaspoonful of pounded sugar
1 teaspoonful of salt
½ teaspoonful of pepper
2 teaspoonfuls of made mustard
vinegar

Mode—Grate the horseradish, and mix it well with the sugar, salt, pepper, and mustard; moisten it with sufficient vinegar to give it the consistency of cream, and serve in a tureen: 3 or 4 tablespoonfuls of cream added to the above, very much improve the appearance and flavour of this sauce. To heat it to serve with hot roast beef, put it in a bain marie or a jar, which place in a saucepan of boiling water; make it hot, but do not allow it to boil, or it will curdle.

Note—This sauce is a great improvement on the old-fashioned way of serving cold-scraped horseradish with hot roast beef. The mixing of the cold vinegar with the warm gravy cools and spoils everything on the plate. Of course, with cold meat, the sauce should be served cold.

> **THE HORSERADISH**—This has been, for many years, a favourite accompaniment of roast beef, and is a native of England. It grows wild in wet ground, but has long been cultivated in the garden, and is, occasionally, used in winter salads and in sauces. On account of the great volatility of its oil, it should never be preserved by drying, but should be kept moist by being buried in sand. So rapidly does its volatile oil evaporate, that even when scraped for the table, it almost immediately spoils by exposure to the air.

MINT SAUCE, to serve with Roast Lamb.

Ingredients

4 dessertspoonfuls of chopped mint
2 dessertspoonfuls of pounded white sugar
¼ pint of vinegar

Mode—Wash the mint, which should be young and fresh-gathered, free from grit; pick the leaves from the stalks, mince them very fine, and put them into a tureen; add the sugar and vinegar, and stir till the former is dissolved. This sauce is better by being made 2 or 3 hours before wanted for table, as the vinegar then becomes impregnated with the flavour of the mint. By many persons, the above proportion of sugar would not be considered sufficient; but as tastes vary, we have given the quantity which we have found to suit the general palate.

Average cost, 3d.

Sufficient to serve with a middling-sized joint of lamb.

Note—Where green mint is scarce and not obtainable, mint vinegar may be substituted for it, and will be found very acceptable in early spring.

> **MINT**—The common mint cultivated in our gardens is known as the *Mentha viridis*, and is employed in different culinary processes, being sometimes boiled with certain dishes, and afterwards withdrawn. It has an agreeable aromatic flavour, and forms an ingredient in soups, and sometimes is used in spring salads. It is valuable as a stomachic and antispasmodic; on which account it is generally served at table with pea-soup. Several of its species grow wild in low situations in the country.

SAUSAGE-MEAT STUFFING, for Turkey.

Ingredients

- 6 oz. of lean pork
- 6 oz. of fat pork
- both weighed after being chopped (beef suet may be substituted for the latter)
- 2 oz. of bread crumbs
- 1 small tablespoonful of minced sage
- 1 blade of pounded mace
- salt and pepper to taste
- 1 egg

Mode—Chop the meat and fat very finely, mix with them the other ingredients, taking care that the whole is thoroughly incorporated.

Moisten with the egg, and the stuffing will be ready for use. Equal quantities of this stuffing and forcemeat, will be found to answer very well, as the herbs, lemon-peel, &c. in the latter, impart a very delicious flavour to the sausage-meat. As preparations, however, like stuffings and forcemeats, are matters to be decided by individual tastes, they must be left, to a great extent, to the discrimination of the cook, who should study her employer's taste in this, as in every other respect.

Average cost, 9d.

Sufficient for a small turkey.

TOMATO SAUCE—HOT, to serve with Cutlets, Roast Meats, &c.

Ingredients

6 tomatoes	1 blade of mace
2 shalots	salt and cayenne to taste
1 clove	¼ pint of gravy, or stock

Mode—Cut the tomatoes in two, and squeeze the juice and seeds out; put them in a stewpan with all the ingredients, and let them simmer *gently* until the tomatoes are tender enough to pulp; rub the whole through a sieve, boil it for a few minutes, and serve. The shalots and spices may be omitted when their flavour is objected to.

Time—1 hour, or rather more, to simmer the tomatoes.

Average cost, for this quantity, 1s.

In full season in September and October.

TOMATO, OR LOVE-APPLE—The plant which bears this fruit is a native of South America, and takes its name from a Portuguese word. The tomato fruit is about the size of a small potato, and is chiefly used in soups, sauces, and gravies. It is sometimes served to table roasted or boiled, and when green, makes a good ketchup or pickle. In its unripe state, it is esteemed as excellent sauce for roast goose or pork, and when quite ripe, a good store sauce may be prepared from it.

CHAPTER XI

GENERAL REMARKS

In Our "INTRODUCTION TO COOKERY" we have described the gradual progress of mankind in the art of cookery, the probability being, that the human race, for a long period, lived wholly on fruits. Man's means of attacking animals, even if he had the desire of slaughtering them, were very limited, until he acquired the use of arms. He, however, made weapons for himself, and, impelled by a carnivorous instinct, made prey of the animals that surrounded him. It is natural that man should seek to feed on flesh; he has too small a stomach to be supported alone by fruit, which has not sufficient nourishment to renovate him. It is possible he might subsist on vegetables; but their preparation needs the knowledge of art, only to be obtained after the lapse of many centuries. Man's first weapons were the branches of trees, which were succeeded by bows and arrows, and it is worthy of remark, that these latter weapons have been found with the natives of all climates and latitudes. It is singular how this idea presented itself to individuals so differently placed.

BRILLAT SAVARIN says, that raw flesh has but one inconvenience,—from its viscousness it attaches itself to the teeth. He goes on to say, that it is not, however, disagreeable; but, when seasoned with salt, that it is easily digested. He tells a story of a Croat captain, whom he invited to dinner in 1815, during the occupation of Paris by the allied troops. This officer was amazed at his host's preparations, and said, "When we are campaigning, and get hungry, we knock over the first animal we find, cut off a steak, powder it with salt, which we always have in the sabretasche, put it under the saddle, gallop over it for half a mile, and then dine like princes." Again, of the huntsmen of Dauphiny it is said, that when they are out shooting in September, they take with them both pepper and salt. If they kill a very fat bird, they pluck and season it, and, after carrying it some time in their caps, eat it. This, they declare, is the best way of serving it up.

IN THIS COUNTRY, plain boiling, roasting, and baking are the usual methods of cooking animal food. To explain the philosophy of these simple culinary operations, we must advert to the effects that are produced by heat on the principal constituents of flesh. When finely-chopped mutton or beef is steeped for some time in a small quantity of clean water, and then subjected to slight pressure, the juice of the meat is extracted, and there is left a white tasteless residue, consisting chiefly of muscular fibres. When this residue is heated to between 158° and 177° Fahrenheit, the fibres shrink together, and become hard and horny. The influence of an elevated temperature on the soluble extract of flesh is not less remarkable. When the watery infusion, which contains all the savoury constituents of the meat, is gradually heated, it soon becomes turbid; and, when the temperature reaches 133°, flakes of whitish matter separate. These flakes are *albumen*, a substance precisely similar, in all its properties, to the white of egg. When the temperature of the watery extract is raised to 158°, the colouring matter of the blood coagulates, and the liquid, which was originally tinged red by this substance, is left perfectly clear, and almost colourless. When evaporated, even at a gentle heat, this residual liquid gradually becomes brown, and acquires the flavour of roast meat.

THESE INTERESTING FACTS, discovered in the laboratory, throw a flood of light upon the mysteries of the kitchen. The fibres of meat are surrounded by a liquid which contains albumen in its soluble state, just as it exists in the unboiled egg. During the operation of boiling or roasting, this substance coagulates, and thereby prevents the contraction and hardening of the fibres. The tenderness of well-cooked meat is consequently proportioned to the amount of albumen deposited in its substance. Meat is underdone when it has been heated throughout only to the temperature of coagulating albumen: it is thoroughly done when it has been heated through its whole mass to the temperature at which the colouring matter of the blood coagulates: it is overdone when the heat has been continued long enough to harden the fibres.

THE JUICE OF FLESH IS WATER, holding in solution many substances besides albumen, which are of the highest possible value as articles of food. In preparing meat for the table, great care should be taken to prevent the escape of this precious juice, as the succulence and sapidity of the meat depend on its retention. The meat to be cooked should be exposed at first to a quick heat, which immediately coagulates the albumen on and near the surface. A kind of shell is thus formed, which effectually retains the whole of the juice within the meat.

DURING THE OPERATIONS OF BOILING, BOASTING, AND BAKING, fresh beef and mutton, when moderately fat, lose, according to Johnston, on an average about—

In boiling. In baking. In roasting.
4 lbs. of beef lose 1 lb. 1 lb. 3 oz. 1 lb. 5 oz.
4 lbs. of mutton lose 14 oz. 1 lb. 4 oz. 1 lb. 6 oz.

BAKING

THE DIFFERENCE BETWEEN ROASTING MEAT AND BAKING IT, may be generally described as consisting in the fact, that, in baking it, the fumes caused by the operation are not carried off in the same way as occurs in roasting. Much, however, of this disadvantage is obviated by the improved construction of modern ovens, and of especially those in connection with the Leamington kitchener, of which we give an engraving here, and a full description of which will be seen at paragraph with the prices at which they can be purchased of Messrs. R. and J. Slack, of the Strand. With meat baked in the generality of ovens, however, which do not possess ventilators on the principle of this kitchener, there is undoubtedly a peculiar taste, which does not at all equal the flavour developed by roasting meat. The chemistry of baking may be said to be the same as that described in roasting.

SHOULD THE OVEN BE VERY BRISK, it will be found necessary to cover the joint with a piece of white paper, to prevent the meat from being scorched and blackened outside, before the heat can penetrate into the inside. This paper should be removed half an hour before the time of serving dinner, so that the joint may take a good colour.

BY MEANS OF A JAR, many dishes, which will be enumerated under their special heads, may be economically prepared in the oven. The principal of these are soup, gravies, jugged hare, beef tea; and this mode of cooking may be advantageously adopted with a ham, which has previously been covered with a common crust of flour and water.

ALL DISHES PREPARED FOR BAKING should be more highly seasoned than when intended to be roasted. There are some dishes which, it may be said, are at least equally well cooked in the oven as by the roaster; thus, a shoulder of mutton and baked potatoes, a fillet or breast of veal, a sucking pig, a hare, well basted, will be received by connoisseurs as well, when baked, as if they had been roasted. Indeed, the baker's oven, or the family oven, may often, as has been said, be substituted for the cook and the spit with greater economy and convenience.

A BAKING-DISH, of which we give an engraving, should not be less than 6 or 7 inches deep; so that the meat, which of course cannot be basted, can stew in its own juices. In the recipe for each dish, full explanations concerning any special points in relation to it will be given.

BOILING

BOILING, or the preparation of meat by hot water, though one of the easiest processes in cookery, requires skilful management. Boiled meat should be tender, savoury, and full of its own juice, or natural gravy; but, through the carelessness and ignorance of cooks, it is too often sent to table hard, tasteless, and innutritious. To insure a successful result in boiling flesh, the heat of the fire must be judiciously regulated, the proper quantity of water must be kept up in the pot, and the scum which rises to the surface must be carefully removed.

MANY WRITERS ON COOKERY assert that the meat to be boiled should be put into cold water, and that the pot should be heated gradually; but Liebig, the highest authority on all matters connected with the chemistry of food, has shown that meat so treated loses some of its most nutritious constituents. "If the flesh," says the great chemist, "be introduced into the boiler when the water is in a state of brisk ebullition, and if the boiling be kept up for a few minutes, and the pot then placed in a warm place, so that the temperature of the water is kept at 158° to 165°, we have the united conditions for giving to the flesh the qualities which best fit it for being eaten." When a piece of meat is plunged into boiling water, the albumen which is near the surface immediately coagulates, forming an envelope, which prevents the escape of the internal juice, and most effectually excludes the water, which, by mixing with this juice, would render the meat insipid. Meat treated thus is juicy and well-flavoured, when cooked, as it retains most of its savoury constituents. On the other hand, if the piece of meat be set on the fire with cold water, and this slowly heated to boiling, the flesh undergoes a loss of soluble and nutritious substances, while, as a matter of course, the soup becomes richer in these matters. The albumen is gradually dissolved from the surface to the centre; the fibre loses, more or less, its quality of shortness or tenderness, and becomes hard and tough: the thinner the piece of meat is, the greater is its loss of savoury constituents. In order to obtain well-flavoured and eatable meat, we must relinquish the idea of making good soup from it, as that mode of boiling which yields the best soup gives the driest, toughest, and most vapid meat. Slow boiling whitens the meat; and, we suspect, that it is on this account that it is in such favour with the cooks. The wholesomeness of food is, however, a matter of much greater moment than the appearance it presents on the table. It should be borne in mind, that the whiteness of meat that has been boiled slowly, is produced by the loss of some important alimentary properties.

THE OBJECTIONS WE HAVE RAISED to the practice of putting meat on the fire in cold water, apply with equal force to the practice of soaking meat before cooking it, which is so strongly recommended by some cooks. Fresh meat ought never to be soaked, as all its most nutritive constituents are soluble in water. Soaking, however, is an operation that cannot be entirely dispensed with in the preparation of animal food. Salted and dried meats require to be soaked for some time in water before they are cooked.

FOR BOILING MEAT, the softer the water is, the better. When spring water is boiled, the chalk which gives to it the quality of hardness, is precipitated. This chalk stains the meat, and communicates to it an unpleasant earthy taste. When nothing but hard water can be procured, it should be softened by boiling it for an hour or two before it is used for culinary purposes.

THE FIRE MUST BE WATCHED with great attention during the operation of boiling, so that its heat may be properly regulated. As a rule, the pot should be kept in a simmering state; a result which cannot be attained without vigilance.

THE TEMPERATURE AT WHICH WATER BOILS, under usual circumstances, is 212° Fahr. Water does not become hotter after it has begun to boil, however long or with whatever violence the boiling is continued. This fact is of great importance in cookery, and attention to it will save much fuel. Water made to boil in a gentle way by the application of a moderate heat is just as hot as when it is made to boil on a strong fire with the greatest possible violence. When once water has been brought to the boiling point, the fire may be considerably reduced, as a very gentle heat will suffice to keep the water at its highest temperature.

THE SCUM WHICH RISES to the surface of the pot during the operation of boiling must be carefully removed, otherwise it will attach itself to the meat, and thereby spoil its appearance. The cook must not neglect to skim during the whole process, though by far the greater part of the scum rises at first. The practice of wrapping meat in a cloth may be dispensed with if the skimming be skillfully managed. If the scum be removed as fast as it rises, the meat will be cooked clean and pure, and come out of the vessel in which it was boiled, much more delicate and firm than when cooked in a cloth.

WHEN TAKEN FROM THE POT, the meat must be wiped with a clean cloth, or, what will be found more convenient, a sponge previously dipped in water and wrung dry. The meat should not be allowed to stand a moment longer than necessary, as boiled meat, as well as roasted, cannot be eaten too hot.

THE TIME ALLOWED FOR THE OPERATION OF BOILING must be regulated according to the size and quality of the meat. As a general rule, twenty minutes, reckoning from the moment when the boiling commences, may be allowed for every pound of meat. All the best authorities, however, agree in this, that the longer the boiling the more perfect the operation.

A FEW OBSERVATIONS ON THE NUTRITIVE VALUE OF SALTED MEAT may be properly introduced in this place. Every housewife knows that dry salt in contact with fresh meat gradually becomes fluid brine. The application of salt causes the fibres of the meat to contract, and the juice to flow out from its pores: as much as one-third of the juice of the meat is often forced out in this manner. Now, as this juice is pure extract of meat, containing albumen, osmazome, and other valuable principles, it follows that meat which has been preserved by the action of salt can never have the nutritive properties of fresh meat.

THE VESSELS USED FOR BOILING should be made of cast-iron, well tinned within, and provided with closely-fitting lids. They must be kept scrupulously clean, otherwise they will render the meat cooked in them unsightly and unwholesome. Copper pans, if used at all, should be reserved for operations that are performed with rapidity; as, by long contact with copper, food may become dangerously contaminated. The kettle in which a joint is dressed should be large enough to allow room for a good supply of water; if the meat be cramped and be surrounded with but little water, it will be stewed, not boiled.

IN STEWING, IT IS NOT REQUISITE to have so great a heat as in boiling. A gentle simmering in a small quantity of water, so that the meat is stewed almost in its own juices, is all that is necessary. It is a method much used on the continent, and is wholesome and economical.

BROILING

GENERALLY SPEAKING, small dishes only are prepared by this mode of cooking; amongst these, the beef-steak and mutton chop of the solitary English diner may be mentioned as celebrated all the world over. Our beef-steak, indeed, has long crossed the Channel; and, with a view of pleasing the Britons, there is in every *carte* at every French restaurant, by the side of *à la Marengo*, and *à la Mayonnaise,—bifteck d'Angleterre*. In order to succeed in a broil, the cook must have a bright, clear fire; so that the surface of the meat may be quickly heated. The result of this is the same as that obtained in roasting; namely, that a crust, so to speak, is formed outside, and thus the juices of the meat are retained. The appetite of an invalid, so difficult to minister to, is often pleased with a broiled dish, as the flavour and sapidity of the meat are so well preserved.

THE UTENSILS USED FOR BROILING need but little description. The common gridiron is the same as it has been for ages past, although some little variety has been introduced into its manufacture, by the addition of grooves to the bars, by means of which the liquid fat is carried into a small trough. One point it is well to bear in mind, viz., that the gridiron should be kept in a direction slanting towards the cook, so that as little fat as possible may fall into the fire. It has been observed, that broiling is the most difficult manual office the general cook has to perform, and one that requires the most unremitting attention; for she may turn her back upon the stewpan or the spit, but the gridiron can never be left with impunity. The revolving gridiron, shown in the engraving, possesses some advantages of convenience, which will be at once apparent.

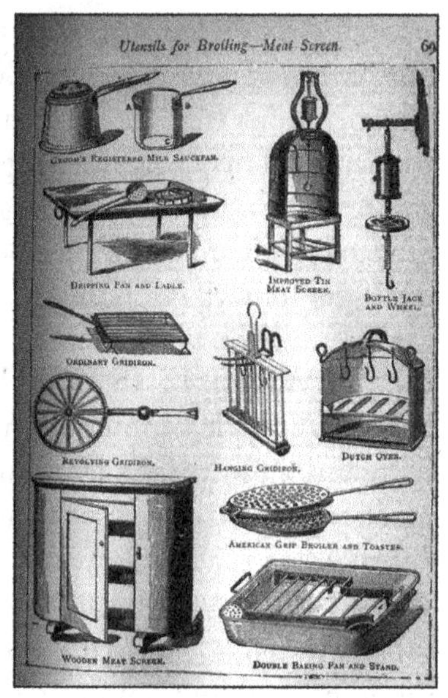

FRYING

THIS VERY FAVOURITE MODE OF COOKING may be accurately described as boiling in fat or oil. Substances dressed in this way are generally well received, for they introduce an agreeable variety, possessing, as they do, a peculiar flavour. By means of frying, cooks can soon satisfy many requisitions made on them, it being a very expeditious mode of preparing dishes for the table, and one which can be employed when the fire is not sufficiently large for the purposes of roasting and boiling. The great point to be borne in mind in frying, is that the liquid must be hot enough to act instantaneously, as all the merit of this culinary operation lies in the invasion of the boiling liquid, which carbonizes or burns, at the very instant of the immersion of the body placed in it. It may be ascertained if the fat is heated to the proper degree, by cutting a piece of bread and dipping it in the frying-pan for five or six seconds; and if it be firm and of a dark brown when taken out, put in immediately what you wish to prepare; if it be not, let the fat be heated until of the right temperature. This having been effected, moderate the fire, so that the action may not be too hurried, and that by a continuous heat the juices of the substance may be preserved, and its flavour enhanced.

THE PHILOSOPHY OF FRYING consists in this, that liquids subjected to the action of fire do not all receive the same quantity of heat. Being differently constituted in their nature, they possess different "capacities for caloric." Thus, you may, with impunity, dip your finger in boiling spirits of wine; you would take it very quickly from boiling brandy, yet more rapidly from water; whilst the effects of the most rapid immersion in boiling oil need not be told. As a consequence of this, heated fluids act differently on the sapid bodies presented to them. Those put in water, dissolve, and are reduced to a soft mass; the result being *bouillon*, stock, &c. Those substances, on the contrary, treated with oil, harden, assume a more or less deep colour, and are finally carbonized. The reason of these different results is, that, in the first instance, water dissolves and extracts the interior juices of the alimentary substances placed in it; whilst, in the second, the juices are preserved; for they are insoluble in oil.

IT IS TO BE ESPECIALLY REMEMBERED, in connection with frying, that all dishes fried in fat should be placed before the fire on a piece of blotting-paper, or sieve reversed, and there left for a few minutes, so that any superfluous greasy moisture may be removed.

THE UTENSILS USED FOR THE PURPOSES OF FRYING are confined to frying-pans, although these are of various sizes; and, for small and delicate dishes, such as collops, fritters, pancakes, &c., the *sauté*pan, of which we give an engraving, is used.

ROASTING

OF THE VARIOUS METHODS OF PREPARING MEAT, ROASTING is that which most effectually preserves its nutritive qualities. Meat is roasted by being exposed to the direct influence of the fire. This is done by placing the meat before an open grate, and keeping it in motion to prevent the scorching on any particular part. When meat is properly roasted, the outer layer of its albumen is coagulated, and thus presents a barrier to the exit of the juice. In roasting meat, the heat must be strongest at first, and it should then be much reduced. To have a good juicy roast, therefore, the fire must be red and vigorous at the very commencement of the operation. In the most careful roasting, some of the juice is squeezed out of the meat: this evaporates on the surface of the meat, and gives it a dark brown colour, a rich lustre, and a strong aromatic taste. Besides these effects on the albumen and the expelled juice, roasting converts the cellular tissue of the meat into gelatine, and melts the fat out of the fat-cells.

IF A SPIT is used to support the meat before the fire, it should be kept quite bright. Sand and water ought to be used to scour it with, for brickdust and oil may give a disagreeable taste to the meat. When well scoured, it must be wiped quite dry with a clean cloth; and, in spitting the meat, the prime parts should be left untouched, so as to avoid any great escape of its juices.

KITCHENS IN LARGE ESTABLISHMENTS are usually fitted with what are termed "smoke-jacks." By means of these, several spits, if required, may be turned at the same time. This not being, of course, necessary in smaller establishments, a roasting apparatus, more economical in its consumption of coal, is more frequently in use.

THE BOTTLE-JACK, of which we here give an illustration, with the wheel and hook, and showing the precise manner of using it, is now commonly used in many kitchens. This consists of a spring inclosed in a brass cylinder, and requires winding up before it is used, and sometimes, also, during the operation of roasting. The joint is fixed to an iron hook, which is suspended by a chain connected with a wheel, and which, in its turn, is connected with the bottle-jack. Beneath it stands the dripping-pan, which we have also engraved, together with the basting-ladle, the use of which latter should not be spared; as there can be no good roast without good basting. "Spare the rod, and spoil the child," might easily be paraphrased into "Spare the basting, and spoil the meat." If the joint is small and light, and so turns unsteadily, this may be remedied by fixing to the wheel one of the kitchen weights. Sometimes this jack is fixed inside a screen; but there is this objection to this apparatus,—that the meat cooked in it resembles the flavour of baked meat. This is derived from its being so completely surrounded with the tin, that no sufficient current of air gets to it. It will be found preferable to make use of a common meat-screen, such as is shown in the woodcut. This contains shelves for warming plates and dishes; and with this, the reflection not being so powerful, and more air being admitted to the joint, the roast may be very excellently cooked.

IN STIRRING THE FIRE, or putting fresh coals on it, the dripping-pan should always be drawn back, so that there may be no danger of the coal, cinders, or ashes falling down into it.

UNDER EACH PARTICULAR RECIPE there is stated the time required for roasting each joint; but, as a general rule, it may be here given, that for every pound of meat, in ordinary-sized joints, a quarter of an hour may be allotted.

WHITE MEATS, AND THE MEAT OF YOUNG ANIMALS, require to be very well roasted, both to be pleasant to the palate and easy of digestion. Thus veal, pork, and lamb, should be thoroughly done to the centre.

MUTTON AND BEEF, on the other hand, do not, generally speaking, require to be so thoroughly done, and they should be dressed to the point, that, in carving them, the gravy should just run, but not too freely. Of course in this, as in most other dishes, the tastes of individuals vary; and there are many who cannot partake, with satisfaction, of any joint unless it is what others would call overdressed.

CHAPTER XII

RECIPES

BAKED BEEF (Cold Meat Cookery)

Ingredients

About 2 lbs. of cold roast beef
2 small onions
1 large carrot or two small ones
1 turnip
a small bunch of savoury herbs
salt and pepper to taste
4 tablespoonfuls of gravy
3 tablespoonfuls of ale
crust or mashed potatoes

ode—Cut the beef in slices, allowing a small amount of fat to each slice; place a layer of this in the bottom of a pie-dish, with a portion of the onions, carrots, and turnips, which must be sliced; mince the herbs, strew them over the meat, and season with pepper and salt. Then put another layer of meat, vegetables, and seasoning; and proceed in this manner until all the ingredients are used. Pour in the gravy and ale (water may be substituted for the former, but it is not so nice), cover with a crust or mashed potatoes, and bake for ½ hour, or rather longer.

Time—Rather more than ½ hour.

Average cost, exclusive of the meat, 6d.

Sufficient for 5 or 6 persons.

Seasonable at any time.

Note—It is as well to parboil the carrots and turnips before adding them to the meat, and to use some of the liquor in which they were boiled as a substitute for gravy; that is to say, when there is no gravy at hand. Be particular to cut the onions in very *thin* slices.

> BEEF—The quality of beef depends on various circumstances; such as the age, the sex, the breed of the animal, and also on the food upon which it has been raised. Bull beef is, in general, dry and tough, and by no means possessed of an agreeable flavour; whilst the flesh of the ox is not only highly nourishing and digestible, but, if not too old, extremely agreeable. The flesh of the cow is, also, nourishing, but it is not so agreeable as that of the ox, although that of a heifer is held in high estimation. The flesh of the smaller breeds is much sweeter than that of the larger, which is best when the animal is about seven years old. That of the smaller breeds is best at about five years, and that of the cow can hardly be eaten too young.

BEEF CAKE

Ingredients

The remains of cold roast beef; to each pound of cold meat allow ¼ lb. of bacon or ham
seasoning to taste of pepper and salt
1 small bunch of minced savoury herbs
1 or 2 eggs

Mode—Mince the beef very finely (if underdone it will be better), add to it the bacon, which must also be chopped very small, and mix well together. Season, stir in the herbs, and bind with an egg, or 2 should 1 not be sufficient. Make it into small square cakes, about ½ inch thick, fry them in hot dripping, and serve in a dish with good gravy poured round them.

Time—10 minutes.

Average cost, exclusive of the cold meat, 6d.

Seasonable at any time.

ROAST RIBS OF BEEF

Ingredients
Beef
a little salt

Mode—The fore-rib is considered the primest roasting piece, but the middle-rib is considered the most economical. Let the meat be well hung (should the weather permit), and cut off the thin ends of the bones, which should be salted for a few days, and then boiled. Put the meat down to a nice clear fire, put some clean dripping into the pan, dredge the joint with a little flour, and keep continually basting the whole time. Sprinkle some fine salt over it (this must never be done until the joint is dished, as it draws the juices from the meat); pour the dripping from the pan, put in a little boiling: water slightly salted, and *strain* the gravy over the meat. Garnish with tufts of scraped horseradish, and send horseradish sauce to table with it. A Yorkshire pudding sometimes accompanies this dish, and, if lightly made and well cooked, will be found a very agreeable addition.

Time—10 lbs. of beef, 2-½ hours; 14 to 16 lbs., from 3-½ to 4 hours.

Average cost, 8-1/2d. per lb.

Sufficient—A joint of 10 lbs. sufficient for 8 or 9 persons.

Seasonable at any time.

ROAST SIRLOIN OF BEEF

Ingredients
Beef
a little salt

Mode—As a joint cannot be well roasted without a good fire, see that it is well made up about ¾ hour before it is required, so that when the joint is put down, it is clear and bright. Choose a nice sirloin, the weight of which should not exceed 16 lbs., as the outside would be too much done, whilst the inside would not be done enough. Spit it or hook it on to the jack firmly, dredge it slightly with flour, and place it near the fire at first, as directed in the preceding recipe. Then draw it to a distance, and keep continually basting until the meat is done. Sprinkle a small quantity of salt over it, empty the dripping-pan of all the dripping, pour in some boiling water slightly salted, stir it about, and *strain* over the meat. Garnish with tufts of horseradish, and send horseradish sauce and Yorkshire pudding to table with it.

Time—A sirloin of 10 lbs., 2-½ hours; 14 to 16 lbs., about 4 or 4-½ hours.

Average cost, 8-½d. per lb.

Sufficient—A joint of 10 lbs. for 8 or 9 persons.

Seasonable at any time.

Note—The above is the usual method of roasting moat; but to have it in perfection and the juices kept in, the meat should at first be laid close to the fire, and when the outside is set and firm, drawn away to a good distance, and then left to roast very slowly; where economy is studied, this plan would not answer, as the meat requires to be at the fire double the time of the ordinary way of cooking; consequently, double the quantity of fuel would be consumed.

ORIGIN OF THE WORD "SIRLOIN."—The loin of beef is said to have been knighted by King Charles II., at Friday Hall, Chingford. The "Merry Monarch" returned to this hospitable mansion for Epping Forest literally "as hungry as a hunter," and beheld, with delight, a huge loin of beef steaming upon the table. "A noble joint!" exclaimed the king. "By St. George, it shall have a title!" Then drawing his sword, he raised it above the meat, and cried, with mock dignity, "Loin, we dub thee knight; henceforward be Sir Loin!" This anecdote is doubtless apocryphal, although the oak table upon which the joint was supposed to have received its knighthood, might have been seen by any one who visited Friday-Hill House, a few years ago. It is, perhaps, a pity to spoil so noble a story; but the interests of truth demand that we declare that *sirloin* is probably a corruption of *surloin*, which signifies the upper part of a loin, the prefix *sur* being equivalent to *over* or *above*. In French we find this joint called *surlonge*, which so closely resembles our *sirloin*, that we may safely refer the two words to a common origin.

BEEF SAUSAGES

Ingredients

To every lb. of suet allow 2 lbs. of lean beef
seasoning to taste of salt, pepper, and mixed spices

Mode—Clear the suet from skin, and chop that and the beef as finely as possible; season with pepper, salt, and spices, and mix the whole well together. Make it into flat cakes, and fry of a nice brown. Many persons pound the meat in a mortar after it is chopped (but this is not necessary when the meat is minced finely.)

Time—10 minutes. *Average cost*, for this quantity, 1s. 6d.

Seasonable at any time.

CHAPTER XIII

GENERAL OBSERVATIONS ON THE COMMON HOG

- THE HOG belongs to the order *Mammalia*, the genus *Sus scrofa*, and the species *Pachydermata*, or thick-skinned; and its generic characters are, a small head, with long flexible snout truncated; 42 teeth, divided into 4 upper incisors, converging, 6 lower incisors, projecting, 2 upper and 2 lower canine, or tusks,—the former short, the latter projecting, formidable, and sharp, and 14 molars in each jaw; cloven feet furnished with 4 toes, and tail, small, short, and twisted; while, in some varieties, this appendage is altogether wanting.

- IT IS A REMARKABLE FACT that, though every one who keeps a pig knows how prone he is to disease, how that disease injures the quality of the meat, and how eagerly he pounces on a bit of coal or cinder, or any coarse dry substance that will adulterate the rich food on which he lives, and by affording soda to his system, correct the vitiated fluids of his body,—yet very few have the judgment to act on what they see, and by supplying the pig with a few shovelfuls of cinders in his sty, save the necessity of his rooting for what is so needful to his health. Instead of this, however, and without supplying the animal with what its instinct craves for, his nostril is bored with a red-hot iron, and a ring clinched in his nose to prevent rooting for what he feels to be absolutely necessary for his health; and ignoring the fact that, in a domestic state at least, the pig lives on the richest of all food,—scraps of cooked animal substances, boiled vegetables, bread, and other items, given in that concentrated essence of aliment for a quadruped called wash, and that he eats to repletion, takes no exercise, and finally sleeps all the twenty-four hours he is not eating, and then, when the animal at last seeks for those medicinal aids which would obviate the evil of such a forcing diet, his keeper, instead of meeting his animal instinct by human reason, and giving him what he seeks, has the inhumanity to torture him by a ring, that, keeping up a perpetual "raw" in the pig's snout, prevents his digging for those corrective drugs which would remove the evils of his artificial existence.

- THE GREAT QUALITY FIRST SOUGHT FOR IN A HOG is a capacious stomach, and next, a healthy power of digestion; for the greater the quantity he can eat, and the more rapidly he can digest what he has eaten, the more quickly will he fatten; and the faster he can be made to increase in flesh, without a material increase of bone, the better is the breed considered, and the more valuable the animal. In the usual order of nature, the development of flesh and enlargement of bone proceed together; but here the object is to outstrip the growth of the bones by the quicker development of their fleshy covering.

- THE CHIEF POINTS SOUGHT FOR IN THE CHOICE OF A HOG are breadth of chest, depth of carcase, width of loin, chine, and ribs, compactness of form, docility, cheerfulness, and general beauty of appearance. The head in a well-bred hog must not be too long, the forehead narrow and convex, cheeks full, snout fine, mouth small, eyes small and quick, ears short, thin, and sharp, pendulous, and pointing forwards; neck full and broad, particularly on the top, where it should join very broad shoulders; the ribs, loin, and haunch should be in a uniform line, and the tail well set, neither too high nor too low; at the same time the back is to be straight or slightly curved, the chest deep, broad, and prominent, the legs short and thick; the belly, when well fattened, should nearly touch the ground, the hair be long, thin, fine, and having few bristles, and whatever the colour, uniform, either white, black, or blue; but not spotted, speckled, brindled, or sandy. Such are the features and requisites that, among breeders and judges, constitute the *beau idéal* of a perfect pig.

- PORK, TO BE PRESERVED, is cured in several ways,—either by covering it with salt, or immersing it in ready-made brine, where it is kept till required; or it is only partially salted, and then hung up to dry, when the meat is called white bacon; or, after salting, it is hung in wood smoke till the flesh is impregnated with the aroma from the wood. The Wiltshire bacon, which is regarded as the finest in the kingdom, is prepared by laying the sides of a hog in large wooden troughs, and then rubbing into the flesh quantities of powdered bay-salt, made hot in a frying-pan. This process is repeated for four days; they are then left for three weeks, merely turning the flitches every other day. After that time they are hung up to dry. The hogs usually killed for purposes of bacon in England average from 18 to 20 stone; on the other hand, the hogs killed in the country for farm-house purposes, seldom weigh less than 26 stone. The legs of boars, hogs, and, in Germany, those of bears, are prepared differently, and called hams.

- THE PRACTICE IN VOGUE FORMERLY in this country was to cut out the hams and cure them separately; then to remove the ribs, which were roasted as "spare-ribs," and, curing the remainder of the side, call it a "gammon of bacon."

Small pork to cut for table in joints, is cut up, in most places throughout the kingdom, as represented in the engraving. The sale is divided with nine ribs to the fore quarter; and the following is an enumeration of the joints in the two respective quarters:—

1. The leg.
2. The loin.
3. The spring, or belly.

4. The hand.
5. The fore-loin.
6. The cheek.

The weight of the several joints of a good pork pig of four stone may be as follows; viz.:—

The leg 8 lbs.
The loin and spring 7 lbs.
The hand 6 lbs.
The chine 7 lbs.
The cheek from 2 to 3 lbs.

Of a bacon pig, the legs are reserved for curing, and when cured are called hams: when the meat is separated from the shoulder-blade and bones and cured, it is called bacon. The bones, with part of the meat left on them, are divided into spare-ribs, griskins, and chines.

CHAPTER XIV

RECIPES: PORK AND HAM

PORK CUTLETS OR CHOPS

Ingredients
Loin of pork
pepper and salt to taste

Mode—Cut the cutlets from a delicate loin of pork, bone and trim them neatly, and cut away the greater portion of the fat. Season them with pepper; place the gridiron on the fire; when quite hot, lay on the chops and broil them for about ¼ hour, turning them 3 or 4 times; and be particular that they are *thoroughly* done, but not dry. Dish them, sprinkle over a little fine salt, and serve plain, or with tomato sauce, sauce piquante, or pickled gherkins, a few of which should be laid round the dish as a garnish.

Time—About ¼ hour. *Average cost*, 10d. per lb. for chops.

Sufficient—Allow 6 for 4 persons.

Seasonable from October to March.

TO BAKE A HAM

Ingredients
Ham
a common crust

Mode—As a ham for baking should be well soaked, let it remain in water for at least 12 hours. Wipe it dry, trim away any rusty places underneath, and cover it with a common crust, taking care that this is of sufficient thickness all over to keep the gravy in. Place it in a moderately-heated oven, and bake for nearly 4 hours. Take off the crust, and skin, and cover with raspings, the same as for boiled ham, and garnish the knuckle with a paper frill. This method of cooking a ham is, by many persons, considered far superior to boiling it, as it cuts fuller of gravy and has a finer flavour, besides keeping a much longer time good.

Time—A medium-sized ham, 4 hours.

Average cost, from 8d. to 10d. per lb. by the whole ham.

Seasonable all the year.

TO BOIL A HAM

Ingredients
Ham
Water
glaze or raspings

Mode—In choosing a ham, ascertain that it is perfectly sweet, by running a sharp knife into it, close to the bone; and if, when the knife is withdrawn, it has an agreeable smell, the ham is good; if, on the contrary, the blade has a greasy appearance and offensive smell, the ham is bad. If it has been long hung, and is very dry and salt, let it remain in soak for 24 hours, changing the water frequently. This length of time is only necessary in the case of its being very hard; from 8 to 12 hours would be sufficient for a Yorkshire or Westmoreland ham. Wash it thoroughly clean, and trim away from the under-side, all the rusty and smoked parts, which would spoil the appearance. Put it into a boiling-pot, with sufficient cold water to cover it; bring it gradually to boil, and as the scum rises, carefully remove it. Keep it simmering very gently until tender, and be careful that it does not stop boiling, nor boil too quickly. When done, take it out of the pot, strip off the skin, and sprinkle over it a few fine bread-raspings, put a frill of cut paper round the knuckle, and serve. If to be eaten cold, let the ham remain in the water until nearly cold: by this method the juices are kept in, and it will be found infinitely superior to one taken out of the water hot; it should, however, be borne in mind that the ham must *not* remain in the saucepan *all* night. When the skin is removed, sprinkle over bread-raspings, or, if wanted particularly nice, glaze it. Place a paper frill round the knuckle, and garnish with parsley or cut vegetable flowers.

Time—A ham weighing 10 lbs., 4 hours to *simmer gently*; 15 lbs., 5 hours; a very large one, about 5 hours.

Average cost, from 8d. to 10d. per lb. by the whole ham.

Seasonable all the year.

Seasonable from September to March.

TO MAKE SAUSAGES

(*Author's Oxford Recipe.*)

Ingredients

1 lb. of pork
fat and lean
without skin or gristle
1 lb. of lean veal
1 lb. of beef suet
½ lb. of bread crumbs
the rind of ½ lemon
1 small nutmeg
6 sage-leaves
1 teaspoonful of pepper
2 teaspoonfuls of salt
½ teaspoonful of savory
½ teaspoonful of marjoram

Mode—Chop the pork, veal, and suet finely together, add the bread crumbs, lemon-peel (which should be well minced), and a small nutmeg grated. Wash and chop the sage-leaves very finely; add these with the remaining ingredients to the sausage-meat, and when thoroughly mixed, either put the meat into skins, or, when wanted for table, form it into little cakes, which should be floured and fried.

Average cost, for this quantity, 2s. 6d.

Sufficient for about 30 moderate-sized sausages.

Seasonable from October to March.

CHAPTER XV

GENERAL OBSERVATIONS ON THE CALF

ANY REMARKS MADE ON THE CALF OR THE LAMB must naturally be in a measure supplementary to the more copious observations made on the parent stock of either. As the calf, at least as far as it is identified with veal, is destined to die young,—to be, indeed, cut off in its comparative infancy,—it may, at first sight, appear of little or no consequence to inquire to what particular variety, or breed of the general stock, his sire or dam may belong. The great art, however, in the modern science of husbandry has been to obtain an animal that shall not only have the utmost beauty of form of which the species is capable, but, at the same time, a constitution free from all taint, a frame that shall rapidly attain bulk and stature, and a disposition so kindly that every *quantum* of food it takes shall, without drawback or procrastination, be eliminated into fat and muscle. The breed, then, is of very considerable consequence in determining, not only the quality of the meat to the consumer, but its commercial value to the breeder and butcher.

UNDER THE ARTIFICIAL SYSTEM adopted in the rearing of domestic cattle, and stock in general, to gratify the arbitrary mandates of luxury and fashion, we can have veal, like lamb, at all seasons in the market, though the usual time in the metropolis for veal to make its appearance is about the beginning of February.

THE COW GOES WITH YOUNG FOR NINE MONTHS, and the affection and solicitude she evinces for her offspring is more human in its tenderness mid intensity than is displayed by any other animal; and her distress when she hears its bleating, and is not allowed to reach it with her distended udders, is often painful to witness, and when the calf has died, or been accidentally killed, her grief frequently makes her refuse to give down her milk. At such times, the breeder has adopted the expedient of flaying the dead carcase, and, distending the skin with hay, lays the effigy before her, and then taking advantage of her solicitude, milks her while she is caressing the skin with her tongue.

IN A STATE OF NATURE, the cow, like the deer, hides her young in the tall ferns and brakes, and the most secret places; and only at stated times, twice or thrice a day, quits the herd, and, hastening to the secret cover, gives suck to her calf, and with the same, circumspection returns to the community.

IT IS SOMETIMES A MATTER OF CONSIDERABLE TROUBLE to induce the blundering calf—whose instinct only teaches him to suck, and that he will do at anything and with anything—acquire the knowledge of imbibition, that for the first few days it is often necessary to fill a bottle with milk, and, opening his mouth, pour the contents down his throat. The manner, however, by which he is finally educated into the mystery of suction, is by putting his allowance of milk into a large wooden bowl; the nurse then puts her hand into the milk, and, by bending her fingers upwards, makes a rude teat for the calf to grasp in his lips, when the vacuum caused by his suction of the fingers, causes the milk to rise along them into his mouth. In this manner one by one the whole family are to be fed three times a day; care being taken, that new-born calves are not, at first, fed on milk from a cow who has some days calved.

AS THE CALF PROGRESSES TOWARDS HIS TENTH WEEK, his diet requires to be increased in quantity and quality; for these

THE STAG. THE HIND.

objects, his milk can be thickened with flour or meal, and small pieces of softened oil-cake are to be slipped into his mouth after sucking, that they may dissolve there, till he grows familiar with, and to like the taste, when it may be softened and scraped down into his milk-and-water. After a time, sliced turnips softened by steam are to be given to him in tolerable quantities; then succulent grasses; and finally, hay may be added to the others. Some farmers, desirous of rendering their calves fat for the butcher in as short a time as possible, forget both the natural weakness of the digestive powers, and the contracted volume of the stomach, and allow the animals either to suck *ad libitum*, or give them, if brought up at the pail or by hand, a larger quantity of milk than they can digest. The idea of overloading the stomach never suggests itself to their minds. They suppose that the more food the young creature consumes, the sooner it will be fat, and they allow it no exercise whatever, for fear it should denude its very bones of their flesh. Under such circumstances, the stomach soon becomes deranged; its functions are no longer capable of acting; the milk, subjected to the acid of the stomach, coagulates, and forms a hardened mass of curd, when the muscles become affected with spasms, and death frequently ensues.

THE MANNER OF CUTTING UP VEAL for the English market is to divide the carcase into four quarters, with eleven ribs to each fore quarter; which are again subdivided into joints as exemplified on the cut.

CHAPTER XVI

RECIPES: VEAL

BAKED VEAL (Cold Meat Cookery).

Ingredients

½ lb. of cold roast veal
a few slices of bacon
1 pint of bread crumbs
½ pint of good veal gravy
½ teaspoonful of minced lemon-peel
1 blade of pounded mace
cayenne and salt to taste
4 eggs

Mode—Mince finely the veal and bacon; add the bread crumbs, gravy, and seasoning, and stir these ingredients well together. Beat up the eggs thoroughly; add these, mix the whole well together, put into a dish, and bake from ¾ to 1 hour. When liked, a little good gravy may be served in a tureen as an accompaniment.

Time—From ¾ to 1 hour.

Average cost, exclusive of the cold meat, 6d.

Sufficient for 3 or 4 persons.

Seasonable from March to October.

ROAST BREAST OF VEAL

Ingredients
Veal
a little flour

Mode—Wash the veal, well wipe it, and dredge it with flour; put it down to a bright fire, not too near, as it should not be scorched. Baste it plentifully until done; dish it, pour over the meat some good melted butter, and send to table with it a piece of boiled bacon and a cut lemon.

Time—From 1-½ to 2 hours.

Average cost, 8-½d. per lb. *Sufficient* for 5 or 6 persons.

Seasonable from March to October.

VEAL CARVING

BREAST OF VEAL

- The carving of a breast of veal is not dissimilar to that of a fore-quarter of lamb, when the shoulder has been taken off. The breast of veal consists of two parts,—the rib-bones and the gristly brisket. These two parts should first be separated by sharply passing the knife in the direction of the lines 1, 2; when they are entirely divided, the rib-bones should be carved in the direction of the lines 5 to 6; and the brisket can be helped by cutting pieces in the direction 3 to 4. The carver should ask the guests whether they have a preference for the brisket or ribs; and if there be a sweetbread served with the dish, as it often is with roast breast of veal, each person should receive a piece.

FILLET OF VEAL

- The carving of this joint is similar to that of a round of beef. Slices, not too thick, in the direction of the line 1 to 2 are cut; and the only point to be careful about is, that the veal be *evenly* carved. Between the flap and the meat the stuffing is inserted, and a small portion of this should be served to every guest. The persons whom the host wishes most to honour should be asked if they like the delicious brown outside slice, as this, by many, is exceedingly relished.

LOIN OF VEAL

- As is the case with a loin of mutton, the careful jointing of a loin of veal is more than half the battle in carving it. If the butcher be negligent in this matter, he should be admonished; for there is nothing more annoying or irritating to an inexperienced carver than to be obliged to turn his knife in all directions to find the exact place where it should be inserted in order to divide the bones. When the jointing is properly performed, there is little difficulty in carrying the knife down in the direction of the line 1 to 2. To each guest should be given a piece of the kidney and kidney fat, which lie underneath, and are considered great delicacies.

CHAPTER XVII

GENERAL OBSERVATIONS ON BIRDS

"Birds, the free tenants of land, air, and ocean,
Their forms all symmetry, their motions grace;
In plumage delicate and beautiful;
Thick without burthen, close as fishes' scales,
Or loose as full-blown poppies to the breeze."

The Pelican Island.

THE DIVISIONS OF BIRDS are founded principally on their habits of life, and the natural resemblance which their external parts, especially their bills, bear to each other. According to Mr. Vigors, there are five orders, each of which occupies its peculiar place on the surface of the globe; so that the air, the forest, the land, the marsh, and the water, has each its appropriate kind of inhabitants. These are respectively designated as BIRDS OF PREY, PERCHERS, WALKERS, WADERS, and SWIMMERS; and, in contemplating their variety, lightness, beauty, and wonderful adaptation to the regions they severally inhabit, and the functions they are destined to perform in the grand scheme of creation, our hearts are lifted with admiration at the exhaustless ingenuity, power, and wisdom of HIM who has, in producing them, so strikingly "manifested His handiwork." Not only these, however, but all classes of animals, have their peculiar ends to fulfil; and, in order that this may be effectually performed, they are constructed in such a manner as will enable them to carry out their conditions. Thus the quadrupeds, that are formed to tread the earth in common with man, are muscular and vigorous; and, whether they have passed into the servitude of man, or are permitted to range the forest or the field, they still retain, in a high degree, the energies with which they were originally endowed. Birds, on the contrary, are generally feeble, and, therefore, timid. Accordingly, wings have been given them to enable them to fly through the air, and thus elude the force which, by nature, they are unable to resist. Notwithstanding the natural tendency of all bodies towards the centre of the earth, birds, when raised in the atmosphere, glide through it with the greatest ease, rapidity, and vigour. There, they are in their natural element, and can vary their course with the greatest promptitude—can mount or descend with the utmost facility, and can light on any spot with the most perfect exactness, and without the slightest injury to themselves.

BIRDS ARE DISTRIBUTED OVER EVERY PART OF THE GLOBE, being found in the coldest as well as the hottest regions, although some species are restricted to particular countries, whilst others are widely dispersed. At certain seasons of the year, many of them change their abodes, and migrate to climates better adapted to their temperaments or modes of life, for a time, than those which they leave. Many of the birds of Britain, directed by an unerring instinct, take their departure from the island before the commencement of winter, and proceed to the more congenial warmth of Africa, to return with the next spring. The causes assigned by naturalists for this peculiarity are, either a deficiency of food, or the want of a secure asylum for the incubation and nourishment of their young. Their migrations are generally performed in large companies, and, in the day, they follow a leader, which is occasionally changed. During the night, many of the tribes send forth a continual cry, to keep themselves together; although one would think that the noise which must accompany their flight would be sufficient for that purpose. The flight of birds across the Mediterranean was noticed three thousand years ago, as we find it said in the book of Numbers, in the Scriptures, that "There went forth a wind from the Lord, and brought quails from the sea, and let them fall upon the camp, and a day's journey round about it, to the height of two cubits above the earth."

IF THE BEAUTY OF BIRDS were not a recommendation to their being universally admired, their general liveliness, gaiety, and song would endear them to mankind. It appears, however, from accurate observations founded upon experiment, that the notes peculiar to different kinds of birds are altogether acquired, and that they are not innate, any more than language is to man. The attempt of a nestling bird to sing has been compared to the endeavour of a child to talk. The first attempts do not seem to possess the slightest rudiments of the future song; but, as the bird grows older and becomes stronger, it is easily perceived to be aiming at acquiring the art of giving utterance to song. Whilst the scholar is thus endeavouring to form his notes, when he is once sure of a passage, he usually raises his tone, but drops it again when he finds himself unequal to the voluntary task he has undertaken. "Many well-authenticated facts," says an ingenious writer, "seem decisively to prove that birds have no innate notes, but that, like mankind, the language of those to whose care they have been committed at their birth, will be their language in after-life." It would appear, however, somewhat unaccountable why, in a wild state, they adhere so steadily to the song of their own species only, when the notes of so many others are to be heard around them. This is said to arise from the attention paid by the nestling bird to the instructions of its own parent only, generally disregarding the notes of all the rest. Persons; however, who have an accurate ear, and who have given their attention to the songs of birds, can frequently distinguish some which have their notes mixed with those of another species; but this is in general so trifling, that it can hardly be considered as more than the mere varieties of provincial dialects.

CHAPTER XVIII

RECIPES: POULTRY AND RABBIT

CHICKEN CUTLETS (an Entree).

Ingredients

2 chickens
seasoning to taste of salt
white pepper, and cayenne
2 blades of pounded mace
egg
bread crumbs
clarified butter
1 strip of lemon-rind
2 carrots
1 onion
2 tablespoonfuls of mushroom ketchup
thickening of butter and flour
1 egg

Mode—Remove the breast and leg bones of the chickens; cut the meat into neat pieces after having skinned it, and season the cutlets with pepper, salt, pounded mace, and cayenne. Put the bones, trimmings, &c., into a stewpan with 1 pint of water, adding carrots, onions, and lemon-peel in the above proportion; stew gently for 1-½ hour, and strain the gravy. Thicken it with butter and flour, add the ketchup and 1 egg well beaten; stir it over the fire, and bring it to the simmering-point, but do not allow it to boil. In the mean time, egg and bread-crumb the cutlets, and give them a few drops of clarified butter; fry them a delicate brown, occasionally turning them; arrange them pyramidically on the dish, and pour over them the sauce.

Time—10 minutes to fry the cutlets. *Average cost*, 2s. each.
Sufficient for an entrée.
Seasonable from April to July.

ROAST DUCKS

Ingredients
A couple of ducks
sage-and-onion stuffing
a little flour

Choosing and Trussing—Choose ducks with plump bellies, and with thick and yellowish feet. They should be trussed with the feet on, which should be scalded, and the skin peeled off, and then turned up close to the legs. Run a skewer through the middle of each leg, after having drawn them as close as possible to the body, to plump up the breast, passing the same quite through the body. Cut off the heads and necks, and the pinions at the first joint; bring these close to the sides, twist the feet round, and truss them at the back of the bird. After the duck is stuffed, both ends should be secured with string, so as to keep in the seasoning.

Mode—To insure ducks being tender, never dress them the same day they are killed; and if the weather permits, they should hang a day or two. Make a stuffing of sage and onion sufficient for one duck, and leave the other unseasoned, as the flavour is not liked by everybody. Put them down to a brisk clear fire, and keep them well basted the whole of the time they are cooking. A few minutes before serving, dredge them lightly with flour, to make them froth and look plump; and when the steam draws towards the fire, send them to table hot and quickly, with a good brown gravy poured *round*, but not *over* the ducks, and a little of the same in a tureen. When in season, green peas should invariably accompany this dish.

Time—Full-grown ducks from ¾ to 1 hour; ducklings from 25 to 35 minutes.

Average cost, from 2s. 3d. to 2s. 6d. each.

Sufficient—A. couple of ducks for 6 or 7 persons.

Seasonable—Ducklings from April to August; ducks from November to February.

Note—Ducklings are trussed and roasted in the same manner, and served with the same sauces and accompaniments. When in season, serve apple sauce.

STEWED RABBIT

Ingredients

1 rabbit
2 large onions
6 cloves
1 small teaspoonful of chopped lemon-peel
a few forcemeat balls
thickening of butter and flour
1 large tablespoonful of mushroom ketchup

Mode—Cut the rabbit into small joints; put them into a stewpan, add the onions sliced, the cloves, and minced lemon-peel. Pour in sufficient water to cover the meat, and, when the rabbit is nearly done, drop in a few forcemeat balls, to which has been added the liver, finely chopped. Thicken the gravy with flour and butter, put in the ketchup, give one boil, and serve.

Time—Rather more than ½ hour. *Average cost*, 1s. to 1s. 6d each.

Sufficient for 4 or 5 persons.

Seasonable from September to February.

POULTRY CARVING

ROAST DUCK

No dishes require so much knowledge and skill in their carving as do game and poultry; for it is necessary to be well acquainted with the anatomy of the bird and animal in order to place the knife at exactly the proper point. A tough fowl and an old goose are sad triers of a carver's powers and temper, and, indeed, sometimes of the good humour of those in the neighbourhood of the carver; for a sudden tilt of the dish may eventuate in the placing a quantity of the gravy in the lap of the right or left-hand supporter of the host. We will endeavour to assist those who are unacquainted with the "gentle art of carving," and also those who are but slightly acquainted with it, by simply describing the rules to follow, and referring to the distinctly-marked Illustrations of each dish, which will further help to bring light to the minds of the uninitiated. If the bird be a young duckling, it may be carved like a fowl, viz., by first taking off the leg and the wing on either side but in cases where the duckling is very small, it will be as well not to separate the leg from the wing, as they will not then form too large a portion for a single serving. After the legs and wings are disposed of, the remainder of the duck will be also carved in the same manner as a fowl; and not much difficulty will be experienced, as ducklings are tender, and the joints are easily broken by a little gentle forcing, or penetrated by the knife. In cases where the duck is a large bird, the better plan to pursue is then to carve it like a goose, that is, by cutting pieces from the breast in the direction indicated by the lines marked from 1 to 2, commencing to carve the slices close to the wing, and then proceeding upwards from that to the breastbone. If more should be wanted than can be obtained from both sides of the breast, then the legs and wings must be attacked, in the same way as is described in connection with carving a fowl. It may be here remarked, that as the legs of a duck are placed far more backward than those of a fowl, their position causing the waddling motion of the bird, the thigh-bones will be found considerably nearer towards the backbone than in a chicken: this is the only difference worth mentioning. The carver should ask each guest if a portion of stuffing would be agreeable; and in order to get at this, a cut should be made below the breast, as shown by the line from 3 to 4, at the part called the "apron," and the spoon inserted. (As described in the recipe, it is an excellent plan, when a couple of ducks are served, to have one with, and the other without stuffing.) As to the prime parts of a duck, it has been said that "the wing of a flier and the leg of a swimmer" are severally the best portions. Some persons are fond of the feet of the duck; and, in trussing, these should never be taken off. The leg, wing, and neckbone are here shown; so that it will be easy to see the shape they should be when cut off.

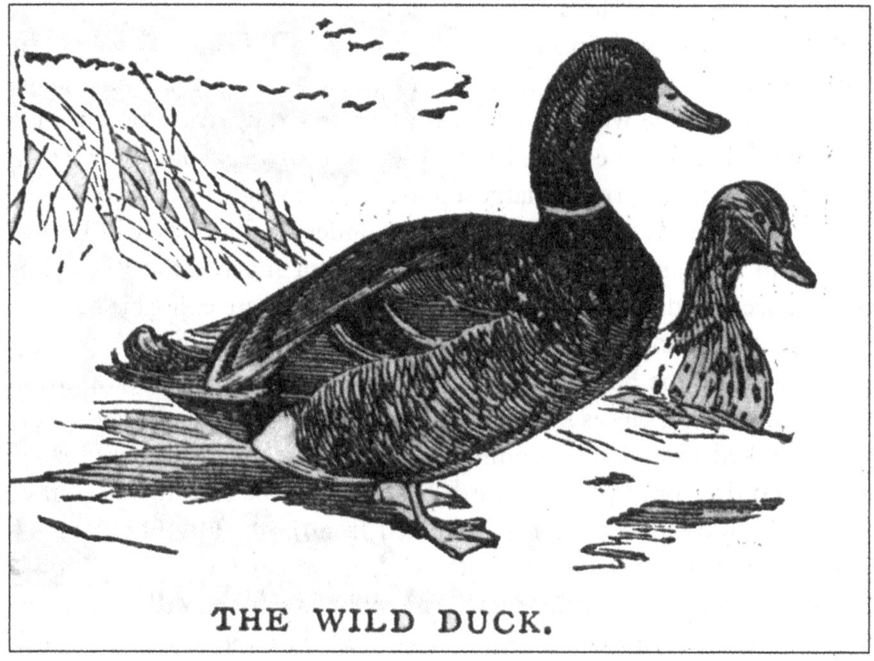

THE WILD DUCK.

RABBITS

In carving a boiled rabbit, let the knife be drawn on each side of the backbone, the whole length of the rabbit, as shown by the dotted line 3 to 4: thus the rabbit will be in three parts. Now let the back be divided into two equal parts in the direction of the line from 1 to 2; then let the leg be taken off, as shown by the line 5 to 6, and the shoulder, as shown by the line 7 to 8. This, in our opinion, is the best plan to carve a rabbit, although there are other modes which are preferred by some.

A roast rabbit is rather differently trussed from one that is meant to be boiled; but the carving is nearly similar, as will be seen by the cut. The back should be divided into as many pieces as it will give, and the legs and shoulders can then be disengaged in the same manner as those of the boiled animal.

ROAST TURKEY

A noble dish is a turkey, roast or boiled. A Christmas dinner, with the middle classes of this empire, would scarcely be a Christmas dinner without its turkey; and we can hardly imagine an object of greater envy than is presented by a respected portly pater-familias carving, at the season devoted to good cheer and genial charity, his own fat turkey, and carving it well. The only art consists, as in the carving of a goose, in getting from the breast as many fine slices as possible; and all must have remarked the very great difference in the large number of people whom a good carver will find slices for, and the comparatively few that a bad carver will succeed in serving. As we have stated in both the carving of a duck and goose, the carver should commence cutting slices close to the wing from, 2 to 3, and then proceed upwards towards the ridge of the breastbone: this is not the usual plan, but, in practice, will be found the best. The breast is the only part which is looked on as fine in a turkey, the legs being very seldom cut off and eaten at table: they are usually removed to the kitchen, where they are taken off, as here marked, to appear only in a form which seems to have a special attraction at a bachelor's supper-table,—we mean devilled: served in this way, they are especially liked and relished.

A boiled turkey is carved in the same manner as when roasted.

CHAPTER XIX

GENERAL OBSERVATIONS ON GAME

THE COMMON LAW OF ENGLAND has a maxim, that goods, in which no person can claim any property, belong, by his or her prerogative, to the king or queen. Accordingly, those animals, those *ferae naturae*, which come under the denomination of game, are, in our laws, styled his or her majesty's, and may therefore, as a matter of course, be granted by the sovereign to another; in consequence of which another may prescribe to possess the same within a certain precinct or lordship. From this circumstance arose the right of lords of manors or others to the game within their respective liberties; and to protect these species of animals, the game laws were originated, and still remain in force. There are innumerable acts of parliament inflicting penalties on persons who may illegally kill game, and some of them are very severe; but they cannot be said to answer their end, nor can it be expected that they ever will, whilst there are so many persons of great wealth who have not otherwise the means of procuring game, except by purchase, and who will have it. These must necessarily encourage poaching, which, to a very large extent, must continue to render all game laws nugatory as to their intended effects upon the rustic population.

THE OBJECT OF THESE LAWS, however, is not wholly confined to the restraining of the illegal sportsman. Even qualified or privileged persons must not kill game at all seasons. During the day, the hours allowed for sporting are from one hour before sunrise till one hour after sunset; whilst the time of killing certain species is also restricted to certain seasons. For example, the season for bustard-shooting is from December 1 to March 1; for grouse, or red grouse, from August 12 to December 10; heath-fowl, or black-game, from August 20 to December 20; partridges from September 1 to February 12; pheasants from October 1 to February 1; widgeons, wild ducks, wild geese, wild fowls, at any time but in June, July, August, and September. Hares may be killed at any time of the year, under certain restrictions defined by an act of parliament of the 10th of George III.

THE THEMES WHICH FORM THE MINSTRELSY OF THE EARLIEST AGES, either relate to the spoils of the chase or the dangers of the battle-field. Even the sacred writings introduce us to Nimrod, the first mighty hunter before the Lord, and tell us that Ishmael, in the solitudes of Arabia, became a skilful bow-man; and that David, when yet young, was not afraid to join in combat with the lion or the bear. The Greek mythology teems with hunting exploits. Hercules overthrows the Nemaean lion, the Erymanthean boar, and the hydra of Lerna; Diana descends to the earth, and pursues the stag; whilst Aesculapius, Nestor, Theseus, Ulysses, and Achilles are all followers of the chase. Aristotle, sage as he was, advises young men to apply themselves early to it; and Plato finds in it something divine. Horace exalts it as a preparative exercise for the path of glory, and several of the heroes of Homer are its ardent votaries. The Romans followed the hunting customs of the Greeks, and the ancient Britons were hunters before Julius Caesar invaded their shores.

ALTHOUGH THE ANCIENT BRITONS FOLLOWED HUNTING, however, they did not confine themselves solely to its pursuit. They bred cattle and tilled the ground, and, to some extent, indicated the rudimentary state of a pastoral and agricultural life; but, in every social change, the sports of the field maintained their place. After the expulsion of the Danes, and during the brief restoration of the Saxon monarchy, these were still followed: even Edward the Confessor, who would join in no other secular amusements, took the greatest delight, says William of Malmesbury, "to follow a pack of swift hounds in pursuit of game, and to cheer them with his voice."

NOR WAS EDWARD the only English sovereign who delighted in the pleasures of the chase. William the Norman, and his two sons who succeeded him, were passionately fond of the sport, and greatly circumscribed the liberties of their subjects in reference to the killing of game. The privilege of hunting in the royal forests was confined to the king and his favourites; and in order that these umbrageous retreats might be made more extensive, whole villages were depopulated, places of worship levelled with the ground, and every means adopted that might give a sufficient amplitude of space, in accordance with the royal pleasure, for the beasts of the chase. King John was likewise especially attached to the sports of the field; whilst Edward III. was so enamoured of the exercise, that even during his absence at the wars in France, he took with him sixty couples of stag-hounds and as many hare-hounds, and every day amused himself either with hunting or hawking. Great in wisdom as the Scotch Solomon, James I., conceited himself to be, he was much addicted to the amusements of hunting, hawking, and shooting. Yea, it is oven asserted that his precious time was divided between hunting, the bottle, and his standish: to the first he gave his fair weather, to the second his dull, and to the third his cloudy. From his days down to the present, the sports of the field have continued to hold their high reputation, not only for the promotion of health, but for helping to form that manliness of character which enters so largely into the composition of the sons of the British soil. That it largely helps to do this there can be no doubt. The late duke of Grafton, when hunting, was, on one occasion, thrown into a ditch. A young curate, engaged in the same chase, cried out, "Lie still, my lord!" leapt over him, and pursued his sport. Such an apparent want of feeling might be expected to have been resented by the duke; but not so. On his being helped up by his attendant, he said, "That man shall have the first good living that falls to my disposal: had he stopped to have given me his sympathy, I never would have given him anything." Such was the manly sentiment of the duke, who delighted in the exemplification of a spirit similarly ardent as his own in the sport, and above the baseness of an assumed sorrow.

THAT HUNTING HAS IN MANY INSTANCES BEEN CARRIED TO AN EXCESS is well known, and the match given by the Prince Esterhazy, regent of Hungary, on the signing of the treaty of peace with France, is not the least extraordinary upon record. On that occasion, there were killed 160 deer, 100 wild boars, 300 hares, and 80 foxes: this was the achievement of one day. Enormous, however, as this slaughter may appear, it is greatly inferior to that made by the contemporary king of Naples on a hunting expedition. That sovereign had a larger extent of ground at his command, and a longer period for the exercise of his talents; consequently, his sport, if it can so be called, was proportionably greater. It was pursued during his journey to Vienna, in Austria, Bohemia, and Moravia; when he killed 5 bears, 1,820 boars, 1,950 deer, 1,145 does, 1,625 roebucks, 11,121 rabbits, 13 wolves, 17 badgers, 16,354 hares, and 354 foxes. In birds, during the same expedition, he killed 15,350 pheasants and 12,335 partridges. Such an amount of destruction can hardly be called sport; it resembles more the indiscriminate slaughter of a battle-field, where the scientific engines of civilized warfare are brought to bear upon defenceless savages.

AS THE INEVITABLE RESULT OF SOCIAL PROGRESS is, at least to limit, if not entirely to suppress, such sports as we have here been treating of, much of the romance of country life has passed away.

This is more especially the case with falconry, which had its origin about the middle of the fourth century, although, lately, some attempts have been rather successfully made to institute a revival of the "gentle art" of hawking. Julius Firmicus, who lived about that time, is, so far as we can find, the first Latin author who speaks of falconers, and the art of teaching one species of birds to fly after and catch others. The occupation of these functionaries has now, however, all but ceased. New and nobler efforts characterize the aims of mankind in the development of their civilization, and the sports of the field have, to a large extent, been superseded by other exercises, it may be less healthful and invigorating, but certainly more elegant, intellectual, and humanizing.

CHAPTER XX

RECIPES: GAME

STEWED VENISON

Ingredients

A shoulder of venison
a few slices of mutton fat
2 glasses of port wine
pepper and allspice to taste
1-½ pint of weak stock or gravy
½ teaspoonful of whole pepper
½ teaspoonful of whole allspice

Mode—Hang the venison till tender; take out the bone, flatten the meat with a rolling-pin, and place over it a few slices of mutton fat, which have been previously soaked for 2 or 3 hours in port wine; sprinkle these with a little fine allspice and pepper, roll the meat up, and bind and tie it securely. Put it into a stewpan with the bone and the above proportion of weak stock or gravy, whole allspice, black pepper, and port wine; cover the lid down closely, and simmer, very gently, from 3-½ to 4 hours. When quite tender, take off the tape, and dish the meat; strain the gravy over it, and send it to table with red-currant jelly. Unless the joint is very fat, the above is the best mode of cooking it.

Time—3-½ to 4 hours.

Average cost, 1s. 4d. to 1s. 6d. per lb.

Sufficient for 10 or 12 persons.

Seasonable—Buck venison, from June to Michaelmas; doe venison, from November to the end of January.

GAME CARVING

ROAST HARE

The "Grand Carver" of olden times, a functionary of no ordinary dignity, was pleased when he had a hare to manipulate, for his skill and grace had an opportunity of display. *Diners à la Russe* may possibly, erewhile, save modern gentlemen the necessity of learning the art which was in auld lang syne one of the necessary accomplishments of the youthful squire; but, until side-tables become universal, or till we see the office of "grand carver" once more instituted, it will be well for all to learn how to assist at the carving of this dish, which, if not the most elegant in appearance, is a very general favourite. The hare, having its head to the left, as shown in the woodcut, should be first served by cutting slices from each side of the backbone, in the direction of the lines from 3 to 4. After these prime parts are disposed of, the leg should next be disengaged by cutting round the line indicated by the figures 5 to 6. The shoulders will then be taken off by passing the knife round from 7 to 8. The back of the hare should now be divided by cutting quite through its spine, as shown by the line 1 to 2, taking care to feel with the point of the knife for a joint where the back may be readily penetrated. It is the usual plan not to serve any bone in helping hare; and thus the flesh should be sliced from the legs and placed alone on the plate. In large establishments, and where men-cooks are kept, it is often the case that the backbone of the hare, especially in old animals, is taken out, and then the process of carving is, of course, considerably facilitated. A great point to be remembered in connection with carving hare is, that plenty of gravy should accompany each helping; otherwise this dish, which is naturally dry, will lose half its flavour, and so become a failure. Stuffing is also served with it; and the ears, which should be nicely crisp, and the brains of the hare, are esteemed as delicacies by many connoisseurs.

HAUNCH OF VENISON

Here is a grand dish for a knight of the carving-knife to exercise his skill upon, and, what will be pleasant for many to know, there is but little difficulty in the performance. An incision being made completely down to the bone, in the direction of the line 1 to 2, the gravy will then be able easily to flow; when slices, not too thick, should be cut along the haunch, as indicated by the line 4 to 3; that end of the joint marked 3 having been turned towards the carver, so that he may have a more complete command over the joint. Although some epicures affect to believe that some parts of the haunch are superior to others, yet we doubt if there is any difference between the slices cut above and below the line. It should be borne in mind to serve each guest with a portion of fat; and the most expeditious carver will be the best carver, as, like mutton, venison soon begins to chill, when it loses much of its charm.

CHAPTER XXI

GENERAL OBSERVATIONS ON VEGETABLES

"Strange there should be found
Who, self-imprison'd in their proud saloons,
Renounce the odours of the open field
For the unscented fictions of the loom;
Who, satisfied with only pencilled scenes,
Prefer to the performance of a God,
Th' inferior wonders of an artist's hand!
Lovely, indeed, the mimic works of art,
But Nature's works far lovelier."
—COWPER.

"THE ANIMAL AND VEGETABLE KINGDOMS," says Hogg, in his Natural History of the Vegetable Kingdom, "may be aptly compared to the primary colours of the prismatic spectrum, which are so gradually and intimately blended, that we fail to discover where the one terminates and where the other begins. If we had to deal with yellow and blue only, the eye would easily distinguish the one from the other; but when the two are blended, and form green, we cannot tell where the blue ends and the yellow begins. And so it is in the animal and vegetable kingdoms. If our powers of observation were limited to the highest orders of animals and plants, if there were only mammals, birds, reptiles, fishes, and insects in the one, and trees, shrubs, and herbs in the other, we should then be able with facility to define the bounds of the two kingdoms; but as we descend the scale of each, and arrive at the lowest forms of animals and plants, we there meet with bodies of the simplest structure, sometimes a mere cell, whose organization, modes of development and reproduction, are so anomalous, and partake so much of the character of both, that we cannot distinguish whether they are plants or whether they are animals."

WHILST IT IS DIFFICULT TO DETERMINE where the animal begins and the vegetable ends, it is as difficult to account for many of the singularities by which numbers of plants are characterized. This, however, can hardly be regarded as a matter of surprise, when we recollect that, so far as it is at present known, the vegetable kingdom is composed of upwards of 92,000 species of plants. Of this amazing number the lichens and the mosses are of the simplest and hardiest kinds. These, indeed, may be considered as the very creators of the soil: they thrive in the coldest and most sterile regions, many of them commencing the operations of nature in the growth of vegetables on the barest rocks, and receiving no other nourishment than such as may be supplied to them by the simple elements of air and rain. When they have exhausted their period in such situations as have been assigned them, they pass into a state of decay, and become changed into a very fine mould, which, in the active spontaneity of nature, immediately begins to produce other species, which in their turn become food for various mosses, and also rot. This process of growth and decay, being, from time to time, continued, by-and-by forms a soil sufficient for the maintenance of larger plants, which also die and decay, and so increase the soil, until it becomes deep enough to sustain an oak, or even the weight of a tropical forest. To create soil amongst rocks, however, must not be considered as the only end of the lichen; different kinds of it minister to the elegant arts, in the form of beautiful dyes; thus the *lichen rocella* is used to communicate to silk and wool, various shades of purple and crimson, which greatly enhance the value of these materials. This species is chiefly imported from the Canary Islands, and, when scarce, as an article of commerce has brought as much as £1000 per ton.

WHEN NATURE HAS FOUND A SOIL, her next care is to perfect the growth of her seeds, and then to disperse them. Whilst the seed remains confined in its capsule, it cannot answer its purpose; hence, when it is sufficiently ripe, the pericardium opens, and lets it out. What must strike every observer with surprise is, how nuts and shells, which we can hardly crack with our teeth, or even with a hammer, will divide of themselves, and make way for the little tender sprout which proceeds from the kernel. There are instances, it is said, such as in the Touch-me-not (*impatiens*), and the Cuckoo-flower (*cardamine*), in which the seed-vessels, by an elastic jerk at the moment of their explosion, cast the seeds to a distance. We are all aware, however, that many seeds—those of the most composite flowers, as of the thistle and dandelion—are endowed with, what have not been inappropriately called, wings. These consist of a beautiful silk-looking down, by which they are enabled to float in the air, and to be transported, sometimes, to considerable distances from the parent plant that produced them. The swelling of this downy tuft within the seed-vessel is the means by which the seed is enabled to overcome the resistance of its coats, and to force for itself a passage by which it escapes from its little prison-house.

IN ACCORDANCE WITH THE PLAN OF THIS WORK, special notices of culinary vegetables will accompany the various recipes in which they are spoken of; but here we cannot resist the opportunity of declaring it as our conviction, that he or she who introduces a useful or an ornamental plant into our island, ought justly to be considered, to a large extent, a benefactor to the country. No one can calculate the benefits which may spring from this very vegetable, after its qualities have become thoroughly known. If viewed in no other light, it is pleasing to consider it as bestowing upon us a share of the blessings of other climates, and enabling us to participate in the luxury which a more genial sun has produced.

CHAPTER XXII

RECIPES: VEGETABLES

STEWED RED CABBAGE

Ingredients

1 red cabbage
a small slice of ham
½ oz. of fresh butter
1 pint of weak stock or broth
1 gill of vinegar
salt and pepper to taste
1 tablespoonful of pounded sugar

Mode—Cut the cabbage into very thin slices, put it into a stewpan, with the ham cut in dice, the butter, ½ pint of stock, and the vinegar; cover the pan closely, and let it stew for 1 hour. When it is very tender, add the remainder of the stock, a seasoning of salt and pepper, and the pounded sugar; mix all well together, stir over the fire until nearly all the liquor is dried away, and serve. Fried sausages are usually sent to table with this dish: they should be laid round and on the cabbage, as a garnish.

Time—Rather more than 1 hour. *Average cost*, 4d. each.

Sufficient for 4 persons.

Seasonable from September to January.

HORSERADISH

This root, scraped, is always served with hot roast beef, and is used for garnishing many kinds of boiled fish. Let the horseradish remain in cold water for an hour; wash it well, and with a sharp knife scrape it into very thin shreds, commencing from the thick end of the root. Arrange some of it lightly in a small glass dish, and the remainder use for garnishing the joint: it should be placed in tufts round the border of the dish, with 1 or 2 bunches on the meat.

Average cost, 2d. per stick.

Seasonable from October to June.

> **THE HORSERADISH**—This belongs to the tribe *Alyssidae*, and is highly stimulant and exciting to the stomach. It has been recommended in chronic rheumatism, palsy, dropsical complaints, and in cases of enfeebled digestion. Its principal use, however, is as a condiment to promote appetite and excite the digestive organs. The horseradish contains sulphur to the extent of thirty per cent, in the number of its elements; and it is to the presence of this quality that the metal vessels in which the radish is sometimes distilled, are turned into a black colour. It is one of the most powerful excitants and antiscorbutics we have, and forms the basis of several medical preparations, in the form of wines, tinctures, and syrups.

Time—½ hour. *Average cost*, from 9d. to 2s. per pint.

Sufficient for 5 or 6 persons.

POTATO SALAD

Ingredients

10 or 12 cold boiled potatoes
4 tablespoonfuls of tarragon or plain vinegar
6 tablespoonfuls of salad-oil
pepper and salt to taste
1 teaspoonful of minced parsley

Mode—Cut the potatoes into slices about ½ inch in thickness; put these into a salad-bowl with oil and vinegar in the above proportion; season with pepper, salt, and a teaspoonful of minced parsley; stir the salad well, that all the ingredients may be thoroughly incorporated, and it is ready to serve. This should be made two or three hours before it is wanted for table. Anchovies, olives, or pickles may be added to this salad, as also slices of cold beef, fowl, or turkey.

Seasonable at any time.

STEWED TOMATOES

Ingredients

8 tomatoes

USES OF THE TRUFFLE—Like the Morel, truffles are seldom eaten alone, but are much used in gravies, soups, and ragoûts. They are likewise dried for the winter months, and, when reduced to powder, form a useful culinary ingredient; they, however, have many virtues attributed to them which they do not possess. Their wholesomeness is, perhaps, questionable, and they should be eaten with moderation.

CHAPTER XXIII

GENERAL OBSERVATIONS ON PUDDINGS AND PASTRY

PUDDINGS AND PASTRY, familiar as they may be, and unimportant as they may be held in the estimation of some, are yet intimately connected with the development of agricultural resources in reference to the cereal grasses. When they began to be made is uncertain; but we may safely presume, that a simple form of pudding was amongst the first dishes made after discovering a mode of grinding wheat into flour. Traditional history enables us to trace man back to the time of the Deluge. After that event he seems to have recovered himself in the central parts of Asia, and to have first risen to eminence in the arts of civilization on the banks of the Nile. From this region, Greece, Carthage, and some other parts along the shores of the Mediterranean Sea, were colonized. In process of time, Greece gave to the Romans the arts which she had thus received from Egypt, and these subsequently diffused them over Europe. How these were carried to or developed in India and China, is not so well ascertained; and in America their ancient existence rests only on very indistinct traditions. As to who was the real discoverer of the use of corn, we have no authentic knowledge. The traditions of different countries ascribe it to various fabulous personages, whose names it is here unnecessary to introduce. In Egypt, however, corn must have grown abundantly; for Abraham, and after him Jacob, had recourse to that country for supplies during times of famine.

THE HABITS OF A PEOPLE, to a great extent, are formed by the climate in which they live, and by the native or cultivated productions in which their country abounds. Thus we find that the agricultural produce of the ancient Egyptians is pretty much the same as that of the present day, and the habits of the people are not materially altered. In Greece, the products cultivated in antiquity were the same kinds of grains and legumes as are cultivated at present, with the vine, the fig, the olive, the apple, and other fruits. So with the Romans, and so with other nations. As to the different modes of artificially preparing those to please the taste, it is only necessary to say that they arise from the universal desire of novelty, characteristic of man in the development of his social conditions. Thus has arisen the whole science of cookery, and thus arose the art of making puddings. The porridge of the Scotch is nothing more than a species of hasty pudding, composed of oatmeal, salt, and water; and the "red pottage" for which Esau sold his birthright, must have been something similar. The barley-gruel of the Lacedaemonians, of the Athenian gladiators and common people, was the same, with the exception of the slight seasoning it had beyond the simplicity of Scottish fare. Here is the ancient recipe for the Athenian national dish:—"Dry near the fire, in the oven, twenty pounds of barley-flour; then parch it; add three pounds of linseed-meal, half a pound of coriander-seed, two ounces of salt, and the quantity of water necessary." To this sometimes a little millet was added, in order to give the paste greater cohesion and delicacy.

HOWEVER GREAT MAY HAVE BEEN THE QUALIFICATIONS of the ancients, however, in the art of pudding-making, we apprehend that such preparations as gave gratification to their palates, would have generally found little favour amongst the insulated inhabitants of Great Britain. Here, from the simple suet dumpling up to the most complicated Christmas production, the grand feature of substantiality is primarily attended to. Variety in the ingredients, we think, is held only of secondary consideration with the great body of the people, provided that the whole is agreeable and of sufficient abundance.

ALTHOUGH FROM PUDDINGS TO PASTRY is but a step, it requires a higher degree of art to make the one than to make the other. Indeed, pastry is one of the most important branches of the culinary science. It unceasingly occupies itself with ministering pleasure to the sight as well as to the taste; with erecting graceful monuments, miniature fortresses, and all kinds of architectural imitations, composed of the sweetest and most agreeable products of all climates and countries. At a very early period, the Orientals were acquainted with the art of manipulating in pastry; but they by no means attained to the taste, variety, and splendour of design, by which it is characterized amongst the moderns. At first it generally consisted of certain mixtures of flour, oil, and honey, to which it was confined for centuries, even among the southern nations of the European continent. At the commencement of the middle ages, a change began to take place in the art of mixing it. Eggs, butter, and salt came into repute in the making of paste, which was forthwith used as an inclosure for meat, seasoned with spices. This advance attained, the next step was to inclose cream, fruit, and marmalades; and the next, to build pyramids and castles; when the summit of the art of the pastry-cook may be supposed to have been achieved.

CHAPTER XXIV

RECIPES: PUDDINGS AND PASTRY

VERY GOOD PUFF-PASTE

Ingredients
To every lb. of flour allow 1 lb. of butter
not quite ½ pint of water

Mode—Carefully weigh the flour and butter, and have the exact proportion; squeeze the butter well, to extract the water from it, and afterwards wring it in a clean cloth, that no moisture may remain. Sift the flour; see that it is perfectly dry, and proceed in the following manner to make the paste, using a very *clean* paste-board and rolling-pin:—Supposing the quantity to be 1 lb. of flour, work the whole into a smooth paste, with not quite ½ pint of water, using a knife to mix it with: the proportion of this latter ingredient must be regulated by the discretion of the cook; if too much be added, the paste, when baked, will be tough. Roll it out until it is of an equal thickness of about an inch; break 4 oz. of the butter into small pieces; place these on the paste, sift over it a little flour, fold it over, roll out again, and put another 4 oz. of butter. Repeat the rolling and buttering until the paste has been rolled out 4 times, or equal quantities of flour and butter have been used. Do not omit, every time the paste is rolled out, to dredge a little flour over that and the rolling-pin, to prevent both from sticking. Handle the paste as lightly as possible, and do not press heavily upon it with the rolling-pin. The next thing to be considered is the oven, as the baking of pastry requires particular attention. Do not put it into the oven until it is sufficiently hot to raise the paste; for the best-prepared paste, if not properly baked, will be good for nothing. Brushing the paste as often as rolled out, and the pieces of butter placed thereon, with the white of an egg, assists it to rise in *leaves* or *flakes*. As this is the great beauty of puff-paste, it is as well to try this method.

Average cost, 1s. 4d. per lb.

BUTTER—About the second century of the Christian era, butter was placed by Galen amongst the useful medical agents; and about a century before him, Dioscorides mentioned that he had noticed that fresh butter, made of ewes' and goats' milk, was served at meals instead of oil, and that it took the place of fat in making pastry. Thus we have undoubted authority that, eighteen hundred years ago, there existed a knowledge of the useful qualities of butter. The Romans seem to have set about making it much as we do; for Pliny tells us, "Butter is made from milk; and the use of this element, so much sought after by barbarous nations, distinguished the rich from the common people. It is obtained principally from cows' milk; that from ewes is the fattest; goats also supply some. It is produced by agitating the milk in long vessels with narrow openings: a little water is added."

COMMON SHORT CRUST

Ingredients

To every pound of flour allow 2 oz. of sifted sugar
3 oz. of butter
about ½ pint of boiling milk

Mode—Crumble the butter into the flour as finely as possible, add the sugar, and work the whole up to a smooth paste with the boiling milk. Roll it out thin, and bake in a moderate oven.

Average cost, 6d. per lb.

> QUALITIES OF SUGAR—Sugars obtained from various plants are in fact, of the same nature, and have no intrinsic difference when they have become equally purified by the same processes. Taste, crystallization, colour, weight, are absolutely identical; and the most accurate observer cannot distinguish the one from the other.

ALMOND PUFFS

Ingredients

2 tablespoonfuls of flour
2 oz. of butter
2 oz. of pounded sugar
2 oz. of sweet almonds
4 bitter almonds

Mode—Blanch and pound the almonds in a mortar to a smooth paste; melt the butter, dredge in the flour, and add the sugar and pounded almonds. Beat the mixture well, and put it into cups or very tiny jelly-pots, which should be well buttered, and bake in a moderate oven for about 20 minutes, or longer should the puffs be large. Turn them out on a dish, the bottom of the puff upper-most, and serve.

Time—20 minutes. *Average cost*, 6d.

Sufficient for 2 or 3 persons. *Seasonable* at any time.

APPLE CHEESECAKES

Ingredients

½ lb. of apple pulp
¼ lb. of sifted sugar
¼ lb. of butter
4 eggs
the rind and juice of 1 lemon

Mode—Pare, core, and boil sufficient apples to make ½ lb. when cooked; add to these the sugar, the butter, which should be melted; the eggs, leaving out 2 of the whites, and take grated rind and juice of 1 lemon; stir the mixture well; line some patty-pans with puff-paste, put in the mixture, and bake about 20 minutes.

Time—About 20 minutes.

Average cost, for the above quantity, with the paste, 1s. 2d.

Sufficient for about 18 or 20 cheesecakes.

Seasonable from August to March.

THE APPLE—The most useful of all the British fruits is the apple, which is a native of Britain, and may be found in woods and hedges, in the form of the common wild crab, of which all our best apples are merely seminal varieties, produced by culture or particular circumstances. In most temperate climates it is very extensively cultivated, and in England, both as regards variety and quantity, it is excellent and abundant. Immense supplies are also imported from the United States and from France. The apples grown in the vicinity of New York are universally admitted to be the finest of any; but unless selected and packed with great care, they are apt to spoil before reaching England.

APPLE TART OR PIE

Ingredients

Puff-paste
apples; to every lb. of unpared apples allow 2 oz. of moist sugar
½ teaspoonful of finely-minced lemon-peel
1 tablespoonful of lemon-juice

Mode—Make ½ lb. of puff-paste by either of the above-named recipes, place a border of it round the edge of a pie-dish, and fill it with apples pared, cored, and cut into slices; sweeten with moist sugar, add the lemon-peel and juice, and 2 or 3 tablespoonfuls of water; cover with crust, cut it evenly round close to the edge of the pie-dish, and bake in a hot oven from ½ to ¾ hour, or rather longer, should the pie be very large. When it is three-parts done, take it out of the oven, put the white of an egg on a plate, and, with the blade of a knife, whisk it to a froth; brush the pie over with this, then sprinkle upon it some sifted sugar, and then a few drops of water. Put the pie back into the oven, and finish baking, and be particularly careful that it does not catch or burn, which it is very liable to do after the crust is iced. If made with a plain crust, the icing may be omitted.

Time—½ hour before the crust is iced; 10 to 15 minutes afterwards.

Average cost, 9d.

Sufficient—Allow 2 lbs. of apples for a tart for 6 persons.

Seasonable from August to March; but the apples become flavourless after February.

Note—Many things are suggested for the flavouring of apple pie; some say 2 or 3 tablespoonfuls of beer, others the same quantity of sherry, which very much improve the taste; whilst the old-fashioned addition of a few cloves is, by many persons, preferred to anything else, as also a few slices of quince.

APRICOT TART

Ingredients
12 or 14 apricots
sugar to taste
puff-paste or short crust

Mode—Break the apricots in half, take out the stones, and put them into a pie-dish, in the centre of which place a very small cup or jar, bottom uppermost; sweeten with good moist sugar, but add no water. Line the edge of the dish with paste, put on the cover, and ornament the pie in any of the usual modes. Bake from ½ to ¾ hour, according to size; and if puff-paste is used, glaze it about 10 minutes before the pie is done, and put it into the oven again to set the glaze. Short crust merely requires a little sifted sugar sprinkled over it before being sent to table.

Time—½ to ¾ hour. *Average cost*, in full season, 1s.

Sufficient for 4 or 5 persons.

Seasonable in August, September, and October; green ones rather earlier.

Note—Green apricots make very good tarts, but they should be boiled with a little sugar and water before they are covered with the crust.

APRICOTS—The apricot is indigenous to the plains of Armenia, but is now cultivated in almost every climate, temperate or tropical. There are several varieties. The skin of this fruit has a perfumed flavour, highly esteemed. A good apricot, when perfectly ripe, is an excellent fruit. It has been somewhat condemned for its laxative qualities, but this has possibly arisen from the fruit having been eaten unripe, or in too great excess. Delicate persons should not eat the apricot uncooked, without a liberal allowance of powdered sugar. The apricot makes excellent jam and marmalade, and there are several foreign preparations of it which are considered great luxuries.

CHERRY TART

Ingredients
1-½ lb. of cherries
2 small tablespoonfuls of moist sugar
½ lb. of short crust

Mode—Pick the stalks from the cherries, put them, with the sugar, into a *deep* pie-dish just capable of holding them, with a small cup placed upside down in the midst of them. Make a short crust with ½ lb. of flour, by either of the recipes 1210 or 1211; lay a border round the edge of the dish; put on the cover, and ornament the edges; bake in a brisk oven from ½ hour to 40 minutes; strew finely-sifted sugar over, and serve hot or cold, although the latter is the more usual mode. It is more economical to make two or three tarts at one time, as the trimmings from one tart answer for lining the edges of the dish for another, and so much paste is not required as when they are made singly. Unless for family use, never make fruit pies in very *large* dishes; select them, however, as deep as possible.

Time—½ hour to 40 minutes.

Average cost, in full season, 8d.

Sufficient for 5 or 6 persons.

Seasonable in June, July, and August.

Note—A few currants added to the cherries will be found to impart a nice piquant taste to them.

> CHERRIES—According to Lucullus, the cherry-tree was known in Asia in the year of Rome 680. Seventy different species of cherries, wild and cultivated, exist,

which are distinguishable from each other by the difference of their form, size, and colour. The French distil from cherries a liqueur Darned *kirsch-waser* (*eau de cérises*); the Italians prepare, from a cherry called marusca, the liqueur named *marasquin*, sweeter and more agreeable than the former. The most wholesome cherries have a tender and delicate skin; those with a hard skin should be very carefully masticated. Sweetmeats, syrups, tarts, entremets, &c., of cherries, are universally approved.

BAKED CUSTARD PUDDING

Ingredients

1-½ pint of milk
¼ lb. of moist sugar
the rind of ¼ lemon
4 eggs

Mode—Put the milk into a saucepan with the sugar and lemon-rind, and let this infuse for about 4 hour, or until the milk is well flavoured; whisk the eggs, yolks and whites; pour the milk to them, stirring all the while; then have ready a pie-dish, lined at the edge with paste ready baked; strain the custard into the dish, grate a little nutmeg over the top, and bake in a *very slow* oven for about ½ hour, or rather longer. The flavour of this pudding may be varied by substituting bitter almonds for the lemon-rind; and it may be very much enriched by using half cream and half milk, and doubling the quantity of eggs.

Time—½ to ¾ hour.

Average cost, 9d.

Sufficient for 5 or 6 persons.

Seasonable at any time.

Note—This pudding is usually served cold with fruit tarts.

FIG PUDDING

Ingredients

2 lbs. of figs
1 lb. of suet
½ lb. of flour
½ lb. of bread crumbs
2 eggs
milk

Mode—Cut the figs into small pieces, grate the bread finely, and chop the suet very small; mix these well together, add the flour, the eggs, which should be well beaten, and sufficient milk to form the whole into a stiff paste; butter a mould or basin, press the pudding into it very closely, tie it down with a cloth, and boil for 3 hours, or rather longer; turn it out of the mould, and serve with melted butter, wine-sauce, or cream.

Time—3 hours, or longer. *Average cost*, 2s.

Sufficient for 7 or 8 persons.

Seasonable—Suitable for a winter pudding.

ALMOND FLOWERS

Ingredients

Puff-paste; to every ½ lb. of paste allow 3 oz. of almonds
sifted sugar
the white of an egg

Mode—Roll the paste out to the thickness of ¼ inch, and, with a round fluted cutter, stamp out as many pieces as may be required. Work the paste up again, roll it out, and, with a smaller cutter, stamp out some pieces the size of a shilling. Brush the larger pieces over with the white of an egg, and place one of the smaller pieces on each. Blanch and cut the almonds into strips lengthwise; press them slanting into the paste closely round the rings; and when they are all completed, sift over some pounded sugar, and bake for about ¼ hour or 20 minutes. Garnish between the almonds with strips of apple jelly, and place in the centre of the ring a small quantity of strawberry jam; pile them high on the dish, and serve.

Time—¼ hour or 20 minutes.

Sufficient—18 or 20 for a dish.

Seasonable at any time.

PLUM TART

Ingredients
½ lb. of good short crust
1-½ pint of plums
¼ lb. of moist sugar

Mode—Line the edges of a deep tart-dish with crust made by recipe; fill the dish with plums, and place a small cup or jar, upside down, in the midst of them. Put in the sugar, cover the pie with crust, ornament the edges, and bake in a good oven from ½ to ¾ hour. When puff-crust is preferred to short crust, use that made by recipe and glaze the top by brushing it over with the white of an egg beaten to a stiff froth with a knife; sprinkle over a little sifted sugar, and put the pie in the oven to set the glaze.

Time—½ to ¾ hour. *Average cost*, 1s.

Sufficient for 5 or 6 persons.

Seasonable, with various kinds of plums, from the beginning of August to the beginning of October.

TO ICE OR GLAZE PASTRY

- To glaze pastry, which is the usual method adopted for meat or raised pies, break an egg, separate the yolk from the white, and beat the former for a short time. Then, when the pastry is nearly baked, take it out of the oven, brush it over with this beaten yolk of egg, and put it back in the oven to set the glaze.

- To ice pastry, which is the usual method adopted for fruit tarts and sweet dishes of pastry, put the white of an egg on a plate, and with the blade of a knife beat it to a stiff froth. When the pastry is nearly baked, brush it over with this, and sift over some pounded sugar; put it back into the oven to set the glaze, and, in a few minutes, it will be done. Great care should be taken that the paste does not catch or burn in the oven, which it is very liable to do after the icing is laid on.

Sufficient—Allow 1 egg and 1-1/8 oz. of sugar to glaze 3 tarts.

BAKED RICE PUDDING

Ingredients

1 small teacupful of rice
4 eggs
1 pint of milk
2 oz. of fresh butter
2 oz. of beef marrow
¼ lb. of currants
2 tablespoonfuls of brand
nutmeg
¼ lb. of sugar
the rind of ½ lemon

Mode—Put the lemon-rind and milk into a stewpan, and let it infuse till the milk is well flavoured with the lemon; in the mean time, boil the rice until tender in water, with a very small quantity of salt, and, when done, let it be thoroughly drained. Beat the eggs, stir to them the milk, which should be strained, the butter, marrow, currants, and remaining ingredients; add the rice, and mix all well together. Line the edges of the dish with puff-paste, put in the pudding, and bake for about ¾ hour in a slow oven. Slices of candied-peel may be added at pleasure, or Sultana raisins may be substituted for the currants.

Time—¾ hour. *Average cost*, 1s. 3d.

Sufficient for 5 or 6 persons.

Seasonable—Suitable for a winter pudding, when fresh fruits are not obtainable.

> **RICE**, with proper management in cooking it, forms a very valuable and cheap addition to our farinaceous food, and, in years of scarcity, has been found eminently useful in lessening the consumption of flour. When boiled, it should be so managed that the grains, though soft, should be as little broken and as dry as possible. The water in which it is dressed should only simmer, and not boil hard. Very little water should be used, as the grains absorb a great deal, and, consequently, swell much; and if they take up too much at first, it is difficult to get rid of it. Baking it in puddings is the best mode of preparing it.

TAPIOCA PUDDING

Ingredients

3 oz. of tapioca
1 quart of milk
2 oz. of butter
¼ lb. of sugar
4 eggs
flavouring of vanilla
grated lemon-rind, or bitter almonds

Mode—Wash the tapioca, and let it stew gently in the milk by the side of the fire for ¼ hour, occasionally stirring it; then let it cool a little; mix with it the butter, sugar, and eggs, which should be well beaten, and flavour with either of the above ingredients, putting in about 12 drops of the essence of almonds or vanilla, whichever is preferred. Butter a pie-dish, and line the edges with puff-paste; put in the pudding, and bake in a moderate oven for an hour. If the pudding is boiled, add a little more tapioca, and boil it in a buttered basin 1-½ hour.

Time—1 hour to bake, 1-½ hour to boil.

Average cost, 1s. 2d.

Sufficient for 5 or 6 persons. *Seasonable* at any time.

> **TAPIOCA**—Tapioca is recommended to the convalescent, as being easy of digestion. It may be used in soup or broth, or mixed with milk or water, and butter. It is excellent food for either the healthy or sick, for the reason that it is so quickly

CHAPTER XXV

GENERAL OBSERVATIONS ON CREAMS, JELLIES, SOUFFLÉS, OMELETS, & SWEET DISHES

CREAMS—The yellowish-white, opaque fluid, smooth and unctuous to the touch, which separates itself from new milk, and forms a layer on its surface, when removed by skimming, is employed in a variety of culinary preparations. The analyses of the contents of cream have been decided to be, in 100 parts—butter, 3.5; curd, or matter of cheese, 3.5; whey, 92.0. That cream contains an oil, is evinced by its staining clothes in the manner of oil; and when boiled for some time, a little oil floats upon the surface. The thick animal oil which it contains, the well-known *butter*, is separated only by agitation, as in the common process of *churning*, and the cheesy matter remains blended with the whey in the state of *buttermilk*. Of the several kinds of cream, the principal are the Devonshire and Dutch clotted creams, the Costorphin cream, and the Scotch sour cream. The Devonshire cream is produced by nearly boiling the milk in shallow tin vessels over a charcoal fire, and kept in that state until the whole of the cream is thrown up. It is used for eating with fruits and tarts. The cream from Costorphin, a village of that name near Edinburgh, is accelerated in its separation from three or four days' old milk, by a certain degree of heat; and the Dutch clotted cream—a coagulated mass in which a spoon will stand upright—is manufactured from fresh-drawn milk, which is put into a pan, and stirred with a spoon two or three times a day, to prevent the cream from separating from the milk. The Scotch "sour cream" is a misnomer; for it is a material produced without cream. A small tub filled with skimmed milk is put into a larger one, containing hot water, and after remaining there all night, the thin milk (called *wigg*) is drawn off, and the remainder of the contents of the smaller vessel is "sour cream."

JELLIES are not the nourishing food they were at one time considered to be, and many eminent physicians are of opinion that they are less digestible than the flesh, or muscular part of animals; still, when acidulated with lemon-juice and flavoured with wine, they are very suitable for some convalescents. Vegetable jelly is a distinct principle, existing in fruits, which possesses the property of gelatinizing when boiled and cooled; but it is a principle entirely different from the gelatine of animal bodies, although the name of jelly, common to both, sometimes leads to an erroneous idea on that subject. Animal jelly, or gelatine, is glue, whereas vegetable jelly is rather analogous to gum. Liebig places gelatine very low indeed in the scale of usefulness. He says, "Gelatine, which by itself is tasteless, and when eaten, excites nausea, possesses no nutritive value; that, even when accompanied by the savoury constituents of flesh, it is not capable of supporting the vital process, and when added to the usual diet as a substitute for plastic matter, does not increase, but, on the contrary, diminishes the nutritive value of the food, which it renders insufficient in quantity and inferior in quality." It is this substance which is most frequently employed in the manufacture of the jellies supplied by the confectioner; but those prepared at home from calves' feet do possess some nutrition, and are the only sort that should be given to invalids. Isinglass is the purest variety of gelatine, and is prepared from the sounds or swimming-bladders of certain fish, chiefly the sturgeon. From its whiteness it is mostly used for making blanc-mange and similar dishes.

THE WHITE OF EGGS is perhaps the best substance that can be employed in clarifying jelly, as well as some other fluids, for the reason that when albumen (and the white of eggs is nearly pure albumen) is put into a liquid that is muddy, from substances suspended in it, on boiling the liquid, the albumen coagulates in a flocculent manner, and, entangling with it the impurities, rises with them to the surface as a scum, or sinks to the bottom, according to their weight.

SOUFFLES, OMELETS, AND SWEET DISHES, in which eggs form the principal ingredient, demand, for their successful manufacture, an experienced cook. They are the prettiest, but most difficult of all entremets. The most essential thing to insure success is to secure the best ingredients from an honest tradesman. The entremets coming within the above classification, are healthy, nourishing, and pleasant to the taste, and may be eaten with safety by persons of the most delicate stomachs.

CHAPTER XXVI

RECIPES: VARIOUS SWEETS

BAKED APPLE CUSTARD

Ingredients

1 dozen large apples
moist sugar to taste
1 small teacupful of cold water
the grated rind of one lemon
1 pint of milk
4 eggs
2 oz. of loaf sugar

Mode—Peel, cut, and core the apples; put them into a lined saucepan with the cold water, and as they heat, bruise them to a pulp; sweeten with moist sugar, and add the grated lemon-rind. When cold, put the fruit at the bottom of a pie-dish, and pour over it a custard, made with the above proportion of milk, eggs, and sugar; grate a little nutmeg over the top, place the dish in a moderate oven, and bake from 25 to 35 minutes. The above proportions will make rather a large dish.

Time—25 to 35 minutes.

Average cost, 1s. 4d.

Sufficient for 6 or 7 persons.

Seasonable from July to March.

THICK APPLE JELLY OR MARMALADE, for Entremets or Dessert Dishes.

Ingredients

Apples; to every lb. of pulp allow ¾ lb. of sugar
½ teaspoonful of minced lemon-peel

Mode—Peel, core, and boil the apples with only sufficient water to prevent them from burning; beat them to a pulp, and to every lb. of pulp allow the above proportion of sugar in lumps. Dip the lumps into water; put these into a saucepan, and boil till the syrup is thick and can be well skimmed; then add this syrup to the apple pulp, with the minced lemon-peel, and stir it over a quick fire for about 20 minutes, or until the apples cease to stick to the bottom of the pan. The jelly is then done, and may be poured into moulds which have been previously dipped in water, when it will turn out nicely for dessert or a side-dish; for the latter a little custard should be poured round, and it should be garnished with strips of citron or stuck with blanched almonds.

Time—From ½ to ¾ hour to reduce the apples to a pulp; 20 minutes to boil after the sugar is added.

Sufficient—1-½ lb. of apples sufficient for a small mould.

Seasonable from July to March; but is best in September, October or November.

CHOCOLATE CREAM

Ingredients

3 oz. of grated chocolate
¼ lb. of sugar
1-½ pint of cream
½ oz. of clarified isinglass
the yolks of 6 eggs

Mode—Beat the yolks of the eggs well; put them into a basin with the grated chocolate, the sugar, and 1 pint of the cream; stir these ingredients well together, pour them into a jug, and set this jug in a saucepan of boiling water; stir it one way until the mixture thickens, but *do not allow it to boil*, or it will curdle. Strain the cream through a sieve into a basin; stir in the isinglass and the other ½ pint of cream, which should be well whipped; mix all well together, and pour it into a mould which has been previously oiled with the purest salad-oil, and, if at hand, set it in ice until wanted for table.

Time—About 10 minutes to stir the mixture over the fire.

Average cost, 4s. 6d, with cream at 1s. per pint.

Sufficient to fill a quart mould. *Seasonable* at any time.

MERINGUES

Ingredients
½ lb. of pounded sugar
the whites of 4 eggs

Mode—Whisk the whites of the eggs to a stiff froth, and, with a wooden spoon, stir in *quickly* the pounded sugar; and have some boards thick enough to put in the oven to prevent the bottom of the meringues from acquiring too much colour. Cut some strips of paper about 2 inches wide; place this paper on the board, and drop a tablespoonful at a time of the mixture on the paper, taking care to let all the meringues be the same size. In dropping it from the spoon, give the mixture the form of an egg, and keep the meringues about 2 inches apart from each other on the paper. Strew over them some sifted sugar, and bake in a moderate oven for ½ hour. As soon as they begin to colour, remove them from the oven; take each slip of paper by the two ends, and turn it gently on the table, and, with a small spoon, take out the soft part of each meringue. Spread some clean paper on the board, turn the meringues upside down, and put them into the oven to harden and brown on the other side. When required for table, fill them with whipped cream, flavoured with liqueur or vanilla, and sweetened with pounded sugar. Join two of the meringues together, and pile them high in the dish, as shown in the annexed drawing. To vary their appearance, finely-chopped almonds or currants may be strewn over them before the sugar is sprinkled over; and they may be garnished with any bright-coloured preserve. Great expedition is necessary in making this sweet dish; as, if the meringues are not put into the oven as soon as the sugar and eggs are mixed, the former melts, and the mixture would run on the paper, instead of keeping its egg-shape. The sweeter the meringues are made, the crisper will they be; but, if there is not sufficient sugar mixed with them, they will most likely be tough. They are sometimes coloured with cochineal; and, if kept well covered in a dry place, will remain good for a month or six weeks.

Time—Altogether, about ½ hour.

Average cost, with the cream and flavouring, 1s.

Sufficient to make 2 dozen meringues. *Seasonable* at any time.

TO MAKE A SOUFFLE

Ingredients

3 heaped tablespoonfuls of potato-flour
rice-flour
arrowroot, or tapioca
1 pint of milk
5 eggs
a piece of butter the size of a walnut
sifted sugar to taste
¼ saltspoonful of salt flavouring

Mode—Mix the potato-flour, or whichever one of the above ingredients is used, with a little of the milk; put it into a saucepan, with the remainder of the milk, the butter, salt, and sufficient pounded sugar to sweeten the whole nicely. Stir these ingredients over the fire until the mixture thickens; then take it off the fire, and let it cool a little. Separate the whites from the yolks of the eggs, beat the latter, and stir them into the soufflé batter. Now whisk the whites of the eggs to the firmest possible froth, for on this depends the excellence of the dish; stir them to the other ingredients, and add a few drops of essence of any flavouring that may be preferred; such as vanilla, lemon, orange, ginger, &c. &c. Pour the batter into a soufflé-dish, put it immediately into the oven, and bake for about ½ hour; then take it out, put the dish into another more ornamental one, such as is made for the purpose; hold a salamander or hot shovel over the soufflé, strew it with sifted sugar, and send it instantly to table. The secret of making a soufflé well, is to have the eggs well whisked, but particularly the whites, the oven not too hot, and to send it to table the moment it comes from the oven. If the soufflé be ever so well made, and it is allowed to stand before being sent to table, its appearance and goodness will be entirely spoiled. Soufflés may be flavoured in various ways, but must be named accordingly. Vanilla is one of the most delicate and recherché flavourings that can be used for this very fashionable dish.

Time—About ½ hour in the oven; 2 or 3 minutes to hold the salamander over.

Average cost, 1s.

Sufficient for 3 or 4 persons.

Seasonable at any time.

TIPSY CAKE

Ingredients

1 moulded sponge-or Savoy-cake
sufficient sweet wine or sherry to soak it
6 tablespoonfuls of brandy, 2 oz. of sweet almonds
1 pint of rich custard

Mode—Procure a cake that is three or four days old,—either sponge, Savoy, or rice answering for the purpose of a tipsy cake. Cut the bottom of the cake level, to make it stand firm in the dish; make a small hole in the centre, and pour in and over the cake sufficient sweet wine or sherry, mixed with the above proportion of brandy, to soak it nicely. When the cake is well soaked, blanch and cut the almonds into strips, stick them all over the cake, and pour round it a good custard, allowing 8 eggs instead of 5 to the pint of milk. The cakes are sometimes crumbled and soaked, and a whipped cream heaped over them, the same as for trifles.

Time—About 2 hours to soak the cake. *Average cost*, 4s. 6d.

Sufficient for 1 dish. *Seasonable* at any time.

CHAPTER XXVII

GENERAL OBSERVATIONS ON PRESERVES, CONFECTIONARY, ICES, AND DESSERT DISHES

PRESERVES

From the nature of vegetable substances, and chiefly from their not passing so rapidly into the putrescent state as animal bodies, the mode of preserving them is somewhat different, although the general principles are the same. All the means of preservation are put in practice occasionally for fruits and the various parts of vegetables, according to the nature of the species, the climate, the uses to which they are applied, &c. Some are dried, as nuts, raisins, sweet herbs, &c.; others are preserved by means of sugar, such as many fruits whose delicate juices would be lost by drying; some are preserved by means of vinegar, and chiefly used as condiments or pickles; a few also by salting, as French beans; while others are preserved in spirits. We have, however, in this place to treat of the best methods of preserving fruits. Fruit is a most important item in the economy of health; the epicurean can scarcely be said to have any luxuries without it; therefore, as it is so invaluable, when we cannot have it fresh, we must have it preserved. It has long been a desideratum to preserve fruits by some cheap method, yet by such as would keep them fit for the various culinary purposes, as making tarts and other similar dishes. The expense of preserving them with sugar is a serious objection; for, except the sugar is used in considerable quantities, the success is very uncertain. Sugar also overpowers and destroys the sub-acid taste so desirable in many fruits: these which are preserved in this manner are chiefly intended for the dessert. Fruits intended for preservation should be gathered in the morning, in dry weather, with the morning sun upon them, if possible; they will then have their fullest flavour, and keep in good condition longer than when gathered at any other time. Until fruit can be used, it should be placed in the dairy, an ice-house, or a refrigerator. In an icehouse it will remain fresh and plump for several days. Fruit gathered in wet or foggy weather will soon be mildewed, and be of no service for preserves.

Having secured the first and most important contribution to the manufacture of preserves,—the fruit, the next consideration is the preparation of the syrup in which the fruit is to be suspended; and this requires much care. In the confectioner's art there is a great nicety in proportioning the degree of concentration of the syrup very exactly to each particular case; and they know this by signs, and express it by certain technical terms. But to distinguish these properly requires very great attention and considerable experience. The principal thing to be acquainted with is the fact, that, in proportion as the syrup is longer boiled, its water will become evaporated, and its consistency will be thicker. Great care must be taken in the management of the fire, that the syrup does not boil over, and that the boiling is not carried to such an extent as to burn the sugar.

The first degree of consistency is called *the thread*, which is subdivided into the little and great thread. If you dip the finger into the syrup and apply it to the thumb, the tenacity of the syrup will, on separating the finger and thumb, afford a thread, which shortly breaks: this is the little thread. If the thread, from the greater tenacity, and, consequently, greater strength of the syrup, admits of a greater extension of the finger and thumb, it is called the great thread. There are half a dozen other terms and experiments for testing the various thickness of the boiling sugar towards the consistency called *caramel*; but that degree of sugar-boiling belongs to the confectioner. A solution of sugar prepared by dissolving two parts of double-refined sugar (the best sugar is the most economical for preserves) in one of water, and boiling this a little, affords a syrup of the right degree of strength, and which neither ferments nor crystallizes. This appears to be the degree called *smooth* by the confectioners, and is proper to be used for the purposes of preserves. The syrup employed should sometimes be clarified, which is done in the following manner:—Dissolve 2 lbs. of loaf sugar in a pint of water; add to this solution the white of an egg, and beat it well. Put the preserving-pan upon the fire with the solution; stir it with a wooden spatula, and, when it begins to swell and boil up, throw in some cold water or a little oil, to damp the boiling; for, as it rises suddenly, if it should boil over, it would take fire, being of a very inflammable nature. Let it boil up again; then take it off, and remove carefully the scum that has risen. Boil the solution again, throw in a little more cold water, remove the scum, and so on for three or four times successively; then strain it. It is considered to be sufficiently boiled when some taken up in a spoon pours out like oil.

Although sugar passes so easily into the state of fermentation, and is, in fact, the only substance capable of undergoing the vinous stage of that process, yet it will not ferment at all if the quantity be sufficient to constitute a very strong syrup: hence, syrups are used to preserve fruits and other vegetable substances from the changes they would undergo if left to themselves. Before sugar was in use, honey was employed to preserve many vegetable productions, though this substance has now given way to the juice of the sugar-cane.

Many fruits, when preserved by boiling, lose much of their peculiar and delicate flavour, as, for instance, pine-apples; and this inconvenience may, in some instances, be remedied by preserving them without heat. Cut the fruit in slices about one fifth of an inch thick, strew powdered loaf sugar an eighth of an inch thick on the bottom of a jar, and put the slices on it. Put more sugar on this, and then another layer of the slices, and so on till the jar is full. Place the jar with the fruit up to the neck in boiling water, and keep it there till the sugar is completely dissolved, which may take half an hour, removing the scum as it rises. Lastly, tie a wet bladder over the mouth of the jar, or cork and wax it.

Any of the fruits that have been preserved in syrup may be converted into dry preserves, by first draining them from the syrup, and then drying them in a stove or very moderate oven, adding to them a quantity of powdered loaf sugar, which will gradually penetrate the fruit, while the fluid parts of the syrup gently evaporate. They should be dried in the stove or oven on a sieve, and turned every six or eight hours, fresh powdered sugar being sifted over them every time they are turned. Afterwards, they are to be kept in a dry situation, in drawers or boxes. Currants and cherries preserved whole in this manner, in bunches, are extremely elegant, and have a fine flavour. In this way it is, also, that orange and lemon chips are preserved.

Marmalades, jams, and fruit pastes are of the same nature, and are now in very general request. They are prepared without difficulty, by attending to a very few directions; they are somewhat expensive, but may be kept without spoiling for a considerable time. Marmalades and jams differ little from each other: they are preserves of a half-liquid consistency, made by boiling the pulp of fruits, and sometimes part of the rinds, with sugar. The appellation of marmalade is applied to those confitures which are composed of the firmer fruits, as pineapples or the rinds of oranges; whereas jams are made of the more juicy berries, such as strawberries, raspberries, currants, mulberries, &c. Fruit pastes are a kind of marmalades, consisting of the pulp of fruits, first evaporated to a proper consistency, and afterwards boiled with sugar. The mixture is then poured into a mould, or spread on sheets of tin, and subsequently dried in the oven or stove till it has acquired the state of a paste. From a sheet of this paste, strips may be cut and formed into any shape that may be desired, as knots, rings, &c. Jams require the same care and attention in the boiling as marmalade; the slightest degree of burning communicates a disagreeable empyreumatic taste, and if they are not boiled sufficiently, they will not keep. That they may keep, it is necessary not to be sparing of sugar.

In all the operations for preserve-making, when the preserving-pan is used, it should not be placed on the fire, but on a trivet, unless the jam is made on a hot plate, when this is not necessary. If the pan is placed close on to the fire, the preserve is very liable to burn, and the colour and flavour be consequently spoiled.

The last-mentioned, but not the least-important preparation of fruit, is the *compôte,* a confiture made at the moment of need, and with much less sugar than would be ordinarily put to preserves. They are most wholesome things, suitable to most stomachs which cannot accommodate themselves to raw fruit or a large portion of sugar: they are the happy medium, and far better than ordinary stewed fruit.

CONFECTIONARY

In speaking of confectionary, it should be remarked that all the various preparations above named come, strictly speaking, under that head; for the various fruits, flowers, herbs, roots, and juices, which, when boiled with sugar, were formerly employed in pharmacy as well as for sweetmeats, were called *confections*, from the Latin word *conficere*, 'to make up;' but the term confectionary embraces a very large class indeed of sweet food, many kinds of which should not be attempted in the ordinary cuisine. The thousand and one ornamental dishes that adorn the tables of the wealthy should be purchased from the confectioner: they cannot profitably be made at home. Apart from these, cakes, biscuits, and tarts, &c., the class of sweetmeats called confections may be thus classified:—1. Liquid confects, or fruits either whole or in pieces, preserved by being immersed in a fluid transparent syrup; as the liquid confects of apricots, green citrons, and many foreign fruits. 2. Dry confects are those which, after having been boiled in the syrup, are taken out and put to dry in an oven, as citron and orange-peel, &c. 3. Marmalade, jams, and pastes, a kind of soft compounds made of the pulp of fruits or other vegetable substances, beat up with sugar or honey; such as oranges, apricots, pears, &c. 4. Jellies are the juices of fruits boiled with sugar to a pretty thick consistency, so as, upon cooling, to form a trembling jelly; as currant, gooseberry, apple jelly, &c. 5. Conserves are a kind of dry confects, made by beating up flowers, fruits, &c., with sugar, not dissolved. 6. Candies are fruits candied over with sugar after having been boiled in the syrup.

DESSERT DISHES

With moderns the dessert is not so profuse, nor does it hold the same relationship to the dinner that it held with the ancients,—the Romans more especially. On ivory tables they would spread hundreds of different kinds of raw, cooked, and preserved fruits, tarts and cakes, as substitutes for the more substantial comestibles with which the guests were satiated. However, as late as the reigns of our two last Georges, fabulous sums were often expended upon fanciful desserts. The dessert certainly repays, in its general effect, the expenditure upon it of much pains; and it may be said, that if there be any poetry at all in meals, or the process of feeding, there is poetry in the dessert, the materials for which should be selected with taste, and, of course, must depend, in a great measure, upon the season. Pines, melons, grapes, peaches, nectarines, plums, strawberries, apples, pears, oranges, almonds, raisins, figs, walnuts, filberts, medlars, cherries, &c. &c., all kinds of dried fruits, and choice and delicately-flavoured cakes and biscuits, make up the dessert, together with the most costly and *recherché* wines. The shape of the dishes varies at different periods, the prevailing fashion at present being oval and circular dishes on stems. The patterns and colours are also subject to changes of fashion; some persons selecting china, chaste in pattern and colour; others, elegantly-shaped glass dishes on stems, with gilt edges. The beauty of the dessert services at the tables of the wealthy tends to enhance the splendour of the plate. The general mode of putting a dessert on table, now the elegant tazzas are fashionable, is, to place them down the middle of the table, a tall and short dish alternately; the fresh fruits being arranged on the tall dishes, and dried fruits, bon-bons, &c., on small round or oval glass plates. The garnishing needs especial attention, as the contrast of the brilliant-coloured fruits with nicely-arranged foliage is very charming. The garnish *par excellence* for dessert is the ice-plant; its crystallized dewdrops producing a marvellous effect in the height of summer, giving a most inviting sense of coolness to the fruit it encircles. The double-edged mallow, strawberry, and vine leaves have a pleasing effect; and for winter desserts, the bay, cuba, and laurel are sometimes used. In town, the expense and difficulty of obtaining natural foliage is great, but paper and composite leaves are to be purchased at an almost nominal price. Mixed fruits of the larger sort are now frequently served on one dish. This mode admits of the display of much taste in the arrangement of the fruit: for instance, a pine in the centre of the dish, surrounded with large plums of various sorts and colours, mixed with pears, rosy-cheeked apples, all arranged with a due regard to colour, have a very good effect. Again, apples and pears look well mingled with plums and grapes, hanging from the border of the dish in a *négligé* sort of manner, with a large bunch of the same fruit lying on the top of the apples. A dessert would not now be considered complete without candied and preserved fruits and confections. The candied fruits may be purchased at a less cost than they can be manufactured at home. They are preserved abroad in most ornamental and elegant forms. And since, from the facilities of travel, we have become so familiar with the tables of the French, chocolate in different forms is indispensable to our desserts.

ICES

Ices are composed, it is scarcely necessary to say, of congealed cream or water, combined sometimes with liqueurs or other flavouring ingredients, or more generally with the juices of fruits. At desserts, or at some evening parties, ices are scarcely to be dispensed with. The principal utensils required for making ice-creams are ice-tubs, freezing-pots, spaddles, and a cellaret. The tub must be large enough to contain about a bushel of ice, pounded small, when brought out of the ice-house, and mixed very carefully with either *salt, nitre,* or *soda.* The freezing-pot is best made of pewter. If it be of tin, as is sometimes the case, the congelation goes on too rapidly in it for the thorough intermingling of its contents, on which the excellence of the ice greatly depends. The spaddle is generally made of copper, kept bright and clean. The cellaret is a tin vessel, in which ices are kept for a short time from dissolving. The method to be pursued in the freezing process must be attended to. When the ice-tub is prepared with fresh-pounded ice and salt, the freezing-pot is put into it up to its cover. The articles to be congealed are then poured into it and covered over; but to prevent the ingredients from separating and the heaviest of them from falling to the bottom of the mould, it is requisite to turn the freezing-pot round and round by the handle, so as to keep its contents moving until the congelation commences. As soon as this is perceived (the cover of the pot being occasionally taken off for the purpose of noticing when freezing takes place), the cover is immediately closed over it, ice is put upon it, and it is left in this state till it is served. The use of the spaddle is to stir up and remove from the sides of the freezing pot the cream, which in the shaking may have washed against it, and by stirring it in with the rest, to prevent waste of it occurring. Any negligence in stirring the contents of the freezing-pot before congelation takes place, will destroy the whole: either the sugar sinks to the bottom and leaves the ice insufficiently sweetened, or lumps are formed, which disfigure and discolour it.

CHAPTER XXVIII

RECIPES: SWEET SAUCES AND JAMS

TO MAKE SYRUP FOR COMPOTES, &c.

Ingredients
To every lb. of sugar allow 1-1/2 pint of water

Mode—Boil the sugar and water together for ¼ hour, carefully removing the scum as it rises: the syrup is then ready for the fruit. The articles boiled in this syrup will not keep for any length of time, it being suitable only for dishes intended to be eaten immediately. A larger proportion of sugar must be added for a syrup intended to keep.

Time—¼ hour.

TO BOIL SUGAR TO CARAMEL

Ingredients
To every lb. of lump sugar allow 1 gill of spring water

Mode—Boil the sugar and water together very quickly over a clear fire, skimming it very carefully as soon as it boils. Keep it boiling until the sugar snaps when a little of it is dropped in a pan of cold water. If it remains hard, the sugar has attained the right degree; then squeeze in a little lemon-juice, and let it remain an instant on the fire. Set the pan into another of cold water, and the caramel is then ready for use. The insides of well-oiled moulds are often ornamented with this sugar, which with a fork should be spread over them in fine threads or network. A dish of light pastry, tastefully arranged, looks very prettily with this sugar spun lightly over it. The sugar must be carefully watched, and taken up the instant it is done. Unless the cook is very experienced and thoroughly understands her business, it is scarcely worth while to attempt to make this elaborate ornament, as it may be purchased quite as economically at a confectioner's, if the failures in the preparation are taken into consideration.

APPLE JAM

Ingredients

To every lb. of fruit weighed after being pared, cored, and sliced, allow 3/4 lb. of preserving-sugar
the grated rind of 1 lemon
the juice of 1/2 lemon

Mode—Peel the apples, core and slice them very thin, and be particular that they are all the same sort. Put them into a jar, stand this in a saucepan of boiling water, and let the apples stew until quite tender. Previously to putting the fruit into the jar, weigh it, to ascertain the proportion of sugar that may be required. Put the apples into a preserving-pan, crush the sugar to small lumps, and add it, with the grated lemon-rind and juice, to the apples. Simmer these over the fire for ½ hour, reckoning from the time the jam begins to simmer properly; remove the scum as it rises, and when the jam is done, put it into pots for use. Place a piece of oiled paper over the jam, and to exclude the air, cover the pots with tissue-paper dipped in the white of an egg, and stretched over the top. This jam will keep good for a long time.

Time—About 2 hours to stew in the jar; ½ hour to boil after the jam begins to simmer.

Average cost, for this quantity, 6s.

Sufficient—7 or 8 lbs. of apples for 6 pots of jam.

Seasonable—Make this in September, October, or November.

TO MAKE CHERRY BRANDY

Ingredients
Morella cherries
good brandy
to every lb. of cherries allow 3 oz. of pounded sugar

Mode—Have ready some glass bottles, which must be perfectly dry. Ascertain that the cherries are not too ripe and are freshly gathered, and cut off about half of the stalks. Put them into the bottles, with the above proportion of sugar to every lb. of fruit; strew this in between the cherries, and, when the bottles are nearly full, pour in sufficient brandy to reach just below the cork. A few peach or apricot kernels will add much to their flavour, or a few blanched bitter almonds. Put corks or bungs into the bottles, tie over them a piece of bladder, and store away in a dry place. The cherries will be fit to eat in 2 or 3 months, and will remain good for years. They are liable to shrivel and become tough if too much sugar be added to them.

Average cost, 1s. to 1s. 6d. per lb.

Sufficient—1 lb. of cherries and about ¼ pint of brandy for a quart bottle. *Seasonable* in August and September.

CHERRY JAM

Ingredients
To every lb. of fruit, weighed before stoning, allow ½ lb. of sugar
to every 6 lbs. of fruit allow 1 pint of red-currant juice
to every pint of juice 1 lb. of sugar

Mode—Weigh the fruit before stoning, and allow half the weight of sugar; stone the cherries, and boil them in a preserving-pan until nearly all the juice is dried up; then add the sugar, which should be crushed to powder, and the currant-juice, allowing 1 pint to every 6 lbs. of cherries (original weight), and 1 lb. of sugar to every pint of juice. Boil all together until it jellies, which will be in from 20 minutes to ½ hour; skim the jam well, keep it well stirred, and, a few minutes before it is done, crack some of the stones, and add the kernels: these impart a very delicious flavour to the jam.

Time—According to the quality of the cherries, from ¾ to 1 hour to boil them; 20 minutes to ½ hour with the sugar.

Average cost, from 7d. to 8d. per lb. pot.

Sufficient—1 pint of fruit for a lb. pot of jam.

Seasonable—Make this in July or August.

RASPBERRY JAM

Ingredients
To every lb. of raspberries allow 1 lb. of sugar
¼ pint of red-currant juice

Mode—Let the fruit for this preserve be gathered in fine weather, and used as soon after it is picked as possible. Take off the stalks, put the raspberries into a preserving-pan, break them well with a wooden spoon, and let them boil for ¼ hour, keeping them well stirred. Then add the currant-juice and sugar, and boil again for ½ hour. Skim the jam well after the sugar is added, or the preserve will not be clear. The addition of the currant juice is a very great improvement to this preserve, as it gives it a piquant taste, which the flavour of the raspberries seems to require.

Time—¼ hour to simmer the fruit without the sugar; ¼ hour after it is added.

Average cost, from 6d. to 8d. per lb. pot.

Sufficient—Allow about 1 pint of fruit to fill a 1-lb. pot.

Seasonable in July and August.

CHAPTER XXIX

GENERAL OBSERVATIONS ON MILK, BUTTER, CHEESE, AND EGGS

MILK

Milk is obtained only from the class of animals called Mammalia, and is intended by Nature for the nourishment of their young. The milk of each animal is distinguished by some peculiarities; but as that of the cow is by far the most useful to us in this part of the world, our observations will be confined to that variety.

Milk, when drawn from the cow, is of a yellowish-white colour, and is the most yellow at the beginning of the period of lactation. Its taste is agreeable, and rather saccharine. The viscidity and specific gravity of milk are somewhat greater than that of water; but these properties vary somewhat in the milk procured from different individuals. On an average, the specific gravity of milk is 1.035, water being 1. The small cows of the Alderney breed afford the richest milk.

From no other substance, solid or fluid, can so great a number of distinct kinds of aliment be prepared as from milk; some forming food, others drink; some of them delicious, and deserving the name of luxuries; all of them wholesome, and some medicinal: indeed, the variety of aliments that seems capable of being produced from milk, appears to be quite endless. In every age this must have been a subject for experiment, and every nation has added to the number by the invention of some peculiarity of its own.

BUTTER

Beckman, in his "History of Inventions," states that butter was not used either by the Greeks or Romans in cooking, nor was it brought upon their tables at certain meals, as is the custom at present. In England it has been made from time immemorial, though the art of making cheese is said not to have been known to the ancient Britons, and to have been learned from their conquerors.

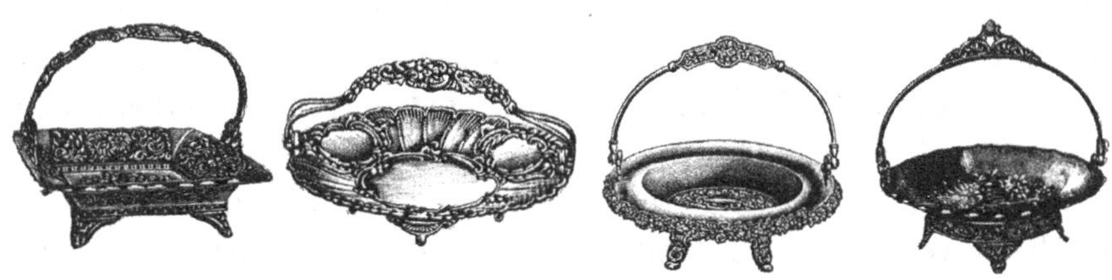

The taste of butter is peculiar, and very unlike any other fatty substance. It is extremely agreeable when of the best quality; but its flavour depends much upon the food given to the cows: to be good, it should not adhere to the knife.

There are two methods pursued in the manufacture of butter. In one, the cream is separated from the milk, and in that state it is converted into butter by churning, as is the practice about Epping; in the other, milk is subjected to the same process, which is the method usually followed in Cheshire. The first method is generally said to give the richest butter, and the latter the largest quantity, though some are of opinion that there is little difference either in quality or quantity.

CHEESE

Cheese is the curd formed from milk by artificial coagulation, pressed and dried for use. Curd, called also casein and caseous matter, or the basis of cheese, exists in the milk, and not in the cream, and requires only to be separated by coagulation. The coagulation, however, supposes some alteration of the curd. By means of the substance employed to coagulate it, it is rendered insoluble in water. When the curd is freed from the whey, kneaded and pressed to expel it entirely, it becomes cheese. This assumes a degree of transparency, and possesses many of the properties of coagulated albumen. If it be well dried, it does not change by exposure to the air; but if it contain moisture, it soon putrefies. It therefore requires some salt to preserve it, and this acts likewise as a kind of seasoning. All our cheese is coloured more or less, except that made from skim milk. The colouring substances employed are arnatto, turmeric, or marigold, all perfectly harmless unless they are adulterated; and it is said that arnatto sometimes contains red lead.

Cheese varies in quality and richness according to the materials of which it is composed. It is made—1. Of entire milk, as in Cheshire; 2. of milk and cream, as at Stilton; 3. of new milk mixed with skimmed milk, as in Gloucestershire; 4. of skimmed milk only, as in Suffolk, Holland, and Italy.

EGGS

There is only one opinion as to the nutritive properties of eggs, although the qualities of those belonging to different birds vary somewhat. Those of the common hen are most esteemed as delicate food, particularly when "new-laid." The quality of eggs depends much upon the food given to the hen. Eggs in general are considered most easily digestible when little subjected to the art of cookery. The lightest way of dressing them is by poaching, which is effected by putting them for a minute or two into brisk boiling water: this coagulates the external white, without doing the inner part too much. Eggs are much better when new-laid than a day or two afterwards. The usual time allotted for boiling eggs in the shell is 3 to 3-¾ minutes: less time than that in boiling water will not be sufficient to solidify the white, and more will make the yolk hard and less digestible: it is very difficult to *guess* accurately as to the time. Great care should be employed in putting them into the water, to prevent cracking the shell, which inevitably causes a portion of the white to exude, and lets water into the egg. Eggs are often beaten up raw in nutritive beverages.

Eggs are employed in a very great many articles of cookery, entrées, and entremets, and they form an essential ingredient in pastry, creams, flip, &c. It is particularly necessary that they should be quite fresh, as nothing is worse than stale eggs. Cobbett justly says, stale, or even preserved eggs, are things to be run from, not after.

CHAPTER XXX

RECIPES: CHEESE AND EGGS

CAYENNE CHEESES

Ingredients

½ lb. of butter
½ lb. of flour
½ lb. of grated cheese
⅓ teaspoonful of cayenne
⅓ teaspoonful of salt
water

Mode—Rub the butter in the flour; add the grated cheese, cayenne. and salt; and mix these ingredients well together. Moisten with sufficient water to make the whole into a paste; roll out, and cut into fingers about 4 inches in length. Bake them in a moderate oven a very light colour, and serve very hot.

Time—15 to 20 minutes. *Average cost*, 1s. 4d.

Sufficient for 6 or 7 persons. *Seasonable* at any time.

TO MAKE A FONDUE

Ingredients

4 eggs
the weight of 2 in Parmesan or good Cheshire cheese
the weight of 2 in butter
pepper and salt to taste

Mode—Separate the yolks from the whites of the eggs; beat the former in a basin, and grate the cheese, or cut it into *very thin* flakes. Parmesan or

Cheshire cheese may be used, whichever is the most convenient, although the former is considered more suitable for this dish; or an equal quantity of each may be used. Break the butter into small pieces, add it to the other ingredients, with sufficient pepper and salt to season nicely, and beat the mixture thoroughly. Well whisk the whites of the eggs, stir them lightly in, and either bake the fondue in a soufflé-dish or small round cake-tin. Fill the dish only half full, as the fondue should rise very much. Pin a napkin round the tin or dish, and serve very hot and very quickly. If allowed to stand after it is withdrawn from the oven, the beauty and lightness of this preparation will be entirely spoiled.

Time—From 15 to 20 minutes. *Average cost*, 10d.

Sufficient for 4 or 5 persons. *Seasonable* at any time.

POACHED EGGS

Ingredients
Eggs
Water
To every pint of water allow 1 tablespoonful of vinegar

Mode—Eggs for poaching should be perfectly fresh, but not quite new-laid; those that are about 36 hours old are the best for the purpose. If quite new-laid, the white is so milky it is almost impossible to set it; and, on the other hand, if the egg be at all stale, it is equally difficult to poach it nicely. Strain some boiling water into a deep clean frying-pan; break the egg into a cup without damaging the yolk, and, when the water boils, remove the pan to the side of the fire, and gently slip the egg into it. Place the pan over a gentle fire, and keep the water simmering until the white looks nicely set, when the egg is ready. Take it up gently with a slice, cut away the ragged edges of the white, and serve either on toasted bread or on slices of ham or bacon, or on spinach, &c. A poached egg should not be overdone, as its appearance and taste will be quite spoiled if the yolk be allowed to harden. When the egg is slipped into the water, the white should be gathered together, to keep it a little in form, or the cup should be turned over it for 1 minute. To poach an egg to perfection is rather a difficult operation; so, for inexperienced cooks, a tin egg-poacher may be purchased, which greatly facilitates this manner of dressing ecgs. Our illustration clearly shows what it is: it consists of a tin plate with a handle, with a space for three perforated cups. An egg should be broken into each cup, and the machine then placed in a stewpan of boiling water, which has been previously strained. When the whites of the eggs appear set, they are done, and should then be carefully slipped on to the toast or spinach, or with whatever they are served. In poaching eggs in a frying-pan, never do more than four at a time; and, when a little vinegar is liked mixed with the water in which the eggs are done, use the above proportion.

Time—2-½ to 3-½ minutes, according to the size of the egg.

Sufficient—Allow 2 eggs to each person.

Seasonable at any time, but less plentiful in winter.

CHAPTER XXXI

GENERAL OBSERVATIONS ON BREAD AND CAKES

BREAD AND BREAD-MAKING

AMONG the numerous vegetable products yielding articles of food for man, the Cereals hold the first place. By means of skilful cultivation, mankind have transformed the original forms of these growths, poor and ill-flavoured as they perhaps were, into various fruitful and agreeable species, which yield an abundant and pleasant supply. Classified according to their respective richness in alimentary elements, the Cereals stand thus:—Wheat, and its varieties, Rye, Barley, Oats, Rice, Indian Corn. Everybody knows it is wheat flour which yields the best bread. Rye-bread is viscous, hard, less easily soluble by the gastric juice, and not so rich in nutritive power. Flour produced from barley, Indian corn, or rice, is not so readily made into bread; and the article, when made, is heavy and indigestible.

On examining a grain of corn from any of the numerous cereals [Footnote: *Cereal,* a corn-producing plant; from Ceres, the goddess of agriculture.] used in the preparation of flour, such as wheat, maize, rye, barley, &c., it will be found to consist of two parts,—the husk, or exterior covering, which is generally of a dark colour, and the inner, or albuminous part, which is more or less white. In grinding, these two portions are separated, and the husk being blown away in the process of winnowing, the flour remains in the form of a light brown powder, consisting principally of starch and gluten. In order to render it white, it undergoes a process called "bolting." It is passed through a series of fine sieves, which separate the coarser parts, leaving behind fine white flour,—the "fine firsts" of the corn-dealer. The process of bolting, as just described, tends to deprive flour of its gluten, the coarser and darker portion containing much of that substance; while the lighter part is peculiarly rich in starch. Bran contains a large proportion of gluten; hence it will be seen why brown broad is so much more nutritious than white; in fact, we may lay it down as a general rule, that the whiter the bread the less nourishment it contains. Majendie proved this by feeding a dog for forty days with white wheaten bread, at the end of which time he died; while another dog, fed on brown bread made with flour mixed with bran, lived without any disturbance of his health. The "bolting" process, then, is rather injurious than beneficial in its result; and is one of the numerous instances where fashion has chosen a wrong standard to go by. In ancient times, down to the Emperors, no bolted flour was known. In many parts of Germany the entire meal is used; and in no part of the world are the digestive organs of the people in a better condition. In years of famine, when corn is scarce, the use of bolted flour is most culpable, for from 18 to 20 per cent, is lost in bran. Brown bread has, of late years, become very popular; and many physicians have recommended it to invalids with weak digestions with great success. This rage for white bread has introduced adulterations of a very serious character, affecting the health of the whole community. Potatoes are added for this purpose; but this is a comparatively harmless cheat, only reducing the nutritive property of the bread; but bone-dust and alum are also put in, which are far from harmless.

Bread-making is a very ancient art indeed. The Assyrians, Egyptians, and Greeks, used to make bread, in which oil, with aniseed and other spices, was an element; but this was unleavened. Every family used to prepare the bread for its own consumption, the *trade* of baking not having yet taken shape. It is said, that somewhere about the beginning of the thirtieth Olympiad, the slave of an archon, at Athens, made leavened bread by accident. He had left some wheaten dough in an earthen pan, and forgotten it; some days afterwards, he lighted upon it again, and found it turning sour. His first thought was to throw it away; but, his master coming up, he mixed this now acescent dough with some fresh dough, which he was working at. The bread thus produced, by the introduction of dough in which alcoholic fermentation had begun, was found delicious by the archon and his friends; and the slave, being summoned and catechised, told the secret. It spread all over Athens; and everybody wanting leavened bread at once, certain persons set up as bread-makers, or bakers. In a short time bread-baking became quite an art, and "Athenian bread" was quoted all over Greece as the best bread, just as the honey of Hyamettus was celebrated as the best honey.

BREAD-MAKING

PANIFICATION, or bread-making, consists of the following processes, in the case of Wheaten Flour. Fifty or sixty per cent. of water is added to the flour, with the addition of some leavening matter, and, preferably, of yeast from malt and hops. All kinds of leavening matter have, however, been, and are still used in different parts of the world: in the East Indies, "toddy," which is a liquor that flows from the wounded cocoa-nut tree; and, in the West Indies, "dunder," or the refuse of the distillation of rum. The dough then undergoes the well-known process called *kneading*. The yeast produces fermentation, a process which may be thus described:— The dough reacting upon the leavening matter introduced, the starch of the flour is transformed into saccharine matter, the saccharine matter being afterwards changed into alcohol and carbonic acid. The dough must be well "bound," and yet allow the escape of the little bubbles of carbonic acid which accompany the fermentation, and which, in their passage, cause the numerous little holes which are seen in light bread.

The yeast must be good and fresh, if the bread is to be digestible and nice. Stale yeast produces, instead of vinous fermentation, an acetous fermentation, which flavours the bread and makes it disagreeable. A poor thin yeast produces an imperfect fermentation, the result being a heavy unwholesome loaf.

When the dough is well kneaded, it is left to stand for some time, and then, as soon as it begins to swell, it is divided into loaves; after which it is again left to stand, when it once more swells up, and manifests, for the last time, the symptoms of fermentation. It is then put into the oven, where the water contained in the dough is partly evaporated, and the loaves swell up again, while a yellow crust begins to form upon the surface. When the bread is sufficiently baked, the bottom crust is hard and resonant if struck with the finger, while the crumb is elastic, and rises again after being pressed down with the finger. The bread is, in all probability, baked sufficiently if, on opening the door of the oven, you are met by a cloud of steam which quickly passes away.

AERATED BREAD—It is not unknown to some of our readers that Dr. Dauglish, of Malvern, has recently patented a process for making bread "light" without the use of leaven. The ordinary process of bread-making by fermentation is tedious, and much labour of human hands is requisite in the kneading, in order that the dough may be thoroughly interpenetrated with the leaven. The new process impregnates the bread, by the application of machinery, with carbonic acid gas, or fixed air. Different opinions are expressed about the bread; but it is curious to note, that, as corn is now reaped by machinery, and dough is baked by machinery, the whole process of bread-making is probably in course of undergoing changes which will emancipate both the housewife and the professional baker from a large amount of labour.

In the production of Aërated Bread, wheaten flour, water, salt, and carbonic acid gas (generated by proper machinery), are the only materials employed. We need not inform our readers that carbonic acid gas is the source of the effervescence, whether in common water coming from a depth, or in lemonade, or any aërated drink. Its action, in the new bread, takes the place of fermentation in the old.

In the patent process, the dough is mixed in a great iron ball, inside which is a system of paddles, perpetually turning, and doing the kneading part of the business. Into this globe the flour is dropped till it is full, and then the common atmospheric air is pumped out, and the pure gas turned on. The gas is followed by the water, which has been aërated for the purpose, and then begins the churning or kneading part of the business.

The following observations are extracted from a valuable work on Bread-making, [Footnote: "The English Bread-Book." By Eliza Acton. London: Longman.] and will be found very useful to our readers:—

The first thing required for making wholesome bread is the utmost cleanliness; the next is the soundness and sweetness of all the ingredients used for it; and, in addition to these, there must be attention and care through the whole process.

An almost certain way of spoiling dough is to leave it half-made, and to allow it to become cold before it is finished. The other most common causes of failure are using yeast which is no longer sweet, or which has been frozen, or has had hot liquid poured over it.

Too small a proportion of yeast, or insufficient time allowed for the dough to rise, will cause the bread to be heavy.

Heavy bread will also most likely be the result of making the dough very hard, and letting it become quite, cold, particularly in winter.

The utensils required for making bread, on a moderate scale, are a kneading-trough or pan, sufficiently large that the dough may be kneaded freely without throwing the flour over the edges, and also to allow for its rising; a hair sieve for straining yeast, and one or two strong spoons.

Yeast must always be good of its kind, and in a fitting state to produce ready and proper fermentation. Yeast of strong beer or ale produces more effect than that of milder kinds; and the fresher the yeast, the smaller the quantity will be required to raise the dough.

Brick ovens are generally considered the best adapted for baking bread: these should be heated with wood faggots, and then swept and mopped out, to cleanse them for the reception of the bread. Iron ovens are more difficult to manage, being apt to burn the surface of the bread before the middle is baked. To remedy this, a few clean bricks should be set at the bottom of the oven, close together, to receive the tins of bread. In many modern stoves the ovens are so much improved that they bake admirably; and they can always be brought to the required temperature, when it is higher than is needed, by leaving the door open for a time.

A FEW HINTS respecting the Making and Baking of CAKES.

Eggs should always be broken into a cup, the whites and yolks separated, and they should always be strained. Breaking the eggs thus, the bad ones may be easily rejected without spoiling the others, and so cause no waste. As eggs are used instead of yeast, they should be very thoroughly whisked; they are generally sufficiently beaten when thick enough to carry the drop that falls from the whisk.

Loaf Sugar should be well pounded, and then sifted through a fine sieve.

Currants should be nicely washed, picked, dried in a cloth, and then carefully examined, that no pieces of grit or stone may be left amongst them. They should then be laid on a dish before the fire, to become thoroughly dry; as, if added damp to the other ingredients, cakes will be liable to be heavy.

Good Butter should always be used in the manufacture of cakes; and if beaten to a cream, it saves much time and labour to warm, but not melt, it before beating.

Less butter and eggs are required for cakes when yeast is mixed with the other ingredients.

The heat of the oven is of great importance, especially for large cakes. If the heat be not tolerably fierce, the batter will not rise. If the oven is too quick, and there is any danger of the cake burning or catching, put a sheet of clean paper over the top. Newspaper, or paper that has been printed on, should never be used for this purpose.

To know when a cake is sufficiently baked, plunge a clean knife into the middle of it; draw it quickly out, and if it looks in the least sticky, put the cake back, and close the oven door until the cake is done.

CHAPTER XXXII

RECIPES: BREADS AND CAKES

TO MAKE YEAST FOR BREAD

Ingredients

1-½ oz. of hops
3 quarts of water
1 lb. of bruised malt
½ pint of yeast

Mode—Boil the hops in the water for 20 minutes; let it stand for about 5 minutes, then add it to 1 lb. of bruised malt prepared as for brewing. Let the mixture stand covered till about lukewarm; then put in not quite ½ pint of yeast; keep it warm, and let it work 3 or 4 hours; then put it into small ½-pint bottles (ginger-beer bottles are the best for the purpose), cork them well, and tie them down. The yeast is now ready for use; it will keep good for a few weeks, and 1 bottle will be found sufficient for 18 lbs. of flour. When required for use, boil 3 lbs. of potatoes without salt, mash them in the same water in which they were boiled, and rub them through a colander. Stir in about ½ lb. of flour; then put in the yeast, pour it in the middle of the flour, and let it stand warm on the hearth all night, and in the morning let it be quite warm when it is kneaded. The bottles of yeast require very careful opening, as it is generally exceedingly ripe.

Time—20 minutes to boil the hops and water, the yeast to work 3 or 4 hours.

Sufficient—½ pint sufficient for 18 lbs. of flour.

TO MAKE GOOD HOME-MADE BREAD

(*Miss Acton's Recipe.*)

Ingredients

1 quartern of flour

1 large tablespoonful of solid brewer's yeast, or nearly 1 oz. of fresh German yeast

1-¼ to 1-½ pint of warm milk-and-water

Mode—Put the flour into a large earthenware bowl or deep pan; then, with a strong metal or wooden spoon, hollow out the middle; but do not clear it entirely away from the bottom of the pan, as, in that case, the sponge (or leaven, as it was formerly termed) would stick to it, which it ought not to do. Next take either a large tablespoonful of brewer's yeast which has been rendered solid by mixing it with plenty of cold water, and letting it afterwards stand to settle for a day and night; or nearly an ounce of German yeast; put it into a large basin, and proceed to mix it, so that it shall be as smooth as cream, with ¾ pint of warm milk-and-water, or with water only; though even a very little milk will much improve the bread. Pour the yeast into the hole made in the flour, and stir into it as much of that which lies round it as will make a thick batter, in which there must be no lumps. Strew plenty of flour on the top; throw a thick clean cloth over, and set it where the air is warm; but do not place it upon the kitchen fender, for it will become too much heated there. Look at it from time to time: when it has been laid for nearly an hour, and when the yeast has risen and broken through the flour, so that bubbles appear in it, you will know that it is ready to be made up into dough. Then place the pan on a strong chair, or dresser, or table, of convenient height; pour into the sponge the remainder of the warm milk-and-water; stir into it as much of the flour as you can with the spoon; then wipe it out clean with your fingers, and lay it aside. Next take plenty of the remaining flour, throw it on the top of the leaven, and begin, with the knuckles of both hands, to knead it well. When the flour is nearly all kneaded in, begin to draw the edges of the dough towards the middle, in order to mix the whole thoroughly; and when it is free from flour and lumps and crumbs, and does not stick to the hands when touched, it will be done, and may again be covered with the cloth, and left to rise a second time. In ¾ hour look at it, and should it have swollen very much, and begin to crack, it will be light enough to bake. Turn it then on to a paste-board or very clean dresser, and with a large sharp knife divide it in two; make it up quickly into loaves, and dispatch it to the oven: make one or two incisions across the tops of the loaves, as they will rise more easily if this be done. If baked in tins or pans, rub them with a tiny piece of butter laid on a piece of clean paper, to prevent the dough from sticking to them. All bread should be turned upside down, or on its side, as soon as it is drawn from the oven: if this be neglected, the under part of the loaves will become wet and blistered from the steam, which cannot then escape from them. *To make the dough without setting a sponge*, merely mix the yeast with the greater part of the warm milk-and-water, and wet up the whole of the flour at once after a little salt has been stirred in, proceeding exactly, in every other respect, as in the directions just given. As the dough will *soften* in the rising, it should be made quite firm at first, or it will be too lithe by the time it is ready for the oven.

MACAROONS

Ingredients

½ lb. of sweet almonds
½ lb. of sifted loaf sugar
the whites of 3 eggs
wafer-paper

Mode—Blanch, skin, and dry the almonds, and pound them well with a little orange-flower water or plain water; then add to them the sifted sugar and the whites of the eggs, which should be beaten to a stiff froth, and mix all the ingredients well together. When the paste looks soft, drop it at equal distances from a biscuit-syringe on to sheets of wafer-paper; put a strip of almond on the top of each; strew some sugar over, and bake the macaroons in rather a slow oven, of a light brown colour when hard and set, they are done, and must not be allowed to get very brown, as that would spoil their appearance. If the cakes, when baked, appear heavy, add a little more white of egg, but let this always be well whisked before it is added to the other ingredients. We have given a recipe for making these cakes, but we think it almost or quite as economical to purchase such articles as these at a good confectioner's.

Time—From 15 to 20 minutes, in a slow oven.

Average cost, 1s. 8d. per lb.

THICK GINGERBREAD

Ingredients

1 lb. of treacle
¼ lb. of butter
¼ lb. of coarse brown sugar
1-½ lb. of flour
1 oz. of ginger
½ oz. of ground allspice
1 teaspoonful of carbonate of soda
¼ pint of warm milk
3 eggs

Mode—Put the flour into a basin, with the sugar, ginger, and allspice; mix these together; warm the butter, and add it, with the treacle, to the other ingredients. Stir well; make the milk just warm, dissolve the carbonate of soda in it, and mix the whole into a nice smooth dough with the eggs, which should be previously well whisked; pour the mixture into a buttered tin, and bake it from ¾ to 1 hour, or longer, should the gingerbread be very thick. Just before it is done, brush the top over with the yolk of an egg beaten up with a little milk, and put it back in the oven to finish baking.

Time—¾ to 1 hour. *Average cost*, 1s. per square.

Seasonable at any time.

POUND CAKE

Ingredients

1 lb. of butter
1-¼ lb. of flour
1 lb. of pounded loaf sugar
1 lb. of currants
9 eggs
2 oz. of candied peel
½ oz. of citron
½ oz. of sweet almonds
when liked, a little pounded mace

Mode—Work the butter to a cream; dredge in the flour; add the sugar, currants, candied peel, which should be cut into neat slices, and the almonds, which should be blanched and chopped, and mix all these well together; whisk the eggs, and let them be thoroughly blended with the dry ingredients. Beat the cake well for 20 minutes, and put it into a round tin, lined at the bottom and sides with a strip of white buttered paper. Bake it from 1-½ to 2 hours, and let the oven be well heated when the cake is first put in, as, if this is not the case, the currants will all sink to the bottom of it. To make this preparation light, the yolks and whites of the eggs should be beaten separately, and added separately to the other ingredients. A glass of wine is sometimes added to the mixture; but this is scarcely necessary, as the cake will be found quite rich enough without it.

Time—1-½ to 2 hours.

Average cost, 3s. 6d.

Sufficient—The above quantity divided in two will make two nice-sized cakes.

Seasonable at any time.

CHAPTER XXXIII

GENERAL OBSERVATIONS ON BEVERAGES

Beverages are innumerable in their variety; but the ordinary beverages drunk in the British isles, may be divided into three classes:—1. Beverages of the simplest kind not fermented. 2. Beverages, consisting of water, containing a considerable quantity of carbonic acid. 3. Beverages composed partly of fermented liquors. Of the first class may be mentioned,—water, toast-and-water, barley-water, eau sucré, lait sucré, cheese and milk whey, milk-and-water, lemonade, orangeade, sherbet, apple and pear juice, capillaire, vinegar-and-water, raspberry vinegar and water.

The beverages composed partly of fermented liquors, are hot spiced wines, bishop, egg-flip, egg-hot, ale posset, sack posset, punch, and spirits-and-water.

We will, however, forthwith treat on the most popular of our beverages, beginning with the one which makes "the cup that cheers but not inebriates."

The beverage called tea has now become almost a necessary of life. Previous to the middle of the 17th century it was not used in England, and it was wholly unknown to the Greeks and Romans. Pepys says, in his Diary,—"September 25th, 1661—I sent for a cup of tea (a China drink), of which I had never drunk before." Two years later it was so rare a commodity in England, that the English East-India Company bought 2 lbs. 2 oz. of it, as a present for his majesty. In 1666 it was sold in London for sixty shillings a pound. From that date the consumption has gone on increasing from 5,000 lbs. to 50,000,000 lbs.

It appears that coffee was first introduced into England by Daniel Edwards, a Turkey merchant, whose servant, Pasqua, a Greek, understood the manner of roasting it. This servant, under the patronage of Edwards, established the first coffee-house in London, in George Yard, Lombard Street. Coffee was then sold at four or five guineas a pound, and a duty was soon afterwards laid upon it of fourpence a gallon, when made into a beverage. In the course of two centuries, however, this berry, unknown originally as an article of food, except to some savage tribes on the confines of Abyssinia, has made its way through the whole of the civilized world. Mahommedans of all ranks drink coffee twice a day; it is in universal request in France; and the demand for it throughout the British isles is daily increasing, the more especially since so much attention has been given to mechanical contrivances for roasting and grinding the berry and preparing the beverage.

Of the various kinds of coffee the Arabian is considered the best. It is grown chiefly in the districts of Aden and Mocha; whence the name of our Mocha coffee. Mocha coffee has a smaller and rounder bean than any other, and likewise a more agreeable smell and taste. The next in reputation and quality is the Java and Ceylon coffee, and then the coffees of Bourbon and Martinique, and that of Berbice, a district of the colony of British Guiana. The Jamaica and St. Domingo coffees are less esteemed.

To have coffee in perfection, it should be roasted and ground just before it is used, and more should not be ground at a time than is wanted for immediate use, or, if it be necessary to grind more, it should be kept closed from the air. Coffee readily imbibes exhalations from other substances, and thus often acquires a bad flavour: brown sugar placed near it will communicate a disagreeable flavour. It is stated that the coffee in the West Indies has often been injured by being laid in rooms near the sugar-works, or where rum is distilled; and the same effect has been produced by bringing over coffee in the same ships with rum and sugar. Dr. Moseley mentions that a few bags of pepper, on board a ship from India, spoiled a whole cargo of coffee.

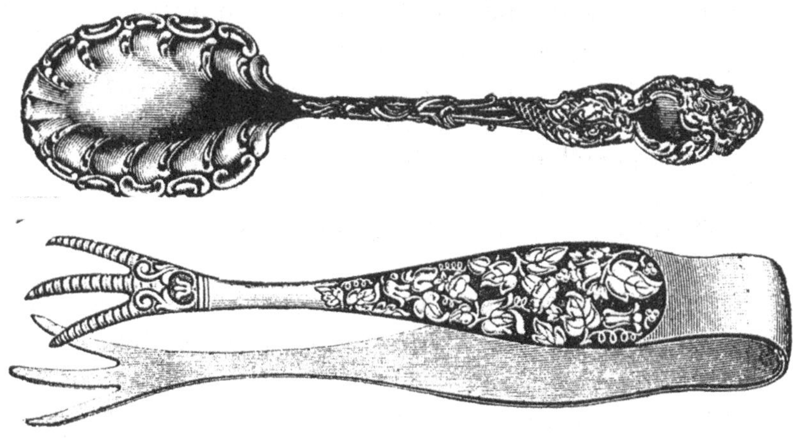

CHAPTER XXXIV

RECIPES: BEVERAGES

TO MAKE CHOCOLATE

Ingredients
Allow ½ oz. of chocolate to each person
to every oz. allow ½ pint of water
½ pint of milk

Mode—Make the milk-and-water hot; scrape the chocolate into it, and stir the mixture constantly and quickly until the chocolate is dissolved; bring it to the boiling-point, stir it well, and serve directly with white sugar. Chocolate prepared with in a mill, as shown in the engraving, is made by putting in the scraped chocolate, pouring over it the boiling milk-and-water, and milling it over the fire until hot and frothy.

Sufficient—Allow ½ oz. of cake chocolate to each person.

> **CHOCOLATE AND COCOA**—Both these preparations are made from the seeds or beans of the cacao-tree, which grows in the West Indies and South America. The Spanish, and the proper name, is cacao, not cocoa, as it is generally spelt. From this mistake, the tree from which the beverage is procured has been often confounded with the palm that produces the edible cocoa-nuts, which are the produce of the cocoa-tree (*Cocos nucifera*), whereas the tree from which chocolate is procured is very different (the *Theobroma cacao*).

The cocoa-tree was cultivated by the aboriginal inhabitants of South America, particularly in Mexico, where, according to Humboldt, it was reared by Montezuma. It was transplanted thence into other dependencies of the Spanish monarchy in 1520; and it was so highly esteemed by Linnaeus receive from him the name now conferred upon it, of Theobroma, a term derived from the Greek, and signifying "*food for gods.*" Chocolate has always been a favourite beverage among the Spaniards and Creoles, and was considered here as a great luxury when first introduced, after the discovery of America; but the high duties laid upon it, confined it long almost entirely to the wealthier classes. Before it was subjected to duty, Mr. Bryan Edwards stated that cocoa plantations were numerous in Jamaica, but that the duty caused their almost entire ruin. The removal of this duty has increased their cultivation.

MALT WINE

Ingredients

5 gallons of water
28 lbs. of sugar
6 quarts of sweet-wort
6 quarts of tun
3 lbs. of raisins
½ lb. of candy
1 pint of brandy

Mode—Boil the sugar and water together for 10 minutes; skim it well, and put the liquor into a convenient-sized pan or tub. Allow it to cool; then mix it with the sweet-wort and tun. Let it stand for 3 days, then put it into a barrel; here it will work or ferment for another three days or more; then bung up the cask, and keep it undisturbed for 2 or 3 months. After this, add the raisins (whole), the candy, and brandy, and, in 6 months' time, bottle the wine off. Those who do not brew, may procure the sweet-wort and tun from any brewer. Sweet-wort is the liquor that leaves the mash of malt before it is boiled with the hops; tun is the new beer after the whole of the brewing operation has been completed.

Time—To be boiled 10 minutes; to stand 3 days after mixing; to ferment 3 days; to remain in the cask 2 mouths before the raisins are added; bottle 6 months after.
Seasonable—Make this in March or October.

GINGER BEER

Ingredients

2-½ lbs. of loaf sugar
1-½ oz. of bruised ginger
1 oz. of cream of tartar
the rind and juice of 2 lemons
3 gallons of boiling water
2 large tablespoonfuls of thick and fresh brewer's yeast

Mode—Peel the lemons, squeeze the juice, strain it, and put the peel and juice into a large earthen pan, with the bruised ginger, cream of tartar, and loaf sugar. Pour over these ingredients 3 gallons of boiling water; let it stand until just warm, when add the yeast, which should be thick and perfectly fresh. Stir the contents of the pan well, and let them remain near the fire all night, covering the pan over with a cloth. The next day skim off the yeast, and pour the liquor carefully into another vessel, leaving the sediment; then bottle immediately, and tie the corks down, and in 3 days the ginger beer will be fit for use. For some tastes, the above proportion of sugar may be found rather too large, when it may be diminished; but the beer will not keep so long good.

Average cost for this quantity, 2s.; or ½d. per bottle.

Sufficient to fill 4 dozen ginger-beer bottles.

Seasonable—This should be made during the summer months.

CHAPTER XXXV

DINNERS AND DINING

Man, it has been said, is a dining animal. Creatures of the inferior races eat and drink; man only dines. It has also been said that he is a cooking animal; but some races eat food without cooking it. A Croat captain said to M. Brillat Savarin, "When, in campaign, we feel hungry, we knock over the first animal we find, cut off a steak, powder it with salt, put it under the saddle, gallop over it for half a mile, and then eat it." Huntsmen in Dauphiny, when out shooting, have been known to kill a bird, pluck it, salt and pepper it, and cook it by carrying it some time in their caps. It is equally true that some races of men do not dine any more than the tiger or the vulture. It is not a *dinner* at which sits the aboriginal Australian, who gnaws his bone half bare and then flings it behind to his squaw. And the native of Terra-del-Fuego does not dine when he gets his morsel of red clay. Dining is the privilege of civilization. The rank which a people occupy in the grand scale may be measured by their way of taking their meals, as well as by their way of treating their women. The nation which knows how to dine has learnt the leading lesson of progress. It implies both the will and the skill to reduce to order, and surround with idealisms and graces, the more material conditions of human existence; and wherever that will and that skill exist, life cannot be wholly ignoble.

Dinner, being the grand solid meal of the day, is a matter of considerable importance; and a well-served table is a striking index of human, ingenuity and resource. "Their table," says Lord Byron, in describing a dinner-party given by Lord and Lady Amundevillo at Norman Abbey,—

"Their table was a board to tempt even ghosts
To pass the Styx for more substantial feasts.
I will not dwell upon ragouts or roasts,
Albeit all human history attests
That happiness for man—the hungry sinner!—
Since Eve ate apples, much depends on dinner."

It has been said, indeed, that great men, in general, are great diners. This, however, can scarcely be true of any great men but men of action; and, in that case, it would simply imply that persons of vigorous constitution, who work hard, eat heartily; for, of course, a life of action *requires* a vigorous constitution, even though there may be much illness, as in such cases as William III. and our brave General Napier. Of men of thought, it can scarcely be true that they eat so much, in a general way, though even they eat more than they are apt to suppose they do; for, as Mr. Lewes observes, "nerve-tissue is very expensive." Leaving great men of all kinds, however, to get their own dinners, let us, who are not great, look after ours. Dine we must, and we may as well dine elegantly as well as wholesomely.

There are plenty of elegant dinners in modern days, and they were not wanting in ancient times. It is well known that the dinner-party, or symposium, was a not unimportant, and not unpoetical, feature in the life of the sociable, talkative, tasteful Greek. Douglas Jerrold said that such is the British humour for dining and giving of dinners, that if London were to be destroyed by an earthquake, the Londoners would meet at a public dinner to consider the subject. The Greeks, too, were great diners: their social and religious polity gave them many chances of being merry and making others merry on good eating and drinking. Any public or even domestic sacrifice to one of the gods, was sure to be followed by a dinner-party, the remains of the slaughtered "offering" being served up on the occasion as a pious *pièce de résistance;* and as the different gods, goddesses, and demigods, worshipped by the community in general, or by individuals, were very numerous indeed, and some very religious people never let a day pass without offering up something or other, the dinner-parties were countless. A birthday, too, was an excuse for a dinner; a birthday, that is, of any person long dead and buried, as well as of a living person, being a member of the family, or otherwise esteemed. Dinners were, of course, eaten on all occasions of public rejoicing. Then, among the young people, subscription dinners, very much after the manner of modern times, were always being got up; only that they would be eaten not at an hotel, but probably at the house of one of the *heterae.* A Greek dinner-party was a handsome, well-regulated affair. The guests came in elegantly dressed and crowned with flowers. A slave, approaching each person as he entered, took off his sandals and washed his feet. During the repast, the guests reclined on couches with pillows, among and along which were set small tables. After the solid meal came the "symposium" proper, a scene of music, merriment, and dancing, the two latter being supplied chiefly by young girls. There was a chairman, or symposiarch, appointed by the company to regulate the drinking; and it was his duty to mix the wine in the "mighty bowl." From this bowl the attendants ladled the liquor into goblets, and, with the goblets, went round and round the tables, filling the cups of the guests.

The elegance with which a dinner is served is a matter which depends, of course, partly upon the means, but still more upon the taste of the master and mistress of the house. It may be observed, in general, that there should always be flowers on the table, and as they form no item of expense, there is no reason why they should not be employed every day.

The variety in the dishes which furnish forth a modern dinner-table, does not necessarily imply anything unwholesome, or anything capricious. Food that is not well relished cannot be well digested; and the appetite of the over-worked man of business, or statesman, or of any dweller in towns, whose occupations are exciting and exhausting, is jaded, and requires stimulation. Men and women who are in rude health, and who have plenty of air and exercise, eat the simplest food with relish, and consequently digest it well; but those conditions are out of the reach of many men. They must suit their mode of dining to their mode of living, if they cannot choose the latter. It is in serving up food that is at once appetizing and wholesome that the skill of the modern housewife is severely tasked; and she has scarcely a more important duty to fulfil. It is, in fact, her particular vocation, in virtue of which she may be said to hold the health of the family, and of the friends of the family, in her hands from day to day. It has been said that "the destiny of nations depends on the manner in which they are fed;" and a great gastronomist exclaims, "Tell me what kind of food you eat, and I will tell you what kind of man you are." The same writer has some sentences of the same kind, which are rather hyperbolical, but worth quoting:—"The pleasures of the table belong to all ages, to all conditions, to all countries, and to all eras; they mingle with all other pleasures, and remain, at last, to console us for their departure. The discovery of a new dish confers more happiness upon humanity than the discovery of a new star."

The gastronomist from whom we have already quoted, has some aphorisms and short directions in relation to dinner-parties, which are well deserving of notice:—"Let the number of your guests never exceed twelve, so that the conversation may be general. [Footnote: We have seen this varied by saying that the number should never exceed that of the Muses or fall below that of the Graces.] Let the temperature of the dining-room be about 68°. Let the dishes be few in number in the first course, but proportionally good. The order of food is from the most substantial to the lightest. The order of drinking wine is from the mildest to the most foamy and most perfumed. To invite a person to your house is to take charge of his happiness so long as he is beneath your roof. The mistress of the house should always be certain that the coffee be excellent; whilst the master should be answerable for the quality of his wines and liqueurs."

BILLS OF FARE

BREAKFASTS

It will not be necessary to give here a long bill of fare of cold joints, &c., which may be placed on the side-board, and do duty at the breakfast-table. Suffice it to say, that any cold meat the larder may furnish, should be nicely garnished, and be placed on the buffet. Collared and potted meats or fish, cold game or poultry, veal-and-ham pies, game-and-Rump-steak pies, are all suitable dishes for the breakfast-table; as also cold ham, tongue, &c. &c.

The following list of hot dishes may perhaps assist our readers in knowing what to provide for the comfortable meal called breakfast. Broiled fish, such as mackerel, whiting, herrings, dried haddocks, &c.; mutton chops and rump-steaks, broiled sheep's kidneys, kidneys à la maître d'hôtel, sausages, plain rashers of bacon, bacon and poached eggs, ham and poached eggs, omelets, plain boiled eggs, oeufs-au-plat, poached eggs on toast, muffins, toast, marmalade, butter, &c. &c.

LUNCHEONS AND SUPPERS

The remains of cold joints, nicely garnished, a few sweets, or a little hashed meat, poultry or game, are the usual articles placed on the table for luncheon, with bread and cheese, biscuits, butter, &c. If a substantial meal is desired, rump-steaks or mutton chops may he served, as also veal cutlets, kidneys, or any dish of that kind. In families where there is a nursery, the mistress of the house often partakes of the meal with the children, and makes it her luncheon. In the summer, a few dishes of fresh fruit should be added to the luncheon, or, instead of this, a compote of fruit or fruit tart, or pudding.

Of suppers we have little to say, as we have already given two bills of fare for a large party, which will answer very well for a smaller number, by reducing the quantity of dishes and by omitting a few. Hot suppers are now very little in request, as people now generally dine at an hour which precludes the possibility of requiring supper; at all events, not one of a substantial kind. Should, however, a bill of fare be required, one of those under the head of DINNERS, with slight alterations, will be found to answer for a hot supper.

BILL OF FARE FOR A PICNIC FOR 40 PERSONS

2149. A joint of cold roast beef, a joint of cold boiled beef, 2 ribs of lamb, 2 shoulders of lamb, 4 roast fowls, 2 roast ducks, 1 ham, 1 tongue, 2 veal-and-ham pies, 2 pigeon pies, 6 medium-sized lobsters, 1 piece of collared calf's head, 18 lettuces, 6 baskets of salad, 6 cucumbers.

2150. Stewed fruit well sweetened, and put into glass bottles well corked; 3 or 4 dozen plain pastry biscuits to eat with the stewed fruit, 2 dozen fruit turnovers, 4 dozen cheesecakes, 2 cold cabinet puddings in moulds, 2 blancmanges in moulds, a few jam puffs, 1 large cold plum-pudding (this must be good), a few baskets of fresh fruit, 3 dozen plain biscuits, a piece of cheese, 6 lbs. of butter (this, of course, includes the butter for tea), 4 quartern loaves of household broad, 3 dozen rolls, 6 loaves of tin bread (for tea), 2 plain plum cakes, 2 pound cakes, 2 sponge cakes, a tin of mixed biscuits, ½ lb, of tea. Coffee is not suitable for a picnic, being difficult to make.

Things not to be forgotten at a Picnic.

A stick of horseradish, a bottle of mint-sauce well corked, a bottle of salad dressing, a bottle of vinegar, made mustard, pepper, salt, good oil, and pounded sugar. If it can be managed, take a little ice. It is scarcely necessary to say that plates, tumblers, wine-glasses, knives, forks, and spoons, must not be forgotten; as also teacups and saucers, 3 or 4 teapots, some lump sugar, and milk, if this last-named article cannot be obtained in the neighbourhood. Take 3 corkscrews.

Beverages—3 dozen quart bottles of ale, packed in hampers; ginger-beer, soda-water, and lemonade, of each 2 dozen bottles; 6 bottles of sherry, 6 bottles of claret, champagne à discrétion, and any other light wine that may be preferred, and 2 bottles of brandy. Water can usually be obtained so it is useless to take it.

CHAPTER XXXVI

THE REARING, MANAGEMENT, AND DISEASES OF INFANCY AND CHILDHOOD

Physiology of Life, as illustrated by Respiration, Circulation, and Digestion.

The infantine management of children, like the mother's love for her offspring, seems to be born with the child, and to be a direct intelligence of Nature. It may thus, at first sight, appear as inconsistent and presumptuous to tell a woman how to rear her infant as to instruct her in the manner of loving it. Yet, though Nature is unquestionably the best nurse, Art makes so admirable a foster-mother, that no sensible woman, in her novitiate of parent, would refuse the admonitions of art, or the teachings of experience, to consummate her duties of nurse. It is true that, in a civilized state of society, few young wives reach the epoch that makes them mothers without some insight, traditional or practical, into the management of infants: consequently, the cases wherein a woman is left to her own unaided intelligence, or what, in such a case, may be called instinct, and obliged to trust to the promptings of nature alone for the well-being of her child, are very rare indeed. Again, every woman is not gifted with the same physical ability for the harassing duties of a mother; and though Nature, as a general rule, has endowed all female creation with the attributes necessary to that most beautiful and, at the same time, holiest function,—the healthy rearing of their offspring,—the cases are sufficiently numerous to establish the exception, where the mother is either physically or socially incapacitated from undertaking these most pleasing duties herself, and where, consequently, she is compelled to trust to adventitious aid for those natural benefits which are at once the mother's pride and delight to render to her child.

In these cases, when obliged to call in the services of hired assistance, she must trust the dearest obligation of her life to one who, from her social sphere, has probably notions of rearing children diametrically opposed to the preconceived ideas of the mother, and at enmity with all her sentiments of right and prejudices of position.

It has justly been said—we think by Hood—that the children of the poor are not brought up, but *dragged up*. However facetious this remark may seem, there is much truth in it; and that children, reared in the reeking dens of squalor and poverty, live at all, is an apparent anomaly in the course of things, that, at first sight, would seem to set the laws of sanitary provision at defiance, and make it appear a perfect waste of time to insist on pure air and exercise as indispensable necessaries of life, and especially so as regards infantine existence.

We see elaborate care bestowed on a family of children, everything studied that can tend to their personal comfort,—pure air, pure water, regular ablution, a dietary prescribed by art, and every precaution adopted that medical judgment and maternal love can dictate, for the well-being of the parents' hope; and find, in despite of all this care and vigilance, disease and death invading the guarded treasure. We turn to the foetor and darkness that, in some obscure court, attend the robust brood who, coated in dirt, and with mud and refuse for playthings, live and thrive, and grow into manhood, and, in contrast to the pale face and flabby flesh of the aristocratic child, exhibit strength, vigour, and well-developed frames, and our belief in the potency of the life-giving elements of air, light, and cleanliness receives a shock that, at first sight, would appear fatal to the implied benefits of these, in reality, all-sufficient attributes of health and life.

But as we must enter more largely on this subject hereafter, we shall leave its consideration for the present, and return to what we were about to say respecting trusting to others' aid in the rearing of children. Here it is that the young and probably inexperienced mother may find our remarks not only an assistance but a comfort to her, in as far as, knowing the simplest and best system to adopt, she may be able to instruct another, and see that her directions are fully carried out.

The human body, materially considered, is a beautiful piece of mechanism, consisting of many parts, each one being the centre of a system, and performing its own vital function irrespectively of the others, and yet dependent for its vitality upon the harmony and health of the whole. It is, in fact, to a certain extent, like a watch, which, when once wound up and set in motion, will continue its function of recording true time only so long as every wheel, spring, and lever performs its allotted duty, and at its allotted time; or till the limit that man's ingenuity has placed to its existence as a moving automaton has been reached, or, in other words, till it has run down.

What the key is to the mechanical watch, air is to the physical man. Once admit air into the mouth and nostrils, and the lungs expand, the heart beats, the blood rushes to the remotest part of the body, the mouth secretes saliva, to soften and macerate the food; the liver forms its bile, to separate the nutriment from the digested aliment; the kidneys perform their office; the eye elaborates its tears, to facilitate motion and impart that glistening to the orb on which depends so much of its beauty; and a dewy moisture exudes from the skin, protecting the body from the extremes of heat and cold, and sharpening the perception of touch and feeling. At the same instant, and in every part, the arteries, like innumerable bees, are everywhere laying down layers of muscle, bones, teeth, and, in fact, like the coral zoophyte, building up a continent of life and matter; while the veins, equally busy, are carrying away the *débris* and refuse collected from where the zoophyte arteries are building,—this refuse, in its turn, being conveyed to the liver, there to be converted into bile.

All these—and they are but a few of the vital actions constantly taking place—are the instant result of one gasp of life-giving air. No subject can be fraught with greater interest than watching the first spark of life, as it courses with electric speed "through all the gates and alleys" of the soft, insensate body of the infant. The effect of air on the new-born child is as remarkable in its results as it is wonderful in its consequence; but to understand this more intelligibly, it must first be remembered that life consists of the performance of *three* vital functions—RESPIRATION, CIRCULATION, and DIGESTION. The lungs digest the air, taking from it its most nutritious element, the *oxygen*, to give to the impoverished blood that circulates through them. The stomach digests the food, and separates the nutriment—*chyle*—from the aliment, which it gives to the blood for the development of the frame; and the blood, which is understood by the term circulation, digests in its passage through the lungs the nutriment—*chyle*—to give it quantity and quality, and the *oxygen* from the air to give it vitality. Hence it will be seen, that, speaking generally, the three vital functions resolve themselves into one,—DIGESTION; and that the lungs are the primary and the most important of the vital organs; and respiration, the first in fact, as we all know it is the last in deed, of all the functions performed by the living body.

THE LUNGS—RESPIRATION

The first effect of air on the infant is a slight tremor about the lips and angles of the mouth, increasing to twitchings, and finally to a convulsive contraction of the lips and cheeks, the consequence of sudden cold to the nerves of the face. This spasmodic action produces a gasp, causing the air to rush through the mouth and nostrils, and enter the windpipe and upper portion of the flat and contracted lungs, which, like a sponge partly immersed in water, immediately expand. This is succeeded by a few faint sobs or pants, by which larger volumes of air are drawn into the chest, till, after a few seconds, and when a greater bulk of the lungs has become inflated, the breast-bone and ribs rise, the chest expands, and, with a sudden start, the infant gives utterance to a succession of loud, sharp cries, which have the effect of filling every cell of the entire organ with air and life. To the anxious mother, the first voice of her child is, doubtless, the sweetest music she ever heard; and the more loudly it peals, the greater should be her joy, as it is an indication of health and strength, and not only shows the perfect expansion of the lungs, but that the process of life has set in with vigour. Having welcomed in its own existence, like the morning bird, with a shrill note of gladness, the infant ceases its cry, and, after a few short sobs, usually subsides into sleep or quietude.

At the same instant that the air rushes into the lungs, the valve, or door between the two sides of the heart-and through which the blood had previously passed-is closed and hermetically sealed, and the blood taking a new course, bounds into the lungs, now expanded with air, and which we have likened to a wetted sponge, to which they bear a not unapt affinity, air being substituted for water. It here receives the *oxygen* from the atmosphere, and the *chyle*, or white blood, from the digested food, and becomes, in an instant, arterial blood, a vital principle, from which every solid and fluid of the body is constructed. Besides the lungs, Nature has provided another respiratory organ, a sort of supplemental lung, that, as well as being a covering to the body, _in_spires air and _ex_pires moisture;—this is the cuticle, or skin; and so intimate is the connection between the skin and lungs, that whatever injures the first, is certain to affect the latter.

Hence the difficulty of breathing experienced after scalds or burns on the cuticle, the cough that follows the absorption of cold or damp by the skin, the oppressed and laborious breathing experienced by children in all eruptive diseases, while the rash is coming to the surface, and the hot, dry skin that always attends congestion of the lungs, and fever.

The great practical advantage derivable from this fact is, the knowledge that whatever relieves the one benefits the other. Hence, too, the great utility of hot baths in all affections of the lungs or diseases of the skin; and the reason why exposure to cold or wet is, in nearly all cases, followed by tightness of the chest, sore throat, difficulty of breathing, and cough. These symptoms are the consequence of a larger quantity of blood than is natural remaining in the lungs, and the cough is a mere effort of Nature to throw off the obstruction caused by the presence of too much blood in the organ of respiration. The hot bath, by causing a larger amount of blood to rush suddenly to the skin, has the effect of relieving the lungs of their excess of blood, and by equalizing the circulation, and promoting perspiration from the cuticle, affords immediate and direct benefit, both to the lungs and the system at large.

THE STOMACH—DIGESTION

The organs that either directly or indirectly contribute to the process of digestion are, the mouth, teeth, tongue, and gullet, the stomach, small intestines, the pancreas, the salivary glands, and the liver. Next to respiration, digestion is the chief function in the economy of life, as, without the nutritious fluid digested from the aliment, there would be nothing to supply the immense and constantly recurring waste of the system, caused by the activity with which the arteries at all periods, but especially during infancy and youth, are building up the frame and developing the body. In infancy (the period of which our present subject treats), the series of parts engaged in the process of digestion may be reduced simply to the stomach and liver, or rather its secretion,—the bile. The stomach is a thick muscular bag, connected above with the gullet, and, at its lower extremity, with the commencement of the small intestines. The duty or function of the stomach is to secrete from the arteries spread over its inner surface, a sharp acid liquid called the *gastric* juice; this, with a due mixture of saliva, softens, dissolves, and gradually digests the food or contents of the stomach, reducing the whole into a soft pulpy mass, which then passes into the first part of the small intestines, where it comes in contact with the bile from the gall-bladder, which immediately separates the digested food into two parts, one is a white creamy fluid called chyle, and the absolute concentration of all nourishment, which is taken up by proper vessels, and, as we have before said, carried directly to the heart, to be made blood of, and vitalized in the lungs, and thus provide for the wear and tear of the system. It must be here observed that the stomach can only digest solids, for fluids, being incapable of that process, can only be *absorbed*; and without the result of digestion, animal, at least human life, could not exist. Now, as Nature has ordained that infantine life shall be supported on liquid aliment, and as, without a digestion the body would perish, some provision was necessary to meet this difficulty, and that provision was found in the nature of the liquid itself, or in other words, THE MILK. The process of making cheese, or fresh curds and whey, is familiar to most persons; but as it is necessary to the elucidation of our subject, we will briefly repeat it. The internal membrane, or the lining coat of a calf's stomach, having been removed from the organ, is hung up, like a bladder, to dry; when required, a piece is cut off, put in a jug, a little warm water poured upon it, and after a few hours it is fit for use; the liquid so made being called *rennet*. A little of this rennet, poured into a basin of warm milk, at once coagulates the greater part, and separates from it a quantity of thin liquor, called *whey*. This is precisely the action that takes place in the infant's stomach after every supply from the breast. The cause is the same in both cases, the acid of the gastric juice in the infant's stomach immediately converting the milk into a soft cheese. It is gastric juice, adhering to the calf's stomach, and drawn out by the water, forming rennet, that makes the curds in the basin. The cheesy substance being a solid, at once undergoes the process of digestion, is separated into *chyle*by the bile, and, in a few hours, finds its way to the infant's heart, to become blood, and commence the architecture of its little frame. This is the simple process of a baby's digestion:-milk converted into cheese, cheese into *chyle*, chyle into blood, and blood into flesh, bone, and tegument-how simple is the cause, but how sublime and wonderful are the effects!

We have described the most important of the three functions that take place in the infant's body-respiration and digestion; the third, namely, circulation, we hardly think it necessary to enter on, not being called for by the requirements of the nurse and mother; so we shall omit its notice, and proceed from theoretical to more practical considerations. Children of weakly constitutions are just as likely to be born of robust parents, and those who earn their bread by toil, as the offspring of luxury and affluence; and, indeed, it is against the ordinary providence of Nature to suppose the children of the hardworking and necessitous to be hardier and more vigorous than those of parents blessed with ease and competence.

All children come into the world in the same imploring helplessness, with the same general organization and wants, and demanding either from the newly-awakened mother's love, or from the memory of motherly feeling in the nurse, or the common appeals of humanity in those who undertake the earliest duties of an infant, the same assistance and protection, and the same fostering care.

THE INFANT

We have already described the phenomena produced on the new-born child by the contact of air, which, after a succession of muscular twitchings, becomes endowed with voice, and heralds its advent by a loud but brief succession of cries. But though this is the general rule, it sometimes happens (from causes it is unnecessary here to explain) that the infant does not cry, or give utterance to any audible sounds, or if it does, they are so faint as scarcely to be distinguished as human accents, plainly indicating that life, as yet, to the new visitor, is neither a boon nor a blessing; the infant being, in fact, in a state of suspended or imperfect vitality,—a state of *quasi* existence, closely approximating the condition of a *still-birth*.

As soon as this state of things is discovered, the child should be turned on its right side, and the whole length of the spine, from the head downwards, rubbed with all the fingers of the right hand, sharply and quickly, without intermission, till the quick action has not only evoked heat, but electricity in the part, and till the loud and sharp cries of the child have thoroughly expanded the lungs, and satisfactorily established its life. The operation will seldom require above a minute to effect, and less frequently demands a repetition. If there is brandy at hand, the fingers before rubbing may be dipped into that, or any other spirit.

While in the bath, the friction along the spine is to be continued, and if the lungs still remain unexpended, while one person retains the child in an inclined position in the water, another should insert the pipe of a small pair of bellows into one nostril, and while the month is closed and the other nostril compressed on the pipe with the hand of the assistant, the lungs are to be slowly inflated by steady puffs of air from the bellows, the hand being removed from the mouth and nose after each inflation, and placed on the pit of the stomach, and by a steady pressure expelling it out again by the mouth. This process is to be continued, steadily inflating and expelling the air from the lungs, till, with a sort of tremulous leap, Nature takes up the process, and the infant begins to gasp, and finally to cry, at first low and faint, but with every gulp of air increasing in length and strength of volume, when it is to be removed from the water, and instantly wrapped (all but the face and mouth) in a flannel. Sometimes, however, all these means will fail in effecting an utterance from the child, which will lie, with livid lips and a flaccid body, every few minutes opening its mouth with a short gasping pant, and then subsiding into a state of pulseless inaction, lingering probably some hours, till the spasmodic pantings growing further apart, it ceases to exist.

The time that this state of negative vitality will linger in the frame of an infant is remarkable; and even when all the previous operations, though long-continued, have proved ineffectual, the child will often rally from the simplest of means—the application of dry heat. When removed from the bath, place three or four hot bricks or tiles on the hearth, and lay the child, loosely folded in a flannel, on its back along them, taking care that there is but one fold of flannel between the spine and heated bricks or tiles. When neither of these articles can be procured, put a few clear pieces of red cinder in a warming-pan, and extend the child in the same manner along the closed lid. As the heat gradually diffuses itself over the spinal marrow, the child that was dying, or seemingly dead, will frequently give a sudden and energetic cry, succeeded in another minute by a long and vigorous peal, making up, in volume and force, for the previous delay, and instantly confirming its existence by every effort in its nature.

We, undoubtedly, believe that crying, to a certain extent, is not only conducive to health, but positively necessary to the full development and physical economy of the infant's being. But though holding this opinion, we are far from believing that a child does not very often cry from pain, thirst, want of food, and attention to its personal comfort; but there is as much difference in the tone and expression of a child's cry as in the notes of an adult's voice; and the mother's ear will not be long in discriminating between the sharp peevish whine of irritation and fever, and the louder intermitting cry that characterizes the want of warmth and sleep. All these shades of expression in the child's inarticulate voice every nurse *should* understand, and every mother will soon teach herself to interpret them with an accuracy equal to language.

There is no part of a woman's duty to her child that a young mother should so soon make it her business to study, as the voice of her infant, and the language conveyed in its cry. The study is neither hard nor difficult; a close attention to its tone, and the expression of the baby's features, are the two most important points demanding attention. The key to both the mother will find in her own heart, and the knowledge of her success in the comfort and smile of her infant. We have two reasons—both strong ones—for urging on mothers the imperative necessity of early making themselves acquainted with the nature and wants of their child: the first, that when left to the entire, responsibility of the baby, after the departure of the nurse, she may be able to undertake her new duties with more confidence than if left to her own resources and mother's instinct, without a clue to guide her through the mysteries of those calls that vibrate through every nerve of her nature; and, secondly, that she may be able to guard her child from the nefarious practices of unprincipled nurses, who, while calming the mother's mind with false statements as to the character of the baby's cries, rather than lose their rest, or devote that time which would remove the cause of suffering, administer, behind the curtains, those deadly narcotics which, while stupefying Nature into sleep, insure for herself a night of many unbroken hours. Such nurses as have not the hardihood to dose their infant charges, are often full of other schemes to still that constant and reproachful cry. The most frequent means employed for this purpose is giving it something to suck,—something easily hid from the mother,—or, when that is impossible, under the plea of keeping it warm, the nurse covers it in her lap with a shawl, and, under this blind, surreptitiously inserts a finger between the parched lips, which possibly moan for drink; and, under this inhuman cheat and delusion, the infant is pacified, till Nature, balked of its desires, drops into a troubled sleep. These are two of our reasons for impressing upon mothers the early, the immediate necessity of putting themselves sympathetically in communication with their child, by at once learning its hidden language as a delightful task.

We must strenuously warn all mothers on no account to allow the nurse to sleep with the baby, never herself to lay down with it by her side for a night's rest, never to let it sleep in the parents' bed, and on no account keep it, longer than absolutely necessary, confined in on atmosphere loaded with the breath of many adults.

The amount of *oxygen* required by an infant is so large, and the quantity consumed by mid-life and age, and the proportion of carbonic acid thrown off from both, so considerable, that an infant breathing the same air cannot possibly carry on its healthy existence while deriving its vitality from so corrupted a medium. This objection, always in force, is still more objectionable at night-time, when doors and windows are closed, and amounts to a condition of poison, when placed between two adults in sleep, and shut in by bed-curtains; and when, in addition to the impurities expired from the lungs, we remember, in quiescence and sleep, how large a portion of mephitic gas is given off from the skin.

THE MILK

As Nature has placed in the bosom of the mother the natural food of her offspring, it must be self-evident to every reflecting woman, that it becomes her duty to study, as far as lies in her power, to keep that reservoir of nourishment in as pure and invigorating a condition as possible; for she must remember that the *quantity* is no proof of the *quality* of this aliment.

The mother, while suckling, as a general rule, should avoid all sedentary occupations, take regular exercise, keep her mind as lively and pleasingly occupied as possible, especially by music and singing. Her diet should be light and nutritious, with a proper sufficiency of animal food, and of that kind which yields the largest amount of nourishment; and, unless the digestion is naturally strong, vegetables and fruit should form a very small proportion of the general dietary, and such preparations as broths, gruels, arrowroot, &c., still less. Tapioca, or ground-rice pudding, made with several eggs, may be taken freely; but all slops and thin potations, such as that delusion called chicken-broth, should be avoided, as yielding a very small amount of nutriment, and a large proportion of flatulence. All purely stimulants should be avoided as much as possible, especially spirits, unless taken for some special object, and that medicinally; but as a part of the dietary they should be carefully shunned. Lactation is always an exhausting process, and as the child increases in size and strength, the drain upon the mother becomes great and depressing. Then something more even than an abundant diet is required to keep the mind and body up to a standard sufficiently healthy to admit of a constant and nutritious secretion being performed without detriment to the physical integrity of the mother, or injury to the child who imbibes it; and as stimulants are inadmissible, if not positively injurious, the substitute required is to be found in *malt liquor*. To the lady accustomed to her Madeira and sherry, this may appear a very vulgar potation for a delicate young mother to take instead of the more subtle and condensed elegance of wine; but as we are writing from experience, and with the avowed object of imparting useful facts and beneficial remedies to our readers, we allow no social distinctions to interfere with our legitimate object.

As regards exercise and amusement, we would certainly neither prohibit a mother's dancing, going to a theatre, nor even from attending an assembly. The first, however, is the best indoor recreation she can take, and a young mother will do well to often amuse herself in the nursery with this most excellent means of healthful circulation. The only precaution necessary is to avoid letting the child suck the milk that has lain long in the breast, or is heated by excessive action.

One of the most common errors that mothers fall into while suckling their children, is that of fancying they are always hungry, and consequently overfeeding them; and with this, the great mistake of applying the child to the breast on every occasion of its crying, without investigating the cause of its complaint, and, under the belief that it wants food, putting the nipple into its crying mouth, until the infant turns in revulsion and petulance from what it should accept with eagerness and joy. At such times, a few teaspoonfuls of water, slightly chilled, will often instantly pacify a crying and restless child, who has turned in loathing from the offered breast; or, after imbibing a few drops, and finding it not what nature craved, throws back its head in disgust, and cries more petulantly than before. In such a case as this, the young mother, grieved at her baby's rejection of the tempting present, and distressed at its cries, and in terror of some injury, over and over ransacks its clothes, believing some insecure pin can alone be the cause of such sharp complaining, an accident that, from her own care in dressing, however, is seldom or ever the case.

The length of time an infant should be suckled must depend much on the health and strength of the child, and the health of the mother, and the quantity and quality of her milk; though, when all circumstances are favourable, it should never be less than *nine*, nor exceed *fifteen* months; but perhaps the true time will be found in the medium between both. But of this we may be sure, that Nature never ordained a child to live on suction after having endowed it with teeth to bite and to grind; and nothing is more out of place and unseemly than to hear a child, with a set of twenty teeth, ask for "the breast."

Though we have said that twelve months is about the medium time a baby should be suckled, we by no means wish to imply that a child should be fed exclusively on milk for its first year; quite the reverse; the infant can hardly be too soon made independent of the mother. Thus, should illness assail her, her milk fail, or any domestic cause abruptly cut off the natural supply, the child having been annealed to an artificial diet, its life might be safely carried on without seeking for a wet-nurse, and without the slightest danger to its system.

All that we have further to say on suckling is an advice to mothers, that if they wish to keep a sound and unchapped nipple, and possibly avoid what is called a "broken breast," never to put it up with a wet nipple, but always to have a soft handkerchief in readiness, and the moment that delicate part is drawn from the child's mouth, to dry it carefully of the milk and saliva that moisten it; and, further, to make a practice of suckling from each breast alternately.

Dress and Dressing, Washing, &c.

As respects the dress and dressing of a new-born infant, or of a child in arms, during any stage of its nursing, there are few women who will require us to give them guidance or directions for their instruction; and though a few hints on the subject may not be out of place here, yet most women intuitively "take to a baby," and, with a small amount of experience, are able to perform all the little offices necessary to its comfort and cleanliness with ease and completeness. We shall, therefore, on this delicate subject hold our peace; and only, from afar, *hint* "at what we would," leaving our suggestions to be approved or rejected, according as they chime with the judgment and the apprehension of our motherly readers.

In these days of intelligence, there are few ladies who have not, in all probability, seen the manner in which the Indian squaw, the aborigines of Polynesia, and even the Lapp and Esquimaux, strap down their baby on a board, and by means of a loop suspend it to the bough of a tree, hang it up to the rafters of the hut, or on travel, dangle it on their backs, outside the domestic implements, which, as the slave of her master, man, the wronged but uncomplaining woman carries, in order that her lord may march in unhampered freedom. Cruel and confining as this system of "backboard" dressing may seem to our modern notions of freedom and exercise, it is positively less irksome, less confining, and infinitely less prejudicial to health, than the mummying of children by our grandmothers a hundred, ay, fifty years ago: for what with chin-stays, back-stays, body-stays, forehead-cloths, rollers, bandages, &c., an infant had as many girths and strings, to keep head, limbs, and body in one exact position, as a ship has halyards.

Children do not so much cry from the washing as from the irritation caused by the frequent change of position in which they are placed, the number of times they are turned on their face, on their back, and on their side, by the manipulations demanded by the multiplicity of articles to be fitted, tacked, and carefully adjusted on their bodies. What mother ever found her girl of six or seven stand quiet while she was curling her hair? How many times nightly has she not to reprove her for not standing still during the process! It is the same with the unconscious infant, who cannot bear to be moved about, and who has no sooner grown reconciled to one position than it is forced reluctantly into another. It is true, in one instance the child has intelligence to guide it, and in the other not; but the *motitory nerves*, in both instances, resent coercion, and a child cannot be too little handled.

On this account alone, and, for the moment, setting health and comfort out of the question, we beg mothers to simplify their baby's dress as much as possible; and not only to put on as little as is absolutely necessary, but to make that as simple in its contrivance and adjustment as it will admit of; to avoid belly-bands, rollers, girths, and everything that can impede or confine the natural expansion of the digestive organs, on the due performance of whose functions the child lives, thrives, and develops its physical being.

REARING BY HAND

As we do not for a moment wish to be thought an advocate for an artificial, in preference to the natural course of rearing children, we beg our renders to understand us perfectly on this head; all we desire to prove is the fact that a child *can* be brought up as well on a spoon dietary as the best example to be found of those reared on the breast; having more strength, indeed, from the more nutritious food on which it lives. It will be thus less liable to infectious diseases, and more capable of resisting the virulence of any danger that may attack it; and without in any way depreciating the nutriment of its natural food, we wish to impress on the mother's mind that there are many cases of infantine debility which might eventuate in rickets, curvature of the spine, or mesenteric disease, where the addition to, or total substitution of, an artificial and more stimulating aliment, would not only give tone and strength to the constitution, but at the same time render the employment of mechanical means totally unnecessary. And, finally, though we would never—where the mother had the strength to suckle her child—supersede the breast, we would insist on making it a rule to accustom the child as early as possible to the use of an artificial diet, not only that it may acquire more vigour to help it over the ills of childhood, but that, in the absence of the mother, it might not miss the maternal sustenance; and also for the parent's sake, that, should the milk, from any cause, become vitiated, or suddenly cease, the child can be made over to the bottle and the spoon without the slightest apprehension of hurtful consequences.

To those persons unacquainted with the system, or who may have been erroneously informed on the matter, the rearing of a child by hand may seem surrounded by innumerable difficulties, and a large amount of personal trouble and anxiety to the nurse or mother who undertakes the duty. This, however, is a fallacy in every respect, except as regards the fact of preparing the food; but even this extra amount of work, by adopting the course we shall lay down, may be reduced to a very small sum of inconvenience; and as respects anxiety, the only thing calling for care is the display of judgment in the preparation of the food. The articles required for the purpose of feeding an infant are a night-lamp, with its pan and lid, to keep the food warm; a nursing-bottle, with a prepared teat; and a small pap saucepan, for use by day. Of the lamp we need hardly speak, most mothers being acquainted with its operation: but to those to whom it is unknown we may observe, that the flame from the floating rushlight heats the water in the reservoir above, in which the covered pan that contains the food floats, keeping it at such a heat that, when thinned by milk, it will be of a temperature suitable for immediate use. Though many kinds of nursing-bottles have been lately invented, and some mounted with India-rubber nipples, the common glass bottle, with the calf's teat, is equal in cleanliness and utility to any; besides, the nipple put into the child's mouth is so white and natural in appearance, that no child taken from the breast will refuse it. The black artificial ones of caoutchouc or gutta-percha are unnatural. The prepared teats can be obtained at any chemist's, and as they are kept in spirits, they will require a little soaking in warm water, and gentle washing, before being tied securely, by means of fine twine, round the neck of the bottle, just sufficient being left projecting for the child to grasp freely in its lips; for if left the full length, or over long, it will be drawn too far into the mouth, and possibly make the infant heave. When once properly adjusted, the nipple need never be removed till replaced by a new one, which will hardly be necessary oftener than once a fortnight, though with care one will last for several weeks. The nursing-bottle should be thoroughly washed and cleaned every day, and always rinsed out before and after using it, the warm water being squeezed through the nipple, to wash out any particles of food that might lodge in the aperture, and become sour. The teat can always be kept white and soft by turning the end of the bottle, when not in use, into a narrow jug containing water, taking care to dry it first, and then to warm it by drawing the food through before putting it into the child's mouth.

Food, and its Preparation.

The articles generally employed as food for infants consist of arrowroot, bread, flour, baked flour, prepared groats, farinaceous food, biscuit-powder, biscuits, tops-and-bottoms, and semolina, or manna croup, as it is otherwise called, which, like tapioca, is the prepared pith of certain vegetable substances. Of this list the least efficacious, though, perhaps, the most believed in, is arrowroot, which only as a mere agent, for change, and then only for a very short time, should ever be employed as a means of diet to infancy or childhood. It is a thin, flatulent, and innutritious food, and incapable of supporting infantine life with energy. Bread, though the universal *régime* with the labouring poor, where the infant's stomach and digestive powers are a reflex, in miniature, of the father's, should never be given to an infant under three months, and, even then, however finely beaten up and smoothly made, is a very questionable diet. Flour, when well boiled, though infinitely better than arrowroot, is still only a kind of fermentative paste, that counteracts its own good by after-acidity and flatulence.

The packets sold as farinaceous food are unquestionably the best aliment that can be given from the first to a baby, and may be continued, with the exception of an occasional change, without alteration of the material, till the child is able to take its regular meals of animal and vegetable food. Some infants are so constituted as to require a frequent and total change in their system of living, seeming to thrive for a certain time on any food given to them, but if persevered in too long, declining in bulk and appearance as rapidly as they had previously progressed. In such cases the food should be immediately changed, and when that which appeared to agree best with the child is resumed, it should be altered in its quality, and perhaps in its consistency.

The food should always be made with water, the whole sweetened at once, and of such a consistency that, when poured out, and it has had time to cool, it will cut with the firmness of a pudding or custard. One or two spoonfuls are to be put into the pap saucepan and stood on the hob till the heat has softened it, when enough milk is to be added, and carefully mixed with the food, till the whole has the consistency of ordinary cream; it is then to be poured into the nursing-bottle, and the food having been drawn through to warm the nipple, it is to be placed in the child's mouth. For the first month or more, half a bottleful will be quite enough to give the infant at one time; but, as the child grows, it will be necessary not only to increase the quantity given at each time, but also gradually to make its food more consistent, and, after the third month, to add an egg to every pint basin of food made. At night the mother puts the food into the covered pan of her lamp, instead of the saucepan—that is, enough for one supply, and, having lighted the rush, she will find, on the waking of her child, the food sufficiently hot to bear the cooling addition of the milk. But, whether night or day, the same food should never be heated twice, and what the child leaves should be thrown away.

The biscuit powder is used in the same manner as the farinaceous food, and both prepared much after the fashion of making starch. But when tops-and-bottoms, or the whole biscuit, are employed, they require soaking in cold water for some time previous to boiling. The biscuit or biscuits are then to be slowly boiled in as much water as will, when thoroughly soft, allow of their being beaten by a three-pronged fork into a fine, smooth, and even pulp, and which, when poured into a basin and become cold, will cut out like a custard. If two large biscuits have been so treated, and the child is six or seven months old, beat up two eggs, sufficient sugar to properly sweeten it, and about a pint of skim milk. Pour this on the beaten biscuit in the saucepan, stirring constantly; boil for about five minutes, pour into a basin, and use, when cold, in the same manner as the other.

TEETHING AND CONVULSIONS

Fits, &c., the consequence of Dentition, and how to be treated—The number and order of the Teeth, and manner in which they are cut—First and Second Set.

About three months after birth, the infant's troubles may be said to begin; teeth commence forming in the gums, causing pain and irritation in the mouth, and which, but for the saliva it causes to flow so abundantly, would be attended with very serious consequences. At the same time the mother frequently relaxes in the punctuality of the regimen imposed on her, and, taking some unusual or different food, excites diarrhoea or irritation in her child's stomach, which not unfrequently results in a rash on the skin, or slight febrile symptoms, which, if not subdued in their outset, superinduce some more serious form of infantine disease. But, as a general rule, the teeth are the primary cause of much of the child's sufferings, in consequence of the state of nervous and functional irritation into which the system is thrown by their formation and progress out of the jaw and through the gums. We propose beginning this branch of our subject with that most fertile source of an infant's suffering—

TEETHING

That this subject may he better understood by the nurse and mother, and the reason of the constitutional disturbance that, to a greater or less degree, is experienced by all infants, may be made intelligible to those who have the care of children, we shall commence by giving a brief account of the formation of the teeth, the age at which they appear in the mouth, and the order in which they pierce the gums. The organs of mastication in the adult consist of 32 distinct teeth, 16 in either jaw; being, in fact, a double set. The teeth are divided into 4 incisors, 2 canine, 4 first and second grinders, and 6 molars; but in childhood the complement or first set consists of only twenty, and these only make their appearance as the development of the frame indicates the requirement of a different kind of food for the support of the system. At birth some of the first-cut teeth are found in the cavities of the jaw, in a very small and rudimentary form; but this is by no means universal. About the third month, the jaws, which are hollow and divided into separate cells, begin to expand, making room for the slowly developing teeth, which, arranged for beauty and economy of space lengthwise, gradually turn their tops upwards, piercing the gum by their edges, which, being sharp, assist in cutting a passage through the soft parts. There is no particular period at which children cut their teeth, some being remarkably early, and others equally late. The earliest age that we have ever ourselves known as a reliable fact was, *six weeks*. Such peculiarities are generally hereditary, and, as in this case, common to a whole family. The two extremes are probably represented by six and sixteen months. Pain and drivelling are the usual, but by no means the general, indications of teething.

About the sixth month the gums become tense and swollen, presenting a red, shiny appearance, while the salivary glands pour out an unusual quantity of saliva. After a time, a white line or round spot is observed on the top of one part of the gums, and the sharp edge of the tooth may be felt beneath if the finger is gently pressed on the part. Through these white spots the teeth burst their way in the following order:—

The Symptoms that generally indicate the cutting of teeth, in addition to the inflamed and swollen state of the gums, and increased flow of saliva, are the restless and peevish state of the child, the hands being thrust into the mouth, and the evident pleasure imparted by rubbing the finger or nail gently along the gum; the lips are often excoriated, and the functions of the stomach or bowels are out of order. In severe cases, occurring in unhealthy or scrofulous children, there are, from the first, considerable fever, disturbed sleep, fretfulness, diarrhoea, rolling of the eyes, convulsive startings, laborious breathing, coma, or unnatural sleep, ending, unless the head is quickly relieved, in death.

The *Treatment* in all cases of painful teething is remarkably simple, and consists in keeping the body cool by mild aperient medicines, allaying the irritation in the gums by friction with a rough ivory ring or a stale crust of broad, and when the head, lungs, or any organ is overloaded or unduly excited, to use the hot bath, and by throwing the body into a perspiration, equalize the circulation, and relieve the system from the danger of a fatal termination.

Though teething is a natural function, and to an infant in perfect health should be unproductive of pain, yet in general it is not only a fertile cause of suffering, but often a source of alarm and danger; the former, from irritation in the stomach and bowels, deranging the whole economy of the system, and the latter, from coma and fits, that may excite alarm in severe cases; and the danger, that eventuates in some instances, from organic disease of the head or spinal marrow.

Convulsions, or Infantine Fits

From their birth till after teething, infants are more or less subject or liable to sudden fits, which often, without any assignable cause, will attack the child in a moment, and while in the mother's arms; and which, according to their frequency, and the age and strength of the infant, are either slight or dangerous.

Whatever may have been the remote cause, the immediate one is some irritation of the nervous system, causing convulsions, or an effusion to the head, inducing coma. In the first instance, the infant cries out with a quick, short scream, rolls up its eyes, arches its body backwards, its arms become bent and fixed, and the fingers parted; the lips and eyelids assume a dusky leaden colour, while the face remains pale, and the eyes open, glassy, or staring. This condition may or may not be attended with muscular twitchings of the mouth, and convulsive plunges of the arms. The fit generally lasts from one to three minutes, when the child recovers with a sigh, and the relaxation of the body. In the other case, the infant is attacked at once with total insensibility and relaxation of the limbs, coldness of the body and suppressed breathing; the eyes, when open, being dilated, and presenting a dim glistening appearance; the infant appearing, for the moment, to be dead.

Treatment-The first step in either case is, to immerse the child in a hot bath up to the chin; or if sufficient hot water cannot be procured to cover the body, make a hip-bath of what can be obtained; and, while the left hand supports the child in a sitting or recumbent position, with the right scoop up the water, and run it over the chest of the patient. When sufficient water can be obtained, the spine should be briskly rubbed while in the bath; when this cannot be done, lay the child on the knees, and with the fingers dipped in brandy, rub the whole length of the spine vigorously for two or three minutes, and when restored to consciousness, give occasionally a teaspoonful of weak brandy and water or wine and water.

An hour after the bath, it may be necessary to give an aperient powder, possibly also to repeat the dose for once or twice every three hours; in which case the following prescription is to be employed. Take of

Powdered scammony 6 grains.
Grey powder 6 grains.
Antimonial powder 4 grains.
Lump sugar 20 grains.

Mix thoroughly, and divide into three powders, which are to be taken as advised for an infant one year old; for younger or weakly infants, divide into four powders, and give as the other. For thirst and febrile symptoms, give drinks of barley-water, or cold water, and every three hours put ten to fifteen drops of spirits of sweet nitre in a dessert-spoonful of either beverage.

CHICKEN-POX, OR GLASS-POX

CHICKEN-POX, or GLASS-POX, may, in strict propriety, be classed as a mild variety of small-pox, presenting all the mitigated symptoms of that formidable disease. Among many physicians it is, indeed, classed as small-pox, and not a separate disease; but as this is not the place to discuss such questions, and as we profess to give only facts, the result of our own practical experience, we shall treat this affection of glass-pox or chicken-pox, as we ourselves have found it, as a distinct and separate disease.

Chicken-pox is marked by all the febrile symptoms presented by small-pox, with this difference, that, in the case of chicken-pox, each symptom is particularly slight. The heat of body is much less acute, and the principal symptoms are difficulty of breathing, headache, coated tongue, and nausea, which sometimes amounts to vomiting. After a term of general irritability, heat, and restlessness, about the fourth day, or between the third and fourth, an eruption makes its appearance over the face, neck, and body, in its first two stages closely resembling small-pox, with this especial difference, that whereas the pustules in small-pox have *flat* and*depressed* centres—an infallible characteristic of small-pox—the pustules in chicken-pox remain *globular*, while the fluid in them changes from a transparent white to a straw-coloured liquid, which begins to exude and disappear about the eighth or ninth day, and, in mild cases, by the twelfth desquamates, or peels off entirely.

Treatment—In all ordinary cases of chicken-pox—and it is very seldom it assumes any complexity—the whole treatment resolves itself into the use of the warm bath, and a course of gentle aperients. The bath should be used when the oppression of the lungs renders the breathing difficult, or the heat and dryness of the skin, with the undeveloped rash beneath the surface, shows the necessity for its use.

HOOPING-COUGH AND DIARRHOEA, WITH THEIR MODE OF TREATMENT

Hooping-Cough

THIS is purely a spasmodic disease, and is only infectious through the faculty of imitation, a habit that all children are remarkably apt to fall into; and even where adults have contracted hooping-cough, it has been from the same cause, and is as readily accounted for, on the principle of imitation, as that the gaping of one person will excite or predispose a whole party to follow the same spasmodic example. If any one associates for a few days with a person who stammers badly, he will find, when released from his company, that the sequence of his articulation and the fluency of his speech are, for a time, gone; and it will be a matter of constant vigilance, and some difficulty, to overcome the evil of so short an association. The manner in which a number of school-girls will, one after another, fall into a fit on beholding one of their number attacked with epilepsy, must be familiar to many. These several facts lead us to a juster notion of how to treat this spasmodic disease. Every effort should, therefore, be directed, mentally and physically, to break the chain of nervous action, on which the continuance of the cough depends.

Symptoms—Hooping-cough comes on with a slight oppression of breathing, thirst, quick pulse, hoarseness, and a hard, dry cough. This state may exist without any change from one to two or three weeks before the peculiar feature of the disease-the *hoop*-sets in. As the characteristics of this cough are known to all, it is unnecessary to enter here, physiologically, on the subject. We shall, therefore, merely remark that the frequent vomiting and bleeding at the mouth or nose are favourable signs, and proceed to the

Treatment, which should consist in keeping up a state of nausea and vomiting. For this purpose, give the child doses of ipecacuanha and antimonial wines, in equal parts, and quantities varying from half to one and a half teaspoonful once a day, or, when the expectoration is hard and difficult of expulsion, giving the following cough mixture every four hours. Take of

Syrup of squills ½ ounce.
Antimonial wine 1 ounce.
Laudanum 15 drops.
Syrup of Toulou 2 drachms.
Water 1-½ ounce.

Mix. The dose is from half a spoonful to a dessertspoonful. When the cough is urgent, the warm bath is to be used, and either one or two leeches applied over the breastbone, or else a small blister laid on the lower part of the throat.

Diarrhoea

The diarrhoea with which children are so frequently affected, especially in infancy, should demand the nurse's immediate attention, and when the secretion, from its clayey colour, indicates an absence of bile, a powder composed of 3 grains of grey powder and 1 grain of rhubarb, should be given twice, with an interval of four hours between each dose, to a child from one to two years, and, a day or two afterwards, an aperient powder containing the same ingredients and quantities, with the addition of 2 or 3 grains of scammony. For the relaxation consequent on an overloaded stomach, or acidity in the bowels, a little magnesia dissolved in milk should be employed two or three times a day.

When much griping and pain attend the diarrhoea, half a teaspoonful of Dalby's Carminative (the best of all patent medicines) should be given, either with or without a small quantity of castor oil to carry off the exciting cause.

CHAPTER XXXVII

THE DOCTOR

"Time," according to the old proverb, "is money;" and it may also, in many cases, and with equal truthfulness, be said to be life; for a few moments, in great emergencies, often turn the balance between recovery and death. This applies more especially to all kinds of poisoning, fits, submersion in water, or exposure to noxious gases; and many accidents. If people knew how to act during the interval that must necessarily elapse from the moment that a medical man is sent for until he arrives, many lives might be saved, which now, unhappily, are lost. Generally speaking, however, nothing is done—all is confusion and fright; and the surgeon, on his arrival, finds that death has already seized its victim, who, had his friends but known a few rough rules for their guidance, might have been rescued. We shall, therefore, in a series of papers, give such information as to the means to be employed in event of accidents, injuries, &c., as, by the aid of a gentleman of large professional experience, we are warranted in recommending.

List of Drugs, &c., necessary to carry out all Instructions.

We append at once A LIST OF DRUGS, &c., and a few PRESCRIPTIONS necessary to carry out all the instructions given in this series of articles. It will be seen that they are few—they are not expensive; and by laying in a little stock of them, our instructions will be of instant value in all cases of accident, &c—The drugs are—Antimonial Wine. Antimonial Powder. Blister Compound. Blue Pill. Calomel. Carbonate of Potash. Compound Iron Pills. Compound Extract of Colocynth. Compound Tincture of Camphor. Epsom Salts. Goulard's

Extract. Jalap in Powder. Linseed Oil. Myrrh and Aloes Pills. Nitre. Oil of Turpentine. Opium, powdered, and Laudanum. Sal Ammoniac. Senna Leaves. Soap Liniment, Opodeldoc. Sweet Spirits of Nitre. Turner's Cerate—To which should be added: Common Adhesive Plaster. Isinglass Plaster. Lint. A pair of small Scales with Weights. An ounce and a drachm Measure-glass. A Lancet. A Probe. A pair of Forceps, and some curved Needles.

The following PRESCRIPTIONS may be made up for a few shillings; and, by keeping them properly labelled, and by referring to the remarks on the treatment of any particular case, much suffering, and, perhaps, some lives, may be saved.

Lotions—1. Mix a dessert-spoonful of Goulard's extract and 2 tablespoonfuls of vinegar in a pint of water—2. Mix 1/2 oz. of sal-ammoniac, 2 tablespoonfuls of vinegar, and the same quantity of gin or whisky, in half a pint of water.

The Common Black Draught—Infusion of senna 10 drachms; Epsom salts 10 drachms; tincture of senna, compound tincture of cardamums, compound spirit of lavender, of each 1 drachm. Families who make black draught in quantity, and wish to preserve it for some time without spoiling, should add about 2 drachms of spirits of hartshorn to each pint of the strained mixture, the use of this drug being to prevent its becoming mouldy or decomposed. A simpler and equally efficacious form of black draught is made by infusing ½ oz. of Alexandrian senna, 3 oz. of Epsom salts, and 2 drachms of bruised ginger and coriander-seeds, for several hours in a pint of boiling water, straining the liquor, and adding either 2 drachms of sal-volatile or spirits of hartshorn to the whole, and giving 3 tablespoonfuls for a dose to an adult.

Fever Mixture—Mix a drachm of powdered nitre, 2 drachms of carbonate of potash, 2 teaspoonfuls of antimonial wine, and a tablespoonful of sweet spirits of nitre, in half a pint of water.

Pills—1. Mix 5 grains of calomel and the same quantity of antimonial powder with a little bread-crumb, and make into two pills. Dose for a full-grown person: two pills—2. Mix 5 grains of blue pill and the same quantity of compound extract of colocynth together, and make into two pills, the dose for a full-grown person.

Powders—Mix a grain of calomel and 4 grains of powdered jalap together.

In all cases, the dose of medicines given is to be regulated by the age of the patient.

BATHS AND FOMENTATIONS

All fluid applications to the body are exhibited either in a hot or cold form; and the object for which they are administered is to produce a stimulating effect over the entire, or a part, of the system; for the effect, though differently obtained, and varying in degree, is the same in principle, whether procured by hot or cold water.

Heat—There are three forms in which heat is universally applied to the body,—that of the tepid, warm, and vapour bath; but as the first is too inert to be worth notice, and the last dangerous and inapplicable, except in public institutions, we shall confine our remarks to the really efficacious and always attainable one—the

Poultices—are only another form of fomentation, though chiefly used for abscesses. The ingredient best suited for a poultice is that which retains heat the longest; of these ingredients, the best are linseed—meal, bran, and bread. Bran sewed into a bag, as it can be reheated, will be found the cleanest and most useful; especially for sore throats.

HOW TO BLEED

In cases of great emergency, such as the strong kind of apoplexy, and when a surgeon cannot possibly be obtained for some considerable time, the life of the patient depends almost entirely upon the fact of his being bled or not. We therefore give instructions how the operation of bleeding is to be performed, but caution the reader only to attempt it in cases of the greatest emergency. Place a handkerchief or piece of tape rather but not too tightly round the arm, about three or four inches above the elbow. This will cause the veins below to swell and become very evident. If this is not sufficient, the hand should be constantly and quickly opened and shut for the same purpose. There will now be seen, passing up the middle of the fore-arm, a vein which, just below the bend of the elbow, sends a branch inwards and outwards, each branch shortly joining another large vein. It is from the *outer* branch—that the person is to be bled. The right arm is the one mostly operated on. The operator should take the lancet in his right hand, between the thumb and first finger, place the thumb of his left hand on the vein below the part where he is going to bleed from, and then gently thrust the tip of the lancet into the vein, and, taking care not to push it too deeply, cut in a gently curved direction, thus and bring it out, point upwards, at about half an inch from the part of the vein into which he had thrust it. The vein must be cut lengthways, and not across. When sufficient blood has been taken away, remove the bandage from above the elbow, and place the thumb of the left hand firmly over the cut, until all the bleeding ceases. A small pad of lint is then to be put over the cut, with a larger pad over it, and the two kept in their places by means of a handkerchief or linen roller bound pretty tightly over them and round the arm.

BLEEDING FROM THE NOSE—Many children, especially those of a sanguineous temperament, are subject to sudden discharges of blood from some part of the body; and as all such fluxes are in general the result of an effort of nature to relieve the system from some overload or pressure, such discharges, unless in excess, and when likely to produce debility, should not be rashly or too abruptly checked. In general, these discharges are confined to the summer or spring months of the year, and follow pains in the head, a sense of drowsiness, languor, or oppression; and, as such symptoms are relieved by the loss of blood, the hemorrhage should, to a certain extent, be encouraged. When, however, the bleeding is excessive, or returns too frequently, it becomes necessary to apply means to subdue or mitigate the amount. For this purpose the sudden and unexpected application of cold is itself sufficient, in most cases, to arrest the most active hemorrhage. A wet towel laid suddenly on the back, between the shoulders, and placing the child in a recumbent posture, is often sufficient to effect the object; where, however, the effusion resists such simple means, napkins wrung out of cold water must be laid across the forehead and nose, the hands dipped in cold water, and a bottle of hot water applied to the feet. If, in spite of these means, the bleeding continues, a little fine wool or a few folds of lint, tied together by a piece of thread, must be pushed up the nostril from which the blood flows, to act as a plug and pressure on the bleeding vessel. When the discharge has entirely ceased, the plug is to be pulled out by means of the thread. To prevent a repetition of the hemorrhage, the body should be sponged every morning with cold water, and the child put under a course of steel wine, have open-air exercise, and, if possible, salt-water bathing. For children, a key suddenly dropped down the back between the skin and clothes, will often immediately arrest a copious bleeding.

BITES AND STINGS.

Bites and stongs may be divided into three kinds:—1. Those of Insects. 2. Those of Snakes. 3. Those of Dogs and other Animals.

The Bites or Stings of Insects, such as gnats, bees, wasps, &c., need cause very little alarm, and are, generally speaking, easily cured. They are very serious, however, when they take place on some delicate part of the body, such as near the eye, or in the throat. *The treatment* is very simple in most cases; and consists in taking out the sting, if it is left behind, with a needle, and applying to the part a liniment made of finely-scraped chalk and olive-oil, mixed together to about the thickness of cream.

Bites of Snakes—These are much more dangerous than the preceding, and require more powerful remedies. The bites of the different kinds of snakes do not all act alike, but affect people in different ways—*Treatment of the part bitten.* The great thing is to prevent the poison getting into the blood; and, if possible, to remove the whole of it at once from the body. A pocket-handkerchief, a piece of tape or cord, or, in fact, of anything that is at hand, should be tied tightly round the part of the body bitten; if it be the leg or arm, immediately *above* the bite, and between it and the heart. The bite should then be sucked several times by any one who is near. There is no danger in this, provided the person who does it has not got the skin taken off any part of his mouth. What has been sucked into the mouth should be immediately spit out again. But if those who are near have sufficient nerve for the operation, and a suitable instrument, they should cut out the central part bitten, and then bathe the wound for some time with warm water, to make it bleed freely. The wound should afterwards be rubbed with a stick of lunar caustic, or, what is better, a solution of this—60 grains of lunar caustic dissolved in an ounce of water—should be dropped into it. The band should be kept on the part during the whole of the time that these means are being adopted. The wound should afterwards be covered with lint dipped in cold water. The best plan, however, to be adopted, if it can be managed, is the following:—take a common wine-glass, and, holding it upside down, put a lighted candle or a spirit-lamp into it for a minute or two. This will take out the air. Then clap the glass suddenly over the bitten part, and it will become attached, and hold on to the flesh. The glass being nearly empty, the blood containing the poison will, in consequence, flow into it from the wound of its own accord. This process should be repeated three or four times, and the wound sucked, or washed with warm water, before each application of the glass. As a matter of course, when the glass is removed, all the blood should be washed out of it before it is applied again—*Constitutional Treatment.* There is mostly at first great depression of strength in these cases, and it is therefore requisite to give some stimulant; a glass of hot brandy-and-water, or twenty drops of sal-volatile, is the best that can be given. When the strength has returned, and if the patient has not already been sick, a little mustard in hot water should be given, to make him so. If, on the other hand, as is often the case, the vomiting is excessive, a large mustard poultice should be placed over the stomach, and a grain of solid opium swallowed in the form of a pill, for the purpose of stopping it. Only one of these pills should be given by a non-professional person. In all cases of bites from snakes, send for a surgeon as quickly as possible, and act according to the above directions until he arrives. If he is within any reasonable distance, content yourself by putting on the band, sucking the wound, applying the glass, and, if necessary, giving a little brandy-and-water.

Bites of Dogs—For obvious reasons, these kinds of bites are more frequently met with than those of snakes. *The treatment* is the same as that for snake-bites, more especially that of the bitten part. The majority of writers on the subject are in favour of keeping the wound open as long as possible. This may be done by putting a few beans on it, and then by applying a large linseed-meal poultice over them.

INJURIES AND ACCIDENTS TO BONES

Dislocation of Bones—When the end of a bone is pushed out of its natural position, it is said to be dislocated. This may be caused by violence, disease, or natural weakness of the parts about a joint—*Symptoms.* Deformity about the joint, with unnatural prominence at one part, and depression at another. The limb may be shorter or longer than usual, and is stiff and unable to be moved, differing in these last two respects from a broken limb, which is mostly shorter, never longer, than usual, and which is always more movable—*Treatment.* So much practical science and tact are requisite in order to bring a dislocated bone into its proper position again, that we strongly advise the reader never to interfere in these cases; unless, indeed, it is altogether impossible to obtain the services of a surgeon. But because any one of us may very possibly be placed in that emergency, we give a few rough rules for the reader's guidance. In the first place make the joint, from which the bone has been displaced, perfectly steady, either by fixing it to some firm object or else by holding it with the hands; then pull the dislocated bone in a direction towards the place from which it has been thrust, so that, if it moves at all from its unnatural position, it may have the best chance of returning to its proper place. Do not, however, pull or press against the parts too violently, as you may, perhaps, by doing so, rupture blood-vessels, and produce most serious consequences. When you *do* attempt to reduce a dislocated bone, do it as quickly as possible after the accident has taken place, every hour making the operation more difficult. When the patient is very strong, he may be put into a warm bath until he feels faint, or have sixty drops of antimonial wine given him every ten minutes until he feels sickish. These two means are of great use in relaxing the muscles. If the bone has been brought back again to its proper place, keep it there by means of bandages; and if there is much pain about the joint, apply a cold lotion to it, and keep it perfectly at rest. The lotion should be, a dessert-spoonful of Goulard's extract, and two tablespoonfuls of vinegar, mixed in a pint of water. Leeches are sometimes necessary. Unless the local pain, or general feverish symptoms, are great, the patient's diet should be the same as usual. Dislocations may be reduced a week, or even a fortnight, after they have taken place. As, therefore, although the sooner a bone is reduced the better, there is no very great emergency, and as the most serious consequences may follow improper or too violent treatment, it is always better for people in these cases to do too little than too much; inasmuch as the good which has not yet may still be done, whereas the evil that *has* been done cannot so easily be undone.

FRACTURES OF BONES—*Symptoms.* 1. Deformity of the part. 2. Unnatural looseness. 3. A grating sound when the two ends of the broken bone are rubbed together. 4. Loss of natural motion and power. In some cases there is also shortening of the limb—Fracture takes place from several causes, as a fall, a blow, a squeeze, and sometimes from the violent action of muscles—*Treatment.* In cases where a surgeon cannot be procured immediately after the accident, the following general rules are offered for the reader's guidance:—The broken limb should be placed and kept as nearly as possible in its natural position. This is to be done by first pulling the two portions of the bone in opposite directions, until the limb becomes as long as the opposite one, and then by applying a splint, and binding it to the part by means of a roller. When there is no deformity, the pulling is of course unnecessary. If there is much swelling about the broken part, a cold lotion is to be applied. This lotion (*which we will call Lotion No. 1*) may be thus made:—Mix a dessert-spoonful of Goulard's extract and two tablespoonfuls of vinegar in a pint of water. When the leg or arm is broken, always, if possible, get it to the same length and form as the opposite limb. The broken part should be kept perfectly quiet. When a broken limb is deformed, and a particular muscle is on the stretch, place the limb in such a position as will relax it. This will in most cases cure the deformity. Brandy-and-water, or sal-volatile and water, are to be given when the Burns and Scalds.

BURNS AND SCALDS being essentially the same in all particulars, and differing only in the manner of their production, may be spoken of together. As a general rule, scalds are less severe than burns, because the heat of water, by which scalds are mostly produced, is not, even when it is boiling, so intense as that of flame; oil, however, and other liquids, whose boiling-point is high, produce scalds of a very severe nature. Burns and scalds have been divided into three classes. The first class comprises those where the burn is altogether superficial, and merely reddens the skin; the second, where the injury is greater, and we get little bladders containing a fluid (called serum) dotted over the affected part; in the third class we get, in the case of burns, a charring, and in that of scalds, a softening or pulpiness, perhaps a complete and immediate separation of the part. This may occur at once, or in the course of a little time. The pain from the second kind of burns is much more severe than that in the other two, although the danger, as a general rule, is less than it is in the third class. These injuries are much more dangerous when they take place on the trunk than when they happen on the arms or legs. The danger arises more from the extent of surface that is burnt than from the depth to which the burn goes. This rule, of course, has certain exceptions; because a small burn on the chest or belly penetrating deeply is more dangerous than a more extensive but superficial one on the arm or leg. When a person's clothes are in flames, the best way of extinguishing them is to wind a rug, or some thick material, tightly round the whole of the body.

CONCUSSION OF BRAIN—STUNNING—This may be caused by a blow or a fall—*Symptoms.* Cold skin; weak pulse; almost total insensibility; slow, weak breathing; pupil of eye sometimes bigger, sometimes smaller, than natural; inability to move; unwillingness to answer when spoken to. These symptoms come on directly after the accident—*Treatment.* Place the patient quietly on a warm bed, send for a surgeon,*and do nothing else for the first four or six hours.* After this time the skin will become hot, the pulse full, and the patient feverish altogether. If the surgeon has not arrived by the time these symptoms have set in, shave the patient's head, and apply the following lotion (No. 2): Mix half an ounce of sal-ammoniac, two tablespoonfuls of vinegar, and the same quantity of gin or whisky, in half a pint of water. Then give this pill (No. 1); Mix five grains of calomel and the same quantity of antimonial powder with a little bread-crumb, and make into two pills. Give a black draught three hours after the pill, and two tablespoonfuls of the above-mentioned fever-mixture every four hours. Keep on low diet. Leeches are sometimes to be applied to the head. These cases are often followed by violent inflammation of the brain. They can, therefore, only be attended to properly throughout by a surgeon. The great thing for people to do in these cases is—nothing; contenting themselves with putting the patient to bed, and waiting the arrival of a surgeon.

TO CURE A COLD—Put a large teacupful of linseed, with ¼ lb. of sun raisins and 2 oz. of stick liquorice, into 2 quarts of soft water, and let it simmer over a slow fire till reduced to one quart; add to it ¼ lb. of pounded sugar-candy, a tablespoonful of old rum, and a tablespoonful of the best white-wine vinegar, or lemon-juice. The rum and vinegar should be added as the decoction is taken; for, if they are put in at first, the whole soon becomes flat and less efficacious. The dose is half a pint, made warm, on going to bed; and a little may be taken whenever the cough is troublesome. The worst cold is generally cured by this remedy in two or three days; and, if taken in time, is considered infallible.

FASTING—It is said by many able physicians that fasting is a means of removing incipient disease, and of restoring the body to its customary healthy sensations. Howard, the celebrated philanthropist (says a writer), used to fast one day in every week. Napoleon, when he felt his system unstrung, suspended his wonted repast, and took his exercise on horseback.

FITS

Fits come on so suddenly, often without even the slightest warning, and may prove fatal so quickly, that all people should be acquainted at least with their leading symptoms and treatment, as a few moments, more or less, will often decide the question between life and death. The treatment, in very many cases at least, to be of the slightest use, should be immediate, as a person in a fit (of apoplexy for instance) may die while a surgeon is being fetched from only the next street. We shall give, as far as the fact of our editing a work for non-professional readers will permit, the peculiar and distinctive symptoms of all kind of fits.

Fainting Fits—are sometimes very dangerous, and at others perfectly harmless; the question of danger depending altogether upon the causes which have produced them, and which are exceedingly various. For instance, fainting produced by disease of the heart is a very serious symptom indeed; whereas, that arising from some slight cause, such as the sight of blood, &c., need cause no alarm whatever. The symptoms of simple fainting are so well known that it would be quite superfluous to enumerate them here. The *treatment* consists in laying the patient at full length upon his back, with his head upon a level with the rest of his body, loosening everything about the neck, dashing cold water into the face, and sprinkling vinegar and water about the mouth; applying smelling-salts to the nose; and, when the patient is able to swallow, in giving a little warm brandy-and-water, or about 20 drops of sal-volatile in water.

Hysterics—These fits take place, for the most part, in young, nervous, unmarried women. They happen much less often in married women; and even (in some rare cases indeed) in men. Young women, who are subject to these fits, are apt to think that they are suffering from "all the ills that flesh is heir to;" and the false symptoms of disease which they show are so like the true ones, that it is often exceedingly difficult to detect the difference. The fits themselves are mostly preceded by great depression of spirits, shedding of tears, sickness, palpitation of the heart, &c. A pain, as if a nail were being driven in, is also often felt at one particular part of the head. In almost all cases, when a fit is coming on, pain is felt on the left side. This pain rises gradually until it reaches the throat, and then gives the patient a sensation as if she had a pellet there, which prevents her from breathing properly, and, in fact, seems to threaten actual suffocation. The patient now generally becomes insensible, and faints; the body is thrown about in all directions, froth issues from the mouth, incoherent expressions are uttered, and fits of laughter, crying, or screaming, take place. When the fit is going off, the patient mostly cries bitterly, sometimes knowing all, and at others nothing, of what has taken place, and feeling general soreness all over the body. *Treatment during the fit.* Place the body in the same position as for simple fainting, and treat, in other respects, as directed in the article on Epilepsy. *Always well loosen the patient's stays*; and, when she is recovering, and able to swallow, give 20 drops of sal volatile in a little water. The *after-treatment* of these cases is very various. If the patient is of a strong constitution, she should live on plain diet, take plenty of exercise, and take occasional doses of castor oil, or an aperient mixture, such as that described as "No. 1," in previous numbers. If, as is mostly the case, the patient is weak and delicate, she will require a different mode of treatment altogether. Good nourishing diet, gentle exercise, cold baths, occasionally a dose of No. 3 myrrh and aloes pills at night, and a dose of compound iron pills twice a day. [As to the myrrh and aloes pills (No. 3), 10 grains made into two pills are a dose for a full-grown person. Of the compound iron pills (No. 4), the dose for a full grown person is also 10 grains, made into two pills.] In every case, amusing the mind, and avoiding all causes of over-excitement, are of great service in bringing about a permanent cure.

PALPITATION OF THE HEART—Where palpitation occurs as symptomatic of indigestion, the treatment must be directed to remedy that disorder; when it is consequent on a plethoric state, purgatives will be effectual. In this case the patient should abstain from every kind of diet likely to produce a plethoric condition of body. Animal food and fermented liquor must be particularly avoided. Too much indulgence in sleep will also prove injurious. When the attacks arise from nervous irritability, the excitement must be allayed by change of air and a tonic diet. Should the palpitation originate from organic derangement, it must be, of course, beyond domestic management. Luxurious living, indolence, and tight-lacing often produce this affection: such cases are to be conquered with a little resolution.

CURE FOR STAMMERING—Where there is no malformation of the organs of articulation, stammering may be remedied by reading aloud with the teeth closed. This should be practised for two hours a day, for three or four months. The advocate of this simple remedy says, "I can speak with certainty of its utility."

SUFFOCATION, APPARENT—Suffocation may arise from many different causes. Anything which prevents the air getting into the lungs will produce it. We shall give the principal causes, and the treatment to be followed in each case.

CURE FOR THE TOOTHACHE—Take a piece of sheet zinc, about the size of a sixpence, and a piece of silver, say a shilling; place them together, and hold the defective tooth between them or contiguous to them; in a few minutes the pain will be gone, as if by magic. The zinc and silver, acting as a galvanic battery, will produce on the nerves of the tooth sufficient electricity to establish a current, and consequently to relieve the pain. Or smoke a pipe of tobacco and caraway-seeds.

WARTS—Eisenberg says, in his "Advice on the Hand," that the hydrochlorate of lime is the most certain means of destroying warts;

the process, however, is very slow, and demands perseverance, for, if discontinued before the proper time, no advantage is gained. The following is a simple cure:—On breaking the stalk of the crowfoot plant in two, a drop of milky juice will be observed to hang on the upper part of the stem; if this be allowed to drop on a wart, so that it be well saturated with the juice, in about three or four dressings the warts will die, and may be taken off with the fingers. They may be removed by the above means from the teats of cows, where they are sometimes very troublesome, and prevent them standing quiet to be milked. The wart touched lightly every second day with lunar caustic, or rubbed every night with blue-stone, for a few weeks, will destroy the largest wart, wherever situated.

WOUNDS—There are several kinds of wounds, which are called by different names, according to their appearance, or the manner in which they are produced. As, however, it would be useless, and even hurtful, to bother the reader's head with too many nice professional distinctions, we shall content ourselves with dividing wounds into three classes.

MEDICAL MEMORANDA

ADVANTAGES OF CLEANLINESS—Health and strength cannot be long continued unless the skin—*all* the skin—is washed frequently with a sponge or other means. Every morning is best; after which the skin should be rubbed very well with a rough cloth. This is the most certain way of preventing cold, and a little substitute for exercise, as it brings blood to the surface, and causes it to circulate well through the fine capillary vessels. Labour produces this circulation naturally. The insensible perspiration cannot escape well if the skin is not clean, as the pores get choked up. It is said that in health about half the aliment we take passes out through the skin.

CAUTIONS IN VISITING SICK-ROOMS—Never venture into a sick-room if you are in a violent perspiration (if circumstances require your continuance there), for the moment your body becomes cold, it is in a state likely to absorb the infection, and give you the disease. Nor visit a sick person (especially if the complaint be of a contagious nature) with *an empty stomach*; as this disposes the system more readily to receive the contagion. In attending a sick person, place yourself where the air passes from the door or window to the bed of the diseased, not betwixt the diseased person and any fire that is in the room, as the heat of the fire will draw the infectious vapour in that direction, and you would run much danger from breathing it.

NECESSITY OF GOOD VENTILATION IN ROOMS LIGHTED WITH GAS—In dwelling-houses lighted by gas, the frequent renewal of the air is of great importance. A single gas-burner will consume more oxygen, and produce more carbonic acid to deteriorate the atmosphere of a room, than six or eight candles. If, therefore, when several burners are used, no provision is made for the escape of the corrupted air and for the introduction of pure air from without, the health will necessarily suffer.

CHAPTER XXXVIII

LEGAL MEMORANDA

Humorists tell us there is no act of our lives which can be performed without breaking through some one of the many meshes of the law by which our rights are so carefully guarded; and those learned in the law, when they do give advice without the usual fee, and in the confidence of friendship, generally say, "Pay, pay anything rather than go to law;" while those having experience in the courts of Themis have a wholesome dread of its pitfalls. There are a few exceptions, however, to this fear of the law's uncertainties; and we hear of those to whom a lawsuit is on agreeable relaxation, a gentle excitement. One of this class, when remonstrated with, retorted, that while one friend kept dogs, and another horses, he, as he had a right to do, kept a lawyer; and no one had a right to dispute his taste. We cannot pretend, in these few pages, to lay down even the principles of law, not to speak of its contrary exposition in different courts; but there are a few acts of legal import which all men—and women too—must perform; and to these acts we may be useful in giving a right direction. There is a house to be leased or purchased, servants to be engaged, a will to be made, or property settled, in all families; and much of the welfare of its members depends on these things being done in proper legal form.

PURCHASING A HOUSE—Few men will venture to purchase a freehold, or even a leasehold property, by private contract, without making themselves acquainted with the locality, and employing a solicitor to examine the titles,; but many do walk into an auction-room, and bid for a property upon the representations of the auctioneer. The conditions, whatever they are, will bind him; for by one of the legal fictions of which we have still so many, the auctioneer, who is in reality the agent for the vendor, becomes also the agent for the buyer, and by putting down the names of bidders and the biddings, he binds him to whom the lot is knocked down to the sale and the conditions,—the falling of the auctioneer's hammer is the acceptance of the offer, which completes the agreement to purchase. In any such transaction you can only look at the written or printed particulars; any verbal statement of the auctioneer, made at the time of the sale, cannot contradict them, and they are implemented by the agreement, which the auctioneer calls on the purchaser to sign after the sale. You should sign no such contract without having a duplicate of it signed by the auctioneer, and delivered to you. It is, perhaps, unnecessary to add, that no trustee or assignee can purchase property for himself included in the trust, even at auction; nor is it safe to pay the purchase money to an agent of the vendor, unless he give a written authority to the agent to receive it, besides handing over the requisite deeds and receipts.

Interest on a purchase is due from the day fixed upon for completing: where it cannot be completed, the loss rests with the party with whom the delay rests; but it appears, when the delay rests with the seller, and the money is lying idle, notice of that is to be given to the seller to make him liable to the loss of interest. In law, the property belongs to the purchaser from the date of the contract; he is entitled to any benefit, and must bear any loss; the seller may suffer the insurance to drop without giving notice; and should a fire take place, the loss falls on the buyer. In agreeing to buy a house, therefore, provide at the same time for its insurance. Common fixtures pass with the house, where nothing is said about them.

There are some well-recognized laws, of what may be called good-neighbourhood, which affect all properties. If you purchase a field or house, the seller retaining another field between yours and the highway, he must of necessity grant you a right of way. Where the owner of more than one house sells one of them, the purchaser is entitled to benefit by all drains leading from his house into other drains, and will be subject to all necessary drains for the adjoining houses, although there is no express reservation as to drains.

THE RELATIONS OF LANDLORD AND TENANT are most important to both parties, and each should clearly understand his position. The proprietor of a house, or house and land, agrees to let it either to a tenant-at-will, a yearly tenancy, or under lease. A tenancy-at-will may be created by parol or by agreement; and as the tenant may be turned out when his landlord pleases, so he may leave when he himself thinks proper; but this kind of tenancy is extremely inconvenient to both parties. Where an annual rent is attached to the tenancy, in construction of law, a lease or agreement without limitation to any certain period is a lease from year to year, and both landlord and tenant are entitled to notice before the tenancy can be determined by the other. This notice must be given at least six months before the expiration of the current year of the tenancy, and it can only terminate at the end of any whole year from the time at which it began; so that the tenant entering into possession at Midsummer, the notice must be given to or by him, so as to terminate at the same term. When once he is in possession, he has a right to remain for a whole year; and if no notice be given at the end of the first half-year of his tenancy, he will have to remain two years, and so on for any number of years.

LEASES—A lease is an instrument in writing, by which one person grants to another the occupation and use of lands or tenements for a term of years for a consideration, the lessor granting the lease, and the lessee accepting it with all its conditions. A lessor may grant the lease for any term less than his own interest. A tenant for life in an estate can only grant a lease for his own life. A tenant for life, having power to grant a lease, should grant it only in the terms of the power, otherwise the lease is void, and his estate may be made to pay heavy penalties under the covenant, usually the only one onerous on the lessor, for quiet enjoyment. The proprietor of a freehold—that is, of the possession in perpetuity of lands or tenements—may grant a lease for 999 years, for 99 years, or for 3 years. In the latter case, the lease may be either verbal or in writing, no particular form and no stamps being necessary, except the usual stamp on agreements; so long as the intention of the parties is clearly expressed, and the covenants definite, and well understood by each party, the agreement is complete, and the law satisfied. In the case of settled estates, the court of Chancery is empowered to authorize leases under the 19 & 20 Vict. c. 120, and 21 & 22 Vict. c. 77, as follows:—

> 21 years for agriculture or occupation. 40 years for water-power. 99 years for building-leases. 60 years for repairing-leases.

A lessor may also grant an under-lease for a term less than his own: to grant the whole of his term would be an assignment. Leases are frequently burdened with a covenant not to underlet without the consent of the landlord: this is a covenant sometimes very onerous, and to be avoided, where it is possible, by a prudent lessee.

A lease for any term beyond three years, whether an actual lease or an agreement for one, must be in the form of a deed; that is, it must be "under seal;" and all assignments and surrenders of leases must be in the same form, or they are *void at law.* Thus an agreement made by letter, or by a memorandum of agreement, which would be binding in most cases, would be valueless when it was for a lease, unless witnessed, and given under hand and seal. The last statute, 8 & 9 Vict. c. 106, under which these precautions became necessary, has led to serious difficulties. "The judges," says Lord St. Leonards, "feel the difficulty of holding a lease in writing, but not by deed, to be altogether void, and consequently decided, that although such a lease is void under the statute, yet it so far regulates the holding, that it creates a tenancy from year to year, terminable by half a year's notice; and if the tenure endure for the term attempted to be created by the void lease, the tenant may be evicted at the end of the term without any notice to quit." An agreement for a lease not by deed has been construed to be a lease for a term of years, and consequently void under the statute; "and yet," says Lord St. Leonards, "a court of equity has held that it may be specifically enforced as an agreement upon the terms stated." The law on this point is one of glorious uncertainty; in making any such agreement, therefore, we should be careful to express that it is an agreement, and not a lease; and that it is witnessed and under seal.

AGREEMENTS—It is usual, where the lease is a repairing one, to agree for a lease to be granted on completion of repairs according to specification. This agreement should contain the names and designation of the parties, a description of the property, and the term of the intended lease, and all the covenants which are to be inserted, as no verbal agreement can be made to a written agreement. It should also declare that the instrument is an agreement for a lease, and not the lease itself. The points to be settled in such an agreement are, the rent, term, and especially covenants for insuring and rebuilding in the event of a fire; and if it is intended that the lessor's consent is to be obtained before assigning or underleasing, a covenant to that effect is required in the agreement. In building-leases, usually granted for 99 years, the tenant is to insure the property; and even where the agreement is silent on that point, the law decides it so. It is otherwise with ordinary tenements, when the tenant pays a full, or what the law terms rack-rent; the landlord is then to insure, unless it is otherwise arranged by the agreement.

INSURANCE—Every lease, or agreement for a lease, should covenant not only who is to pay insurance, but how the tenement is to be rebuilt in the event of a fire; for if the house were burnt down, and no provision made for insurance, the tenant, supposing there was the ordinary covenant to repair in the lease, would not only have to rebuild, but to pay rent while it was being rebuilt. More than this, supposing, under the same lease, the landlord had taken the precaution of insuring, he is not compelled to lay out the money recovered in rebuilding the premises. Sir John Leach lays it down, that "the tenant's situation could not be changed by a precaution, on the part of the landlord, with which he had nothing to do." This decision Lord Campbell confirmed in a more recent case, in which an action was brought against a lessee who was not bound to repair, and neither he nor the landlord bound to insure; admitting an equitable defence, the court affirmed Sir John Leach's decision, holding that the tenant was bound to pay the rent, and could not require the landlord to lay out the insurance money in rebuilding. This is opposed to the opinion of Lord St. Leonards, who admits, however, that the decision of the court must overrule his *dictum*. Such being the state of the law, it is very important that insurance should be provided for, and that the payment of rent should be made to depend upon rebuilding the house in the event of a fire. Care must be taken, however, that this is made a covenant of the lease, as well as in the agreement, otherwise the tenant must rebuild the house.

BREAKS IN THE LEASE—Where a lease is for seven, fourteen, or twenty-one years, the option to determine it at the end of the first term is in the tenant, unless it is distinctly agreed that the option shall be mutual, according to Lord St. Leonards.

TAXES—Land-tax, sewers-rate, and property-tax, are landlord's taxes; but by 30 Geo. II. c. 2, the occupier is required to pay all rates levied, and deduct from the rent such taxes as belong to the landlord. Many landlords now insert a covenant, stipulating that land-tax and sewers-rate are to be paid by the tenants, and not deducted: this does not apply to the property-tax. All other taxes and rates are payable by the occupier.

NOTICE TO QUIT—In the case of leasing for a term, no notice is necessary; the tenant quits, as a matter of course, at its termination; or if, by tacit consent, he remains paying rent as heretofore, he becomes a tenant at sufferance, or from year to year. Half a year's notice now becomes necessary, as we have already seen, to terminate the tenancy; except in London, and the rent is under forty shillings, when a quarter's notice is sufficient. Either of these notices may be given verbally, if it can be proved that the notice was definite, and given at the right time. Form of notice is quite immaterial, provided it is definite and clear in its purport.

RECOVERY OF RENT—The remedies placed in the hands of landlords are very stringent. The day after rent falls due, he may proceed to recover it, by action at law, by distress on the premises, or by action of ejectment, if the rent is half a year in arrear. Distress is the remedy usually applied, the landlord being authorized to enter the premises, seize the goods and chattels of his tenant, and sell them, on the fifth day, to reimburse himself for all arrears of rent and the charges of the distress. There are a few exceptions; but, generally, all goods found on the premises may be seized. The exceptions are—dogs, rabbits, poultry, fish, tools and implements of a man's trade actually in use, the books of a scholar, the axe of a carpenter, wearing apparel on the person, a horse at the plough, or a horse he may be riding, a watch in the pocket, loose money, deeds, writings, the cattle at a smithy forge, corn sent to a mill for grinding, cattle and goods of a guest at an inn; but, curiously enough, carriages and horses standing at livery at the same inn may be taken. Distress can only be levied in the daytime, and if made after the tender of arrears, it is illegal. If tender is made after the distress, but before it is *impounded*, the landlord must abandon the distress and bear the cost himself. Nothing of a perishable nature, which cannot be restored in the same condition—as milk, fruit, and the like, must be taken.

The law does not regard a day as consisting of portions. The popular notion that a notice to quit should be served before noon is an error. Although distraint is one of the remedies, it is seldom advisable in a landlord to resort to distraining for the recovery of rent. If a tenant cannot pay his rent, the sooner he leaves the premises the better. If he be a rogue and won't pay, he will probably know that nine out of ten distresses are illegal, through the carelessness, ignorance, or extortion of the brokers who execute them. Many, if not most, of the respectable brokers will not execute distresses, and the business falls into the hands of persons whom it is by 2722. When a tenant deserts premises, leaving one half-year's rent in arrear, possession may be recovered by means of the police-court. The rent must not exceed £20 per annum, and must be at least three-fourths of the value of the premises. In cases in which the tenant has not deserted the premises, and where notice to quit has been given and has expired, the landlord must give notice to the tenant of his intended application. The annual rent in this case, also, must not exceed £20.

APPRENTICES—By the statute 5 Eliz. cap. 4, it is enacted that, in cases of ill-usage by masters towards apprentices, or of neglect of duty by apprentices, the complaining party may apply to a justice of the peace, who may make such order as equity may require. If, for want of conformity on the part of the master, this cannot be done, then the master may be bound to appear at the next sessions. Authority is given by the act to the justices in sessions to discharge the apprentice from his indentures. They are also empowered, on proof of misbehaviour of the apprentice, to order him to be corrected or imprisoned with hard labour.

HUSBAND AND WIFE—Contrary to the vulgar opinion, second cousins, as well as first, may legally marry. When married, a husband is liable for his wife's debts contracted before marriage. A creditor desirous of suing for such a claim should proceed against both. It will, however, be sufficient if the husband be served with process, the names of both appearing therein, thus:—John Jones and Ann his wife. A married woman, if sued alone, may plead her marriage, or, as it is called in law, coverture. The husband is liable for debts of his wife contracted for necessaries while living with him. If she voluntarily leaves his protection, this liability ceases. He is also liable for any debts contracted by her with his authority. If the husband have abjured the realm, or been transported by a sentence of law, the wife is liable during his absence, as if she were a single woman, for debts contracted by her.

In civil cases, a wife may now give evidence on behalf of her husband in criminal cases she can neither be a witness for or against her husband. The case of assault by him upon her forms an exception to this rule.

The law does not at this day admit the ancient principle of allowing moderate correction by a husband upon the person of his wife. Although this is said to have been anciently limited to the use of "a stick not bigger than the thumb," this barbarity is now altogether exploded. He may, notwithstanding, as has been recently shown in the famous Agapemone case, keep her under restraint, to prevent her leaving him, provided this be effected without cruelty.

By the Divorce and Matrimonial Causes Act, 1857, a wife deserted by her husband may apply to a magistrate, or to the petty sessions, for an order to protect her lawful earnings or property acquired by her after such desertion, from her husband and his creditors. In this case it is indispensable that such order shall, within ten days, be entered at the county court of the district within which she resides. It will be seen that the basis of an application for such an order is *desertion*. Consequently, where the parties have separated by common consent, such an order cannot be obtained, any previous cruelty or misconduct on the husband's part notwithstanding.

When a husband allows his wife to invest money in her own name in a savings-bank, and he survives her, it is sometimes the rule of such establishments to compel him to take out administration in order to receive such money, although it is questionable whether such rule is legally justifiable. Widows and widowers pay no legacy-duty for property coming to them through their deceased partners.

WILLS—The last proof of affection which we can give to those left behind, is to leave their worldly affairs in such a state as to excite neither jealousy, nor anger, nor heartrendings of any kind, at least for the immediate future. This can only be done by a just, clear, and intelligible disposal of whatever there is to leave. Without being advocates for every man being his own lawyer, it is not to be denied that the most elaborately prepared wills have been the most fruitful sources of litigation, and it has even happened that learned judges left wills behind them which could not be carried out. Except in cases where the property is in land or in leases of complicated tenure, very elaborate details are unnecessary; and we counsel no man to use words in making his will of which he does not perfectly understand the meaning and import.

By the act of 1852 it was enacted that no will shall be valid unless signed at the foot or end thereof by the testator, or by some person in his presence, and by his direction; but a subsequent act proceeds to say that every will shall, as far only as regards the position of the signature of the testator, or of the person signing for him, be deemed valid if the signature shall be so placed at, or after, or following, or under, or beside, or opposite to the end of the will, that it shall be apparent on the face of it that the testator intended to give it effect by such signature. Under this clause, a will of several sheets, all of which were duly signed, except the last one, has been refused probate; while, on the other hand, a similar document has been admitted to probate where the last sheet only, and none of the other sheets, was signed. In order to be perfectly formal, however, each separate sheet should be numbered, signed, and witnessed, and attested on the last sheet. This witnessing is an important act: the witnesses must subscribe it in the presence of the testator and of each other; and by their signature they testify to having witnessed the signature of the testator, he being in sound mind at the time. Wills made under any kind of coercion, or even importunity may become void, being contrary to the wishes of the testator. Fraud or imposition also renders a will void, and where two wills made by the same person happen to exist, neither of them dated, the maker of the wills is declared to have died intestate.

INDEX

Account-book, 9
Accounts, of housekeeper, 28
Aerated bread, 220–221
After-dinner invitations, 22
Air, 244–245
Albumen, 60–61, 114
Almond flowers, 182–183
Almond puffs, 176
Announcement, of guests, 24
Apple, 177
Apple cheesecakes, 176–177
Apple custard, 190
Apple jam, 206–207
Apple marmalade, 191
Apple pie, 177–178
Apple sauce, 104
Apple tart, 177–178
Apprentices, 293
Apricots, 179
Apricot tart, 178–179
April, 40
Arrival, of guests, 23
Asparagus sauce, 104–105
Aspic, 50–51
Assiette, 51–52
Assiette volante, 51
Au-bleu, 52
August, 42

Baillie, Joanna, 4
Bain marie, 52, 106
Baked apple custard, 190
Baked beef, 127–128
Baked custard pudding, 181
Baked haddocks, 93–94
Baked ham, 136–137
Baked pike, 95–96
Baked rice pudding, 184–185
Baked sole, 97–98
Baked veal, 144
Baking, of meat, 115–117
Baking-dish, 117
Barley soup, 68–69
Baths, 272
Béchamel, 52
Beef
 baked, 127–128
 cake, 128–129
 roasting of, 126
 roast ribs of, 129
 roast sirloin of, 130
 sausage, 131
Beef stock, 61
Beer, ginger, 234
Benevolence, 7–8
Beverages, classes of, 229
Bill of fare
 for breakfast, 239
 for luncheons, 240
 for picnic for 40 persons, 240–241
 for suppers, 240
Birds, 147–149. *See also* Poultry
Birth, 249–250
Biscuit powder, 261

Bites, 274–276
Blanch, 52
Blanquette, 52
Bleeding, 272–273
Boiled ham, 137–138
Boiled sole, 101
Boiling, of meat, 117–121
Bolting, 218
Bone dislocation, 276–277
Bone fractures, 278
Bones, in soups, 61
Bottle feeding, 258–259
Bottle-jack, 125
Bouilli, 52
Bouillie, 52
Bouillon, 52
Brain concussion, 279–280
Braise, 52
Braisière, 52
Brandy, cherry, 207
Brass, 36
Bread, 217–222
  aerated, 220–221
  gingerbread, 227
  home-made, 225–226
Bread crumbs, fried, 105–106
Bread-making, 219–222
Breakfast, 12, 29
  bill of fare for, 239
  cook at, 48
Breastfeeding, 253–255
Brider, 52
Broiling, of meat, 121–122
Bronze, 35–36
Brown gravy, 107–108
Browning, for stock, 67–68
Brown sauces, 103
Buffet, 24
Burns, 278–279
Butter, 175, 187, 211, 222
Buttermilk, 187

Cabbage, stewed, 168
Cabbage soup, 69
Cake(s)
  butter in, 222
  eggs in, 222
  pound, 228
  tipsy, 195
Calf, 140–143
Calls, 14–18
Caramel, 53, 198, 205–206
Carving
  of duck, 153–154
  of fish, 100–101
  of game, 163–164
  of poultry, 153–156
  of rabbit, 155
  of turkey, 155–156
Casserole, 53
Caviar, 84
Cayenne cheeses, 214
Cereals, 217–218
Chantilly soup, 69–70
Charcoal, 37–38
Charity, 7–8
Cheese, 211–212, 214–215
Cheesecake, 176–177
Cherries, 180–181
Cherry brandy, 207
Cherry jam, 207–208
Cherry tart, 180
Chestnut, 71
Chestnut soup, 70–71
Chicken cutlets, 150
Chicken-pox, 265–266
Chocolate, 232–233
Chocolate (beverage), 232

Chocolate cream, 191–192
Churning, 187
Chyle, 248–249
Cleanliness, 2, 284
Clotted cream, 187
Cloves, 107–108
Coal, 38
Cocoa, 232–233
Cocoa-nut, 72–73
Cocoa-nut soup, 72–73
Codfish, 91–92
Coffee, 230–231
Cold (illness), 280
Common black draught, 271
Common short crust, 175–176
Compôte, 53, 200, 205
Concussion, 279–280
Condolences, 16–17
Confectionary, 200–201
Consommé, 53
Conversation, 4–5
Convulsions, in infants, 264–265
Cook
  at breakfast, 48
  in dinner, 49–50
  duties of, 47–48
  housekeeper and, 29
Costorphin cream, 187
Crab, 91–92
Cream(s), 187–188
  chocolate, 191–192
Croquette, 53
Croutons, 53
Crust, common short, 175–176
Cry, of infant, 251–252
Curd, 211–212
Currants, 222
Custard, apple, 190
Custard sauce, 105

Daubière, 53
December, 44
Désosser, 53
Dessert, 21
Dessert dishes, 201–203
Dessert-spoonful, 47
Diarrhea, 267–268
Digestion, 247–249
Dinner, 235–239
  after, 21–22
  announcement, 20
  cook and, 49–50
  family, 25–26
  half-hour before, 19
  housekeeper duties after, 30–31
  invitation, 18–19
  seating at, 20–21
Dog bites, 276
Drachm, 47
Dress
  of infant, 256
  of mistress, 5–7
Drop, 47
Drugs, 269–270
Duck, 151–152, 153–154

Early rising, 2
Economy, 3
Eel-pout, 84
Eggs, 212–213
  in cakes, 222
  poached, 215–216
Egg whites, 188–189
Egypt, 83–84, 171
Entrées, 53
Entremets, 53
Escalopes, 53

Fainting fits, 281

Falconry, 161
Family dinner, 25–26
Farinaceous food, 260
Fashion, 5–7
Fasting, 280
February, 39
Feeding, of infant, 258–259
Feuilletage, 53
Fever mixture, 271
Fig pudding, 182
Fillet of veal, 146
Fish
    body parts of, 79–80
    bones of, 81
    in Britain, 86
    broiled, 89–90
    carving, 100–101
    choosing, 90, 91
    conformation of, 79
    death of, 82–83
    diet of, 81–82
    dressing, 88–90
    in Egypt, 83–84
    as food, 83–88
    in France, 86
    fried, 89
    garnishing, 89
    in Greece, 84
    longevity of, 82
    preservation of, 88
    recipes, 91–101
    respiration of, 80–81
    in Rome, 84–85
    in season, 38–44, 87
    stock, 77
Fish cake, 93
Fits, 280–282
Flamber, 53
Flour, 217
Fomentations, 272
Foncer, 53
Fondue, 214–215
France, fish in, 86
Fried bread crumbs, 105–106
Fried smelt, 97
Fried sole, 101
Friendship, 3–4
Friendship visits, 15–16
Frugality, 3
Fruit
    presentation of, 202–203
    preserves, 196–200
    in season, 38–44
Fruit pastes, 199–200
Frying, of meat, 122–124
Fuel, in kitchen, 37–38

Galette, 54
Game
    carving of, 163–164
    in history, 157–161
    recipes, 162–164
    in season, 38–44
Gas lighting, 285
Gastric juice, 247–248
Gâteau, 54
Gelatine, 60, 188
Ginger beer, 234
Gingerbread, 227
Glacer, 54
Glass-pox, 265–266
Glazing, of pastry, 184
Good temper, 5
Gravy(ies)
    basis of, 102–103
    brown, 107–108
    stock for, 106
Greece, 84, 237

Gridiron, 121–122
Gruel, 172
Guests
  announcement of, 24
  arrival of, 23

Haddock, 93–94
Ham
  baked, 136–137
  boiled, 137–138
Hare, 163. *See also* Rabbit
Haunch of venison, 164
Hawking, 161
Heart palpitation, 282–283
Heat, 272
Hog
  body parts of, 132
  choice of, 133–134
  ring in snout of, 132–133
  rooting by, 132
Home-made bread, 225–226
Hooping cough, 266–267
Hors-d'oeuvres, 54
Horseradish, 109, 168–169
Horseradish sauce, 108–109
Hospitality, 4
Housekeeper
  inventory by, 32
  in kitchen, 28–29
  qualifications of, 27–28
Housekeeper's room, 29, 30
House purchase, 286–288
Hysterics, 281–282

Ice-plant, 202
Ices, 203–204
Icing, of pastry, 184
Infant, 249–265
Infantile fits, 264–265
Insurance, 290–291
Inventory, 32
Invitation
  after-dinner, 22
  dinner, 18–19
Irving, Washington, 4

Jam(s), 199–200
  apple, 206–207
  cherry, 207–208
  raspberry, 208–209
January, 38
Jelly(ies), 188–189
  apple, 191
Jerrold, Douglas, 236
July, 41–42
June, 41

Kitchen
  features of, 33
  fuel in, 37–38
  housekeeper in, 28–29
  utensils, 35–36
Kneading, 219

Lady's maid, in housekeeper's room, 30
Landlord-tenant relations, 288
Leases, 288–293
Lichen, 166
Lighting, by gas, 285
Lit, 54
Lobster, 94–95
Loin of veal, 146
Lotas, 84
Lotions, 271
Love-apple, 111–112
Luncheon, 14, 240
Lungs, 245–247

Macaroons, 226–227
Maigre, 54
Malt wine, 233–234
March, 39–40
Marmalade, 199–200
  apple, 191
Marriage, 293–295
Matelote, 54
May, 40–41
Mayonnaise, 54
Measures, 47
Meat
  baking, 115–117
  boiling of, 117–121
  broiling of, 121–122
  frying of, 122–124
  roasting of, 124–126
  salted, 120
  in season, 38–44
  for soups, 56, 60
  for stocks, 61–62
Meat fibers, 114–115
Medical memoranda, 284–285
Medium stock, 66
Meringue, 54, 192–193
Milk, 210, 248, 253–257
Minim, 47
Mint, 110
Mint sauce, 109–110
Miroton, 54
Morning calls
  making, 16
  receiving, 17
Moss, 166
Mouiller, 54
Mutton, roasting of, 126

Nosebleed, 273–274
November, 43–44
Nurse, 251–252

October, 43
Omelets, 189
Onion, 74
Onion soup, 74
Osmazome, 60

Palpitation of heart, 282–283
Paner, 54
Parsley, 70
Pastes, fruit, 199–200
Pastry, 171–173
Pea soup, 75
Peat, 37
Picnic, 240–241
Pie, apple, 177–178
Pig. *See* Hog
Pigeon, 61
Pike, 95–96
Pills, 271
Piquer, 54
Plum tart, 183
Poached eggs, 215–216
Poêlée, 55
Pork. *See also* Ham; Hog
  chops, 136
  cut for table, 134–135
  preservation of, 134
Pork sausage, 138–139
Porridge, 172
Potato salad, 170
Pots, for boiling meat, 120–121
Poultices, 272
Poultry
  carving, 153–156
  recipes, 150–152
  in season, 38–44
Pound cake, 228

Powders, 272
Prawns, 96
Prescriptions, 271–272
Preserves, 196–200
Pudding(s), 171–173
baked custard, 181
fig, 182
rice, 184–185
tapioca, 185–186
Puff-pastry, 174–175
Purée, 55

Quitting of lease, 292

Rabbit, 152, 155. *See also* Hare
Ragout, 55
Raspberry jam, 208–209
Rearing by hand, 257–261
Red mullet, 84
Remoulade, 55
Rennet, 248
Rent, recovery of, 292–293
Respiration, 245–247, 253
Ribs, beef, 129
Rice pudding, 184–185
Rissoles, 55
Roast breast of veal, 145
Roast duck, 151–152, 153–154
Roast hare, 163
Roasting, of meat, 124–126
Roast ribs of beef, 129
Roast sirloin of beef, 130
Roast turkey, 155–156
Rome, 84–85, 172
Roux, 55

Salad, potato, 170
Salmi, 55
Salmon, 100–101
Salted meat, 120
Sauce(s)
apple, 104
asparagus, 104–105
basis of, 102–103
brown, 103
custard, 105
horseradish, 108–109
mint, 109–110
tomato, hot, 111–112
Sauce piquante, 55
Sausage
beef, 131
pork, 138–139
Sausage-meat stuffing, 110–111
Sauter, 55
Savarin, Brillat, 99, 113
Scalds, 278–279
Scales, 36
Scum, 62, 119
Seasoning
of baked meat, 116
of soups, 58
Seasons, 38–44, 157–158
Seating, at dinner, 20–21
Seeds, 167
September, 42–43
Servants, hiring of, 9–12
Shopping, 8–9
Short crust, 175–176
Shrimp, 96
Sick-rooms, 285
Sirloin, 130
Skimming, 62
Smelt, 97
Smoke-jacks, 124
Smoothness, in preserves, 198
Snake bites, 275–276
Sole, 97–98, 101

Soufflés, 189, 193–194
Soup(s)
barley, 68–69
bones in, 61
cabbage, 69
Chantilly, 69–70
chemistry of, 59–64
chestnut, 70–71
cocoa-nut, 72–73
economy of, 59–64
meat for, 56, 60
onion, 74
pea, 75
seasoning of, 58
stew, 76
stock in, 59–60
vegetable, 76
vegetables in, 57–58
water in, 57
Soup a la julienne, 73
Sour cream, 187
Spit, for roasting, 124
Stammering, 283
Stewed rabbit, 152
Stewed red cabbage, 168
Stewed tomatoes, 170
Stewed venison, 162
Stew soup, 76
Still-room, 31
Stings, 274
Stock, 59–60, 61–64, 66–68, 106
Stomach, 247–249
Stuffing, sausage-meat, 110–111
Stunning, 279–280
Sturgeon, 84
Suffocation, 283
Supper, 240
Sweet dishes, 189
Syrup, 205

Table-spoonful, 47
Tamis, 55
Tapioca, 186
Tapioca pudding, 185–186
Tart
apple, 177–178
apricot, 178–179
cherry, 180
plum, 183
Taxes, 291–292
Tea, 229
Tea-spoonful, 47
Teething, 261–263
Temper, 5
Tenant-landlord relations, 288
Thread, in preserves, 198
Tipsy cake, 195
Tomato, 111–112
Tomato, stewed, 170
Tomato sauce, hot, 111–112
Toothache, 283
Tourte, 55
Trifling occurrences, 4–5
Trousser, 55
Truffle, 170
Trussing, duck, 151
Turkey, 155–156

Utensils
for broiling, 121–122
for drying, 123–124
kitchen, 35–36

Veal, 140–141, 140–143
baked, 144
carving, 145–146
fillet of, 146
loin of, 146

roast breast of, 145
Vegetable jelly, 188
Vegetable preserves, 196–200
Vegetables
recipes for, 168–170
in season, 38–44
seeds of, 167
in soups, 57–58, 63–64
Vegetable soup, 76
Venison
carving, 164
haunch of, 164
stewed, 162
Ventilation, 285
Vessels, for boiling meat, 120–121
Visits, 14–18
Vol-au-vent, 55

Wages, of domestic servants, 10–12
Waking, 2
Warts, 283–284
Washing, of infant, 256–257
Water
in baby food, 260
for boiling of meat, 117–118
in soups, 57
Weighing machines, 36–37
Whey, 248
White stock, 67
Whooping cough, 266–267
Wills, 295–296
Wine, malt, 233–234
Wounds, 284

Yeast, 219–220, 221, 224